OUT OF THE SHADOWS

Women of the Restoration Movement

Angela L. Mabe

Charleston, AR:
COBB PUBLISHING
2024

Out of the Shadows: Women of the Restoration Movement
is copyright © 2024 by Angela Mabe. All rights reserved.

No portion of this book may be duplicated in any way, regardless of means or method without the prior written permission of the author or publisher, except for small quotations used in a review.

Scripture quotations marked KJV are from the Holy Bible, King James Version.

Scripture quotations marked NKJV are from the Holy Bible, New King James Version. Used by permission.

Scripture quotations marked ESV are from the Holy Bible, English Standard Version. Used by Permission.

Published in the United States of America by:
Cobb Publishing
704 E. Main St
Charleston, AR 72933
CobbPublishing.com
Editor@CobbPublishing.com
479.747.8372

ISBN: 978-1-965789-88-9

Dedicated to my dad,
Herman Edward Jones
For instilling in me a love for
Restoration history

And

In memory of Carole Childers
for being a woman of encouragement

TABLE OF CONTENTS

Preface i

Chapter 1 1
   Looking Back 1

Chapter 2 17
   Elizabeth Rogers: A Woman of Submission (1792- 1868) 17

Chapter 3 31
   Nancy Hurt Smith: A Woman of Character (1792-1861) 31

Chapter 4 50
   Emily Harvey Thomas Tubman: A Woman Who Gave (1794-1885) 50

Chapter 5 63
   Selina Campbell: A Woman of Usefulness (1802-1897) 63

Chapter 6 83
   Charlotte Fall Fanning: A Woman Who Loved to Teach (1809-1896) 83

Chapter 7 98
   Nancy Larimore: A Woman of Motherly Love (1813-1902) 98

Chapter 8 109
   Margaret Lipscomb: A Woman of Invention (1842-1926) 109

Chapter 9 124
   Julia Esther Larimore: A Woman with a Song in her Heart (1845-1907) 124

Chapter 10 140
   Mattie Carr: A Woman on a Mission (1846-1907) 140

Chapter 11 156
Influential Mothers of the Restoration 156
MARY J. DUNN POTTER 156
MARGARET LINGOW ELAM 161
MARY LUMPKIN BARNES (MISS. POLLY) 164
LUCY JANE B. McCALEB 168
ELIZA BALLOU GARFIELD 172
JANE BREEDEN LIPSCOMB 177

Chapter 12 184
Influential Wives of the Restoration 184
MARY CATHERINE CONN GANO 184
SARAH I. TURNER SEWELL and
   ELIZABETH A. SEWELL 189
ELIZABETH CAMPBELL STONE and
   CELIA WILSON BOWEN STONE 193
MARGARET E. VICK HOLBROOK 196

Chapter 13 207
Wives of Influence Continued 207
HETTY DE SPAIN CLARK 207
LAVINIA CAMPBELL PENDLETON 213
ANNIE BACON FALL 216
OTWAYANNA FRANCES HIX MCGARVEY 217

Chapter 14 227
Influential Aunts, Mother-in-laws, Sister-in-laws, Sisters,
   Grandmothers, Adopted Moms, Daughters and Close Friends . 227
MARY GOFORTH GANO (Aunt and Mother-in-law) 227
ANNA LIPSCOMB (Sister-in-law) 228
DOROTHEA CAMPBELL BRYANT and JANE CAMPBELL
   MCKEEVER (Sisters) 229
ANN DAY LIPSCOMB (Grandmother) 234
LUCINDA KUYKENDALL SEWELL
   (Adopted Mother or Adopted Aunt) 236
LAVINIA CAMPBELL AND HER SISTERS (Daughters) 238

    LOULIE MCGARVEY (Daughter) 238
    MRS. DABNEY (A Friend) 239

Chapter 15 .... **245**
    "Faults They Had, But Faults Have We" (Alexander Campbell). 245
    MARY PERSONETT FRANKLIN 245
    LUCRETIA RUDOLPH GARFIELD 248
    ELIZA SANDIDGE SCOTT 250
    SUSAN MITCHUM BALL HALL 252
    SOPHIA LEWIS JOHNSON 255

Chapter 16: **259**
    Conclusion: Looking Forward 259

References **265**

A special Thank you **279**

Final Notes **280**

PREFACE

The Restoration Movement was a plea for unity: a unity to be achieved by returning to the Bible and the pattern of New Testament Christianity. The men and women of the Restoration Movement showed great zeal in pursuing this goal. However, Satan never tires of pulling people away from the Scriptures and misguiding their focus on returning to the Scriptures. The fight against division is ever-present. Dr. James Maxwell, former professor of Religious Studies at Southwestern Christian College, says that many people in today's church do not seek a return to God's truths, choosing to "remain on the inside and are apparently seeking to change the Church from the inside out… Instead of making serious efforts to restore New Testament Christianity, many emphasize restoring the Restoration Movement."[1] There should not be a glorified celebration of the movement of the 18th and 19th centuries; it is the Restoration PLEA alone which needs to be rekindled. My good friend, Scott Harp, says, "Understanding what the Restoration plea is will help the church that Jesus built grow in any generation."[2] If we understand that plea and act upon it with zeal we can unite many to Christ.

In this book, it is not my intention to discuss Restoration women in a way that puts them or their words on the level of divine authority. Again, it is the Restoration **PLEA** that needs rekindling, not the movement. It is my hope, however, that highlighting the lives of these noteworthy women and bringing them out of the shadows will encourage contemporary women to match—or even surpass—their zeal in pursuing that Restoration plea.

---

[1] Maxwell, *Let's Go Back...Way Back!: Black Presence in the Restoration Movement*, p. xv.
[2] Harp, "Adhering to the Restoration Plea," *Gospel Advocate*, July 2012, p. 19.

Chapter 1

Looking Back

There is a time and a place for looking back. Growing up the daughter of a George Jones fan, I often heard my dad break out with one or two lines of spontaneous lyrical memories that brought a smile to any face that witnessed it. When Dad smiled his playful smile and pointed his finger at me, these lyrics usually followed, "I was looking back to see if you were looking back to see if I was looking back to see if you were looking back at me." Reflecting upon these lyrics, I've thought that the boy would never have known if the girl was interested in him if he had never looked back.

On the other hand, many of our inspirational quotes say we must "<u>never</u> look back." In the sense of putting an old life behind you and pressing on towards your goal, that is certainly true. That is what Jesus is teaching in Luke 9:62 when He speaks of the farmer who should not look back once he puts his hand to the plow, in order to keep the furrows straight. Now, I know you shouldn't look back *while* you're plowing, but do you think the farmer ever stopped his horse, took out his handkerchief, wiped his brow and looked back to gauge his progress? If his furrows were not as straight as he originally thought, don't you think he is going to want to know why? Philosopher George Santayana famously observed, "Those who cannot remember the past are condemned to repeat it."[1] In other words, looking back can be very beneficial. Remember, "hindsight is 20/20," and sometimes a clearer perspective can be gained and lessons can be learned by considering the past.

---

[1] Santayana, *The Life of Reason: Reason in Common Sense vol. 1,* 1905, Ch. 12, para. 19.

History is exciting to me. I know that some of you might not have enjoyed history in school, but if you will stay with me I'll try to make it as painless as I possibly can. I've taught at a Christian school on and off for nearly seventeen years. One of my greatest joys was costuming children in historical period clothing and acting out history lessons. My sixth graders enjoyed baking flat bread in the ground while studying the time of Abraham. They also enjoyed wearing Egyptian garb and mummifying a chicken or a turkey each year. Due to its unforgettable smell this unit was not our principal's favorite. During my first attempt at mummification our principal was showing visitors around the school, and he came to the conclusion that there was something wrong with the bathrooms. I eventually had to take the smelly turkey home for Christmas break, and my husband was none too happy. I really get into history, so much so that my youngest child declared more than once, "I'm not stepping foot in another old house." My teenage son would tell his friends that his mother was strange, because she loves to visit old dead preachers in cemeteries. My children also bonded in embarrassment when their mother would break out singing Johnny Horton history songs when their friends were in the car. I've always found history exciting, and it is especially exciting when it is connected to me.

In this study, we are going to look back into the past, but before we do, one thing I always like to point out that history is really HIS STORY. So many now are calling it "social studies," meaning the study of man. HIS STORY is God's story from creation on, and we are still part of His on-going story. God should not be left out of the picture or out of our world view. Hopefully, you will become part of God's ongoing history as women of restoration. Today's world is all about the here and now and focusing on how to please yourself. Our culture is clearly not teaching us to look back to what it considers an archaic book—the Bible—

to search out a truth that it believes is nonexistent. As a mother, I'm worried that my children are being infiltrated by every screen, device, billboard and peer to be tolerant and accepting of messages like these. I want my children to know that God's word is truth. Jesus says in John 8:32, "And you shall know the truth, and the truth shall make you free" (NKJV). I want them to love truth, thirst for it, and search it out. I believe we all need to take a pause from our plowing and consider what benefits we can gain from the past to equip ourselves against the troubled culture in which we live. Let's look at five reasons why we should look back.

We Look Back to Find Truth.

The world often ridicules looking back at a book that was written so long ago. However, we know that God is truth, and His inspired word is truth (John 17:17). We look to the Bible and the Bible alone as our only rule of faith. The truth has always been with us and will always be with us. The Bible says, "The grass withers, the flower fades, but the word of our God stands forever" (Isaiah 40:8). In His word, God has given us "all things that pertain to life and godliness, through the knowledge of Him who called us by glory and virtue" (2 Peter 1:3). In order to equip ourselves against our troubled culture, we need to continually look back at God's truths, study them and know them: then we can always be ready with an answer (1 Peter 3:15). We must be restorers of truth.

The word "restore" indicates a sense of looking back and bringing something back to its original state (Merriam-Webster). However, when we use the word "restore," we need to understand it in terms of restoring submission to God's truth and His perfect will for us. God's truths have no need to be restored in and of themselves. It is man's obedience and practice of His truths that need restoring. Never in history has the Church on Earth been perfect. In reference to God's correction of the Corinthians through Paul, Owen said this:

> God wants His people to repent when they leave His expressed will and make a genuine effort to return to His will. While the word 'restoration' may be imperfect, the idea of a return to God's will is at the core of what God has always called His people to do.[1]

Therefore, we must follow Romans 12:2, "And do not be conformed to this world, but be transformed by the renewing of your mind, that you may prove what is that good and acceptable and perfect, will of God." God has called us to be <u>agents</u> of His perfect will. We are to be <u>instruments of God</u> (Rom. 6:13), <u>ambassadors for Christ</u> (2 Cor. 5:20) and restorers of His truth to the world. This purpose from God is an ongoing process and a privilege to effect. Are we looking back to God's Word in preparation of this mission?

We Look Back to Observe Satan's Strategies.

The Bible says that Satan is our enemy or adversary (1 Peter 5:8). One of the most effective ways to prepare ourselves for our mission to restore is to look back in history and study our enemy and his strategies to see what we are up against.

Have you ever wondered why there are so many denominations and where they all came from? These are valid questions, especially since God's word says there is only one body or one

---

[1] Owen, "Is 'Restoration' Still a Valid Principle?" *Gospel Advocate*, January 2006, p. 38.

church (Eph. 4:4). When I was a teenager, my Bible class teacher drew a chart on the board every Wednesday night.

This chart cleared up a lot of questions for me as a young person. The line at the top represented the Church that was started on the day of Pentecost. This is the one Church that Paul was talking about in Ephesians 4:4-5. Everything in the Old Testament points to this Church. Jesus spent His time on Earth preparing the apostles so they would be ready to begin this Church. We find the pattern that God wanted for His Church in the book of Acts and the letters of the New Testament. This is the Church that we want to emulate and the Church of which we want to be a part. This is the Church God intended, but soon after the deaths of the apostles, the Church began to deviate from the inspired pattern. On the chart this fact was indicated by other lines that branched off from the top one. The devil did what he does best, gradually but effectively corrupting men's knowledge of the truth. Paul had warned in Acts 20:29-30, "After my departure savage wolves will come in among you, not sparing the flock. Also from among yourselves men will rise up, speaking perverse things, to draw away the disciples after themselves."

Like savage wolves, many were coming in from outside the Church and trying to change or take over the Church. Pagan influences were threatening the early church from the outside, and they gained great strides in 313 A.D., with the introduction of Constantine's Edict of Toleration. This edict ended governmental persecution against Christians, which would seem like a good thing; however, in 325 A.D., the first creed—the Nicene Creed—was adopted by Constantine's universal council meeting to settle controversy over doctrine. Christianity held hands with the government to become a state religion. "Many passed from heathenism to Christianity by no other conversion than a mere change of name."[1] Pagan influences mixing with compromises on Jesus's teachings resulted in a watered-down Christianity.

Inside the church, some were incorporating practices from Judaism. Do you remember how often Paul warned the Church against Judaizing teachers? Their influence resulted in calling members of the clergy "priests," which resulted in the clergy being treated as superior to the laity, or common individuals. Paul also warned that those "among yourselves" would cause trouble, speaking specifically to elders in Acts 20:28. In the second century, members of many of the autonomous congregations in the Church started to hold up one elder above the others. These exalted elders, or "bishops," in turn began meeting in councils or synods. Those who presided over these meetings started to meet in other councils, creating a hierarchy.[2] Finally, in A.D. 606 A.D., one man was placed over the whole hierarchy with the title of "Pope." Beginning with Innocent III, the Pope was considered by many to be the "Vicegerent of God" and the "Vicar of Christ."[3] Wow! How far is that from the truth in the Bible? Sometimes we think the devil only works <u>outside</u> the Church. Quite the contrary, <u>inside</u> the Church is one of his favorite places to spread all his lies and pull us away from God's truths. We learn from the past what happens to a church when that old devil gradually pulls us away from the truth.

We Look Back to Learn What Not to Repeat.

History is not just fun for me; it deepens my faith. Paul affirms that the world is full of the evidence of God's existence

---

[1] Cox, *A Concise Account of Church History*, p. 37.
[2] Walker, Norris, Lotz, & Handy, *A History of the Christian Church*.
[3] Cox, *A Concise Account of Church History*, pp. 43-44.

when he asserts, "Since the creation of the world His invisible attributes, His eternal power and divine nature, have been clearly seen, being understood through what has been made, so that they are without excuse" (Rom. 1:19-20). For some, the study of science deepens their faith. Animals, plants, the earth, and the human body all point to God. In fact, increasing numbers are beginning to recognize signs of a designer in nature. However, the pages of history are where I find the answers to my questions. I learn from historians and archaeologists who look deeper into the history surrounding the events of the Bible, and attain overwhelming evidence that support its accuracy. I also learn lessons from the missteps of others. I can look back at history and see where man went wrong and started digressing away from God. Further, I can clearly see where men began adding to and taking away from God's inspired word.

Over a period of a few hundred years, the devil pulled the Church so far away from the New Testament pattern that it was barely recognizable. Paul warned believers that "in latter times some will depart from the faith, giving heed to deceiving spirits and doctrines of demons, speaking lies in hypocrisy, having their own conscience seared with a hot iron, forbidding to marry, and commanding to abstain from foods which God created to be received with thanksgiving by those who believe and know the truth" (1 Tim. 4:1-3). History demonstrates the accuracy of Paul's prediction. Much of this digression resulted from all those council meetings. Year after year new rules of faith were added that were not a part of the New Testament pattern. See what I mean about the value of studying history? You can tell if a practice has authority from God in His word or if it originated in the minds of men.

It's important to always remember that our mission to restore is both a God-given privilege and a responsibility. Paul said,

"But even if we, or an angel from heaven, preach any other gospel to you than what we have preached to you, let him be accursed. As we have said before, so now I say again, if anyone preaches any other gospel to you than what you have received, let him be accursed" (Gal. 1:8-9). The apostle Paul says to "Be diligent to present yourself approved to God, a worker who does not need to be ashamed, rightly dividing the word of truth" (II Tim. 2:15). As God's agents on a mission to restore, we need to carefully do our part in the restoration process, whether by planting a seed or by guiding someone to the truths in God's word. Restoring God's truths to the world is our goal. God will add people to the Church, but we must do our part in spreading His word. Satan thoroughly enjoys it when people add, take away, water down, or ignore God's truths. God needs our time and our diligence. He entrusted us with the truth; we have no right to mishandle it.

The *Reformation* was a movement in the 16th and 17th centuries that involved men who tried to bring disregarded truth from the Scriptures back to the light. A monk by the name of Martin Luther secured a copy of the Bible and basically began to say many of the religious practices of the time were not found in that book. Luther was soon followed by other brave men that went up against civil and ecclesiastical authority to speak up for a return to the Bible. However, these men and their followers often did not go far enough, wanting only to reform their given church instead of restoring the New Testament Church. In fact, many of their followers began to identify themselves by taking the name of their preferred Reformation leader, much to the dismay of the leaders themselves. Luther pleaded, "I pray you, leave my name alone, and do not call yourselves Lutherans but Christians..."[1]

---

[1] Schaff, *History of the Christian Church*, vol. 8, ch. 5.

John Wesley said, "I wish the name 'Methodist' might never be mentioned more, but lost in eternal oblivion."[1] Still the seeds of denominationalism were sown, ultimately resulting in hundreds of denominations. Satan was very active during the Reformation Movement. The last thing Satan wanted then and wants today is for people to return to God's truth; he works against every true restorer out there.

We Look Back to Observe Those Who Fought for Truth Before Us.

The "Restoration Movement" refers to a time during American history when people were again calling for a return to the Bible. However, this time it was with more force. The movement started near the end of the 1700's but had its greatest impact in the 1800's. I've always loved the 1800's. My family constantly accuses me of watching too much Little House on the Prairie. And my dad and I have always enjoyed swapping books and stories about preachers from the Restoration Movement. It's a connection we have. My dad promoted a love of truth in me through the stories of these people that fought so hard for the Restoration plea. In high school, a beloved teacher led me to a series of books on the Restoration called the *Search for the Ancient Order*, which I still read over and over. Restoration history even paved the way to meeting my husband: he was curious about a girl that loved to read about old preachers.

In addition to studying Restoration history, I love to find the graves of many of the preachers from the movement. It's like researching genealogy, except in this case it involves your Church family's genealogy. One of my favorite family trips was to

---

[1] Coombs, *The Basis of Christian Unity*, fig. 331.

Durham, North Carolina, where we were looking for the grave of James O'Kelly. He was an early American preacher who along with Rice Haggard, said that men should just call themselves Christians. The grave was located in a nice neighborhood nestled between some of the houses. My husband was afraid to park our old, worn-out van, covered with hail dents, anywhere near the houses, so we parked in an outlying cul-de-sac and traipsed down a path to the old grave. To me, that's a fun trip! On another trip to Fall Creek Falls, my children saw signs on the trail we were hiking that said, "Restoration in Progress." At the time, I did not realize that my children only knew the word "restoration" in association with my reading and grave-hunting hobby. They both asked why there were signs about old dead preachers at the top of Fall Creek Falls!

The Restoration Movement involved men such as Thomas Campbell, Alexander Campbell, Barton W. Stone, Walter Scott, Raccoon John Smith, and many more. These men called for Christians to "speak where the Bible speaks and be silent where the Bible is silent." They felt that human creeds should be abolished and that the Bible alone should be our guide. Congregations should again be autonomous, emulating the example of the New Testament. These and other principles led to a return to the New Testament pattern. I will note here that these principles were not being stressed only in a Restoration Movement limited to America. My uncle, a missionary to India, often reminds me that these principles were surfacing all over the world, calling for a return to the Bible. The Restoration preachers took many closer to the truth in God's word, but meanwhile, Satan did not go on vacation. He kept working throughout the Restoration Movement, and he is still working against all restorers today. He tries constantly to pull us away from the truth. Now more than ever, it is so important to understand how vital restoration is. Today Satan has a post-modern generation believing in tolerance. Our society tells us, "You believe what you believe, and I'll believe what I believe." The devil tells people to just have their own devotion. Some people will say, "I'm spiritual; I'm just not religious." He makes them believe that they don't need the Church to support and encourage them. In probably his greatest victory so far, the devil has this post-modern generation not believing in absolute truth. How dangerous is that! Ladies, we need the determination and the zeal that it takes to go up against our enemy the devil. We need to be restorers with a similar zeal as the Restoration leaders of the 1800's. Selina Campbell, one of the women from the Restoration Movement, said, "Old ways become new ways when long lost sight of and new things become old in one generation. But truth is eternal and unchangeable."[1]

In this book, I am going to take you back to the Restoration Movement. You may question my purpose in doing this if all we need is to go back to the truths in God's word. A friend of mine from college who had grown up under a denominational creed, but had come to the decision to follow the Bible alone, was worried about me. He just did not understand why I liked reading about old preachers and their wives. He worried because he knew that we should not look to a man or woman for truth, only to the inspired word of God. Putting any of these Restoration figures on a pedestal is not my intent. They had struggles as well as we do. We are all human; therefore, we all need to be discerning of who we look to as an example. Once I told my fourth-grade class they needed to be like the Bereans (Acts 17:11) and check their Bibles because even our preachers can slip. Little Janie with the cute little red pig tails went home and did exactly that. Monday came, and Janie's mother met me at the door to my classroom asking,

---

[1] Campbell, *Home Life and Reminisces of Alexander Campbell*, p. 331.

"Why did you have Janie checking on her daddy's preaching?" I explained, and we had a good laugh. Janie was a great example to us all: she was checking her Scriptures, and for that I was proud. The reason I want to take you back to the Restoration Movement is for you to catch a sense of the spirit of sacrifice and undying love, the dedicated commitment and the awe-inspiring zeal these Restoration figures had towards bringing truth to others. This is the zeal we need to have. This is the zeal towards truth we want our children to possess. This is my purpose in looking back at the Restoration Movement.

The author (and children) at the grave of James O'Kelly, Durham, North Carolina (11/2011)

We Look Back to Be Ever Mindful of Our Mission to Restore.

Do we keep our mission to restore at the forefront of our minds? We can't influence others unless our mission is ever before us. Reading about women who have fought for truth ahead of us may be one way that helps you keep the need for restoration in mind.

Former Restoration leaders and biographers of the Restoration Movement believed that it is important to look at the lives of those who have lived before us. James E. Scobey said this about Charlotte Fanning:

> The influence of a life so consecrated to the good of mankind does not lose its power because one may die. It flows on and on, with, or maybe, not so intensive a force, but with ever-broadening waves, toward the shores of eternity.[1]

Scobey also said:

> For what she was and did her name and fame should be cherished by us now living, and we trust it will still be revered by many yet unborn. It is a pleasing labor to recount the noble attributes of our loved and lost.[2]

Alexander Campbell said:

> I have just been concluding that we ought more frequently to reflect upon those of our acquaintance, who are gone before us, recall their images, contemplate their virtues, moralize upon their frailties and whenever their excellences occur to our memory endeavor to make them our own.[3]

---

[1] Larimore, *The Life Work of Mrs. Charlotte Fanning*, p. 5.
[2] Scobey, *Franklin College and Its Influences*, p. 344.
[3] Richardson, *Memoirs of Alexander Campbell*, vol. 2, p. 652.

Hebrews 11:4, referring to Abel, reminds us that "he being dead still speaks."

Now, what do I mean by the title of this book, *Out of the Shadows*? Well, who did the restoring in the Restoration Movement? Was it just the men? The Bible tells us in Matthew 5:13-14 that <u>all</u> Christians are the salt and the light of the earth. Like salt, we are to preserve God's truth, and as light, we are to illuminate the world and restore truth in ourselves as well as in all those we can reach. Yet few books have been written about women restorers; their stories remain in the shadows.

I have enjoyed many teacher field trips with the East Tennessee Historical Society, and it seems that at almost every historical site we visited in East Tennessee, there was a plaque stating that a group of ladies restored or kept that site from ruin. Fort Loudon and Blount Mansion are two places in Knoxville that have been restored because of the efforts of women. Like these determined ladies restoring historical sites, determined ladies can be wonderful and very effective restorers of truth as long as it's within the parameters God has given us. Our role is not to be in the limelight leading a worship service, but God still gave us a mission to restore His truth in so many other ways. He has equipped us with special talents for our mission; however, some women do not realize what those talents are or how important they are. We need to recognize these talents and put them to use restoring this generation. I believe women especially can bring something very effective to the table in reaching this post-modern generation. Charlotte Fanning, one of our Restoration ladies, realized this as well about women of her generation. She said:

> Let the Bible have its influence in our everyday life. Lay up the precepts of God's word in your hearts, and let it mold your character. Teach its truths with earnestness and

simplicity. The life of women should be earnest. They are capable of doing good that others cannot effect.[1]

For women to realize what we can do on our mission to restore, I want to take you back in history to meet some of our Restoration women. I want to show you some of our sisters' talents and their effective ways of being female restorers as we discerningly take from their lives what we need to encourage us to be Restoration Women in today's world. Let's bring these women out of the shadows and observe how they sacrificed themselves for the Restoration cause through encouraging their husbands, running their farms, caring for their children and teaching the truth through their submissive examples, all the while not knowing when their husbands would return from their own crusades to teach the truth.[2] These women were quite remarkable. Let's pull them out of the shadows and spread their stories and their examples, so we may gain a portion of the zeal they possessed to help us on our own mission to be Women of Restoration today.

QUESTIONS

1. What are the benefits of looking back and studying the women of the Restoration Movement?
2. Why should we look back in history and study our enemy, Satan?

---

[1] Larimore, *The Life Work of Mrs. Charlotte Fanning*, p. 10.
[2] Phillips, *A Medley of the Restoration*.

3. What is the author's purpose for you in studying the women of the Restoration?
4. What is our mission as Christians today?
5. Is there still a need for the Restoration Plea?

Chapter 2

Elizabeth Rogers: A Woman of Submission (1792-1868)

In today's world, the word "submission" is very unpopular. In the 1990s, my husband and I toured the CNN building in Atlanta, and our tickets included admission to seats in the audience of a talk show called "Talk Back Live." The topic was on the (then) most recent statement put out by the Southern Baptists that women should submit to their husbands. Most of the audience that interjected into the discussion described submission as archaic. When my husband described the Biblical definition and the workings of submission within our family, one man was appalled and showed anger towards him. That day was an eye opener for us both.

The Greek word for submission is *hupotasso* which means, "to arrange under," "to subject to" and "to obey."[1] While the

---

[1] *Thayer's Greek-English Lexicon* (2003 edition), p. 645.

word "submission" may cause many women to crease their foreheads in disapproval, Scripture teaches that men and women—though equal in God's eyes—have certain roles. Even Jesus, our greatest example of submission, has a certain role. He has authority over the angels, yet He is in subjection to His Father. Part of our role as women is to submit to our husbands (Ephesians 5:22-24).

Those who think negatively on a woman's role to submit forget that Scripture also teaches that husbands are to love their wives as Jesus loved the Church (Ephesians 5:25). This is what helps the God-given roles run smoothly. If only the world understood this divine system! Submission seems hard and unfair when faced with an overbearing husband. Many wives then become frustrated, or even defiant, at God's command to submit. Some in these bad situations serve their overbearing husbands, but view their service as directed to God. These women are being the examples their husbands need, but it is a hard row to hoe.

It is a breath of fresh air to see a husband such as Samuel Rogers carrying out his role and loving his wife as Jesus loved the Church. It is also good for us to read about a woman like Elizabeth serving her Lord through submission to her husband. Elizabeth Rogers was a great woman of submission. She was submissive to her husband but ultimately to her Lord.

In order to get a glimpse of Elizabeth's submissive life, let's first look at the life of the man to whom she submitted. Samuel Rogers, born in Charlotte County, Virginia in 1789, became one of our early Restoration Movement preachers that proclaimed the simple gospel message and baptized 7000.[1] Rogers grew up with only the religious influence of his mother, a pious Methodist. When the Rogers family moved from Kentucky to Missouri (then

---

[1] Garrett, *The Stone-Campbell Movement*.

under Spanish rule), Rogers' father tried to get his wife to leave behind her Bible. Instead, she sewed it up in a feather bed to keep Spanish priests from finding the precious book she needed to read to her children.[1]

When Rogers became a young man, he started listening to sermons from various faiths. It wasn't until after his family's return to Kentucky and after his marriage in 1812 that he finally heard sermons to his liking from a man named Barton W. Stone. Samuel was about 19 years old when he heard Stone preach.[2] Stone is the Restoration leader known for having an "active part in the Cane Ridge and other camp meeting revivals of 1800-1803."[3] He is also known for signing the *Last Will and Testament of the Springfield Presbytery*.[4] This document declared that the presbytery of which Stone was a member would dissolve. Stone and the other signers decided that the presbytery's creeds would be put away, and the Bible alone would be accepted as their guide. It was also decided that they would only take the name, "Christians."[5]

Elizabeth, like Stone, had a strong spiritual influence on Samuel. Elizabeth was the youngest daughter of Andrew Irvin. Her family lived in Cane Ridge in Bourbon County, Kentucky, around the time of the Cane Ridge Revival. They were greatly influenced by Stone and others who were involved in writing the *Last Will and Testament of the Springfield Presbytery*. The Irvins soon turned from their Presbyterian background and decided to renounce the Westminster Confession of Faith and take the Bible

---

[1] Rogers, *Toils and Struggles of the Olden Times*.
[2] Richardson, *Memoirs...* vol. 2; Rogers, *Toils and Struggles of the Olden Times*.
[3] Ferguson, *Church History: Reformation and Modern*, p. 69.
[4] *Ibid.*
[5] Williams, "Stone, Barton Warren," in *Encyclopedia of the Stone-Campbell Movement*, pp. 709-710.

alone as their guide.[1] After meeting her future husband, Elizabeth, who was grounded in her faith based on Bible truths alone, began to pray for him. In his autobiography, Rogers later gave credit to his wife for leading him to the simple teachings of the Bible:

> But my young wife was especially pious. She was greatly interested for my salvation, and, by prayerful and continued efforts, was not long in leading me to the cross of that savior who had given her abounding life and peace.[2]

Elizabeth continued to be there for her husband during the War of 1812. Samuel Rogers fought under Major John T. Johnson, a man that would also become a great Restoration preacher. He made it through the war alive even after experiencing one skirmish that left him with seven bullet holes in his clothes.[3] Roger's soldiering years proved tough on him spiritually, causing him to leave the Lord for a time, but through her quiet submission Elizabeth helped her husband during this time of spiritual despondency and tough family decisions. Rogers wrote that it was Elizabeth and her love for the New Testament that renewed his interest in religion and influenced him to serve his Savior through preaching.[4]

Leading with quiet submission can be so powerful. When it came time for Rogers to leave on one of his first preaching tours, he described the scene this way:

> My faithful Christian wife approached me with tearful eyes, but a heavenly and triumphant smile lighted up her face as she said. "My dear husband, why are you so

---

[1] Rogers, *Toils and Struggles of the Olden Times*.
[2] *Ibid.*, p. 27.
[3] Garrett, *The Stone-Campbell Movement*.
[4] Rogers, *Toils and Struggles of the Olden Times*.

desponding, and what occasion do you now have to weep? Did you not leave me, and enlist to fight the battles of your country, with little hope of even earthly reward? How much better is it now, that you go, with a brave heart to fight the battles of king Jesus, with the promise of the life that now is and of that which is to come!" With such words of encouragement, I felt my manhood return, and, after we had all bowed in prayer and exchanged a few words of parting, we set out upon our journey…[1]

Elizabeth Rogers followed the same motto that her husband did: "My Master first, then others." Rogers learned this lesson from a slave he once met by a spring. When he asked for a drink from his cup, the slave said, "If you please, sir, when I have served my master."[2] Elizabeth and her husband made this concept the rule in both their lives.

Elizabeth also demonstrated her submissiveness by truly listening to her husband when discussing family moves, keeping in mind her Lord and Savior's will at all times. After one preaching tour Rogers came home and recounted each event for his wife:

> My wife listened with profound attention to the detailed account of my journey and the providence attending it, and at once expressed herself as agreeing with me in conclusion that the Lord had really called me and was directing my course.[3]

The couple discussed a move from Bourbon County, Kentucky, to a work in Ohio. Rogers later wrote, "She said she was

---

[1] *Ibid*, p. 40.
[2] Garrett, *The Stone-Campbell Movement*, p. 292.
[3] Rogers, *Toils and Struggles of the Olden Times*, p. 46.

willing to go with me to my new field of labor—counting all things but loss for Christ."[1]

Elizabeth was submissive despite her circumstances. Upon moving to Ohio, she found herself in a "common" log cabin, chinked and daubed with clay. Samuel described it in his autobiography as "rough" but "comfortable," and went on to say, "We had no right to complain of our humble dwelling, for many of the old prophets had not one half as good as ours, and our Redeemer had none at all."[2]

Through Elizabeth's submission to her husband and her Lord, she won great respect from her husband. Rogers bragged on his wife extensively in his writings:

> [Elizabeth] did more than all the rest to support me in my struggles in this holy warfare... When she found me in the least desponding, she had always words of encouragement to offer. I do not now remember to have heard, in all my life, an unpleasant or discouraging word from her lips. No matter how long I might have been absent, or how much I had overstayed my time, she had no word of reproach at our meeting, but always a smile and a cordial welcome.[3]

Rogers boasted of his wife's talents. He thought her to be a diligent spinner and weaver even with difficult material. She was very talented in making all the clothing for her large family and in managing the household. Rogers used the word "industrious" to describe Elizabeth's ability to "support a large family" as well as he could himself.[4] Nevertheless, she must have felt blessed

---

[1] *Ibid.*
[2] *Ibid.*, p. 47.
[3] *Ibid.*, p. 54.
[4] *Ibid.*

when brethren would gift extra bushels of grain or made contributions to the preacher's family at hog killing or sugar-making time.[1] Samuel also bragged of Elizabeth's insight in managing guests. She always knew what their company needed. Samuel said:

> I am inclined to think that he [Brother Raines] was partial to my house because my wife understood better than most women the kind of entertainment a young preacher ought to have. She knew that he enjoyed his books and needed some time alone, so she didn't try to entertain him every minute of his stay.[2]

In Rogers's eyes, Elizabeth was also an excellent mother to her ten children. He believed deeply in the potential for women to change the world. He said:

> We should remember that the effects of a mother's training and influence are not felt alone in the limits of her own household, but also far and wide in society, and extend to all generations, and into boundless eternity.[3]

The Rogers' boys loved their mama but were also afraid to disobey her will. Samuel described Elizabeth's ability to guide their boys as a "rare faculty."[4]

Another way Elizabeth chose to submit to her husband was by providing what he needed during his ailments of body, heart, and mind. Rogers describes how, during one period of sickness, his wife helped to prop him up in bed and held a candle for him so he could write poetry during one of his irresistible urges to

---

[1] Garrett, *The Stone-Campbell Movement*.
[2] Rogers, *Toils and Struggles of the Olden Times*, p. 125.
[3] *Ibid.*, p. 113.
[4] *Ibid.*, p. 54.

compose. Another time, when Rogers was thrown from his horse, he expressed that, while Elizabeth truly felt sorry for his pain, he was proud to say she looked for the hand of God even in his affliction.[1] When Rogers' humble disposition led him to struggle with feeling that he was unworthy to preach God's word, Elizabeth was there for him: "My faithful wife with ever vigilant eye, discovered my despondency, and administered to my poor heart the very consolations that I had administered to others."[2] Elizabeth said:

> Why should we be cast down? Has not the Lord done great things for us; whereof, we should be glad? Has not his gospel been powerful to our salvation? Have not multitudes been brought to repentance by your preaching? What more should you expect from the Lord than what he has done? Suppose you have been deceived as to your impressions; what of that? Are not all men liable to be deceived? The Lord has not deceived you. Man may have done so, or you may have done so yourself. You know that the promises of God are yea and amen. Has any promise failed you? Besides, you are not your own, but are bought, even with the precious blood of Christ; and therefore, you are to serve Him. You are called to be a doer of good; to let your light shine; to improve your talents, whether one or five: to teach; to warn, to exhort. This much, in his Word, God calls on you to do, and, on the great day, he may ask you, should you now give up your work, "Why have you been all the day idle?"[3]

At times Rogers also struggled between his heartfelt duty to preach and his duty to his family, but Elizabeth's quiet submissiveness was always there. Referring to a time in their lives when

---

[1] *Ibid.*
[2] *Ibid.*, p. 92.
[3] *Ibid.*

they were struggling financially, Rogers said, "My family more needful of my attention than ever before—what was I to do? This question became the subject of my most earnest prayers. No man ever toiled, day after day, under greater embarrassment, than I did for more than a year."[1] Rogers had to turn down many pressing calls to preach to take care of his family during that year.[2] Elizabeth was there for him through it all, submitting to her husband and her Lord whether her husband was called to be at home or out reaping souls in the field.

In his writings, Rogers occasionally points out the admirable qualities of women he knew. The Rogers were close to the family of another great Restoration preacher by the name of Ben Franklin. Rogers said this of Ben Franklin's mother in regards to her intellect:

> Indeed, she was no ordinary woman. There were very few women in her day who had a better acquaintance with the Bible than she, or who had so bright an intellect. Her husband was sensible of this, and, when hard pressed in a controversy, had a happy way of getting out of trouble by calling to his aid his wife, who, with wonderful skill could turn the shafts of any common adversary.[3]

Rogers appreciated Elizabeth's intellect as well. He gave credit to women as being able to match or surpass men in intelligence. He would have probably understood reasons why women have pushed for their rights beginning in the 1920's up through the present. However, I think he may have also foreseen the negative consequences of the feminist movement for today's world. He once said:

---

[1] *Ibid*, p. 146.
[2] *Ibid*.
[3] *Ibid.*, p. 146.

> Talk of women's rights and privileges! All other rights and privileges sink into nothingness when compared with that of rearing warriors for the army of the Lord. Had Sister Franklin and my dear wife gone out into the world to occupy the public pulpit, the chances are that the six preachers whom they reared would never have been heard of, my sisters.... Think not that you are in any mean business when you are bringing up your children in the fear of the Lord. No! this is the noblest work in the world; and a mission a thousand times nobler than any known by those who are constantly croaking about women's rights.[1]

Many women today have forgotten that it is a privilege to bring up a child in the Lord because they are so consumed with the rat race. Elizabeth and her husband both knew that it's more about God-given roles than about women's inherent capabilities or intelligence.

Now, some may question Roger's view of the father's role in all of this, and surely he would not forget about the father's share of the responsibility. However, he believed that a mother's Christian role was indispensable. He said that experiences of life had taught him to

> ...look hopefully upon those children who have a pious and intelligent mother to instruct them and to look with distrust upon those children whose mothers are wanting in religious intelligence and Christian deportment. No matter how accomplished, how religious, the father may be; this cannot compensate for the defects of the mother.[2]

---

[1] *Ibid.*, p. 147.
[2] *Ibid.*, p. 112.

It is apparent in Rogers' life that he took fatherhood duties seriously, but he most definitely held motherhood and its duties in a lofty place of honor.

At a later point in Roger's career, he was pressed to stay longer on a preaching tour in Missouri. He loved his work in the open frontier and sometimes would be gone six months to a year on his trips to Missouri. It really troubled him to leave churches with no one to look after them.[1] He wrote:

> I knew not what to do: for I felt the force of their arguments, and appreciated their plea. But my family was large and needed my presence every day, and my poor wife had lived almost like a widow more than half her life. The fact that she had always been willing for me to go where the Lord called, did not relieve me, for I felt that I was imposing upon good nature. It was also true, on the other hand, that my family was among friends tried and true, who were ready to give any assistance needed, and that my wife, with the help of the older children, managed affairs about as well as I could have done; yet I was needed at home…[2]

Elizabeth listened to her husband's predicament and told him that she had decided long ago to leave his Christian duty up to him. She did not want to be a stumbling block in his path, but she did say that it would make her happy if he felt he could serve God's kingdom just as well at home. Then they prayed and talked some more until Samuel felt that his wife was pushing him to go and help the people of Missouri who so badly needed it. As Samuel left, Elizabeth said, "Go now, and the Lord be with you; but I hope you may, upon your return, be able to say, I have come

---

[1] Garrett, *The Stone-Campbell Movement*.
[2] Rogers, *Toils and Struggles of the Olden Times*, p. 169.

home to stay." Then she added, "The will of the Lord be done."[1] Again, Elizabeth always served her Heavenly Master foremost.

When the time came to leave Missouri again to go home, Rogers told the Christians there he would only return with his wife and family.[2]

> With this petition, I returned home, and was almost ashamed to show it to my wife, or to intimate that I thought we ought to consider it favorably, so gracefully and cheerfully had she heretofore yielded to every demand of a like nature. In due time however, I handed her the petition, and after a most solemn and prayerful consideration of it, shall I say she decided it to be our duty to go? Yes, to the praise of that woman, be it said: that woman whose first and highest aim always was to have the smiles and approbation of her God: that woman I owe more than to all others; that woman to whom the world is indebted more than can ever be repaid. Her comfort, her convenience, her pleasure, she was never known to bring into the account against her duty to God.[3]

The only change that Elizabeth made to the plans was suggesting they should stay two years instead of one to make sure that the work was in a good condition to be left.[4] Elizabeth Rogers was a true example of a woman of submission. Yes, she did have a husband that loved her as Jesus loved the Church, and we know that is not the case for all women. However, it is nice to see an example of a couple that understood God's roles for each of them and to witness their process in joint decision-making. But

---

[1] *Ibid.*, p. 171.
[2] *Ibid.*
[3] *Ibid.*, p. 206.
[4] *Ibid.*

most importantly, in Elizabeth we've seen a wife who submitted to her husband because she first chose to serve her King.

Rogers wrote these words just before he died in 1873:

> I shall greet first of all my Father, whose hand has led me all the journey, and my Savior whose grace has been sufficient for me in every day of trial. And next I shall look around for her whose love and goodness have imposed on me a debt of gratitude I can never repay. When we meet, shall we not gather of the children and grandchildren and sit down under the shade of the throne and rest?[1]

When God and His will is the motivation for our submission, like Elizabeth Rogers, we will reach far more people with the light of the Gospel than we could ever imagine.

---

[1] Phillips, *A Medley of the Restoration*, p. 33.

QUESTIONS

1. What does Scripture teach us about submission for men and women?
2. Compare your views and the world's views on submission to what Scripture teaches us.
3. How did Elizabeth's submission affect her husband and her marriage?
4. What was Elizabeth's motto?
5. Do we try to follow Elizabeth's motto today, or do we just talk ourselves into thinking we do?

Grave of Elizabeth Rogers, Old Cynthiana Cemetery, Cynthiana, KY (6/29/2024)

CHAPTER 3

Nancy Hurt Smith: A Woman of Character (1792-1861)

One might say that the majority of the Restoration women described in this book are women of character, but there is one who stands above all others. Nancy Hurt Smith, the wife of Raccoon John Smith, exemplified a character that was strong enough to shine through the story of her husband despite the fact that only a small amount of material has ever been recorded about her. Her husband, Raccoon John Smith, was one of the most prominent men of the Restoration Movement. In fact, many people today like to read about Smith's character (in a different sense of the word), his many antics and his crucial involvement in the Restoration Movement. Nancy was the bulwark of character Smith needed: she was the woman behind the man. She was the one who took a broken man and helped to restore the strength, wit and love that shaped his spirit—a spirit that almost single-handedly spread the gospel throughout the state of Kentucky.[1]

To understand Nancy's story, we first need to know the man she married. John Smith was born in East Tennessee in 1784, a time when the people called that area the State of Franklin. Due to restlessness and a desire for peace away from the unrest going on between the people of the short-lived State of Franklin and the State of North Carolina, Smith's father moved his large family several times. First, they moved to Powell Valley and then to

---

[1] Shields, "Smith, 'Raccoon' John," in *Encyclopedia of the Stone-Campbell Movement*.

Stockton's Valley near the Cumberland in Kentucky.[1] Smith's parents were hard-working people that taught their children to be the same. Smith followed his father around the farm helping with chores that went with pioneer life.[2] He was never in school more than six months out of his whole life, but he taught himself constantly through his intense hunger for knowledge and through his love for oratory.[3]

Smith grew up in a family with strong Calvinistic ideals belonging to the Baptist faith. After being taught that he needed to "experience" or feel the Holy Spirit touch him to become a member of the faith and to be sure he was of the elect, he waited and waited for his moment.[4] Smith eventually drove himself into intense despair over the pursuit of this sign from God. He just wasn't sure what he was looking for in an experience, and he was reluctant to accept anything that wasn't an obvious, outward show of the Holy Spirit. However, he wasn't quite sure about all this shaking, rolling, and running into trees like he saw at area revivals.[5]

When Smith moved into Wayne County near his brother, there came a day when he was at his favorite praying spot in a thicket, lying face down in the dirt, and felt a sense of peace come over him after praying fervently. Although still in doubt, Smith was encouraged by his brother to relate this experience to the Clear Fork Baptist Church and became a member. Smith then felt a deep desire to preach and once even exhorted in his sleep, only to be hushed by his mother warning him that he had not been called yet. Later, when he had a few close calls involving a

---

[1] West, *The Search for the Ancient Order*, vol. 1.
[2] Donaldson, *Raccoon John Smith: Frontiersman and Reformer*.
[3] Shields, "Smith, 'Raccoon' John."
[4] *Ibid.*
[5] Williams, *Life of Elder John Smith*.

rattlesnake and a runaway bull, Smith considered these near-misses to be signs and began to preach.[1]

Not long before this, Smith had met a vision of beauty, Anna Townsend, at a prayer meeting. John was not in the least skilled in the art of courting. At the age of twenty-two his encounters with girls consisted of possibly two attempts at talking with them. Nevertheless, Smith married Anna Townsend on December 9, 1806 and moved her into his drafty, unsealed log cabin in Wayne County. In 1814, after he and Anna had been blessed with four children, Smith hoped to better his financial situation by moving his family to Hickory Flats, Alabama. Instead, tragedy hit.[2]

One day while Smith was away from home visiting with old friends of his father's, Anna was also called away to tend a sick neighbor; she left her three older children with her brother and sister who had traveled with them to Alabama. Anna was unaware of anything being wrong until her eyes caught the glimpse of a blaze through the woods.[3] She rushed home only to find out that her oldest two, Eli and Elvira had perished in the fire "in the very bed where, at twilight, they had fallen asleep in each other's arms, with a mother's goodnight kiss upon their lips."[4]

Even after building a new cabin and trying to move on with their lives, Anna found the agony was too much to bear, and she was soon buried near her precious children. Smith also lost all of his money except for a few coins that he found in the ashes. On top of this, he and his remaining two children took sick. Friends carried the children away to nurse them in their homes while

---

[1] *Ibid.*
[2] *Ibid.*
[3] *Ibid.*
[4] *Ibid.*, p. 101.

Smith lay alone in his newly built cabin for months, praying for the Lord to let him die.[1]

What would have happened to John Smith if it wasn't for a young neighbor lady, Anna Miller, who came by the cabin and tended to him faithfully?[2] When the sickness got to the point where the young lady's father moved Smith to his house to die, John made it to the man's house just on the sheer hope of being able to drink a little water, which he had been denied on doctor's orders. Upon quenching his thirst, Smith fell into a deep sleep and thought that he had passed on from this life. However, he awoke the next morning and began to regain his strength. He had to be fed like a child for a while and developed a palsy that would stay with him throughout his life, but he did eventually recover.[3]

Smith blamed his experiences on his own desire for material wealth. When he grew well enough, he left his children in the homes of friends and traveled back to Kentucky a broken man, lacking the spirit he once possessed. Having already questioned the subject of God's elect and the process of election before the loss of his precious children, Smith now agonized over it.[4] Soon after arriving in Kentucky, Smith was urged to attend the Tate's Creek Association meeting. Upon arrival John Smith

> …wore a pair of homespun pantaloons, striped with copperas—loose enough, but far too short for him—a cotton coat, once checked with blue and white, but now of undistinguishable colors; they had been given to him in Alabama. His shapeless hat was streaked with sweat and dust. His socks, too large for his shrunken ankles hung down upon his foxy shoes. His shirt was coarse and dirty

---

[1] *Ibid.*
[2] Donaldson, *Raccoon John Smith: Frontiersman and Reformer.*
[3] Williams, *Life of Elder John Smith.*
[4] *Ibid.*

and unbuttoned at the neck; his white cravax was in the coffin of his wife.[1]

When Smith rose to speak a few words to the assembly, only a few recognized him, and others started to leave at the sight of the "uncouth" man.[2] Therefore, Smith resorted to a tactic that may remind you of the ringleader at a circus: "Stay friends, and hear what the great Augustine said!" he proclaimed.[3] Some in the audience smiled at John but still attempted to leave. Smith raised his voice louder than before and asked, "Will you not stay and hear what the great Cato said?"[4] Eventually there was a glimmer of recognition on more and more of the faces in the crowd. Smith said:

> I am John Smith from Stockton's Valley. In more recent years I have lived in Wayne, among the rocks and hills of the Cumberland. Down there, saltpeter caves abound, and raccoons make their homes. On that wild frontier, we never had good schools, nor many books; consequently, I stand before you today a man without an education. But, my brethren, even in that ill-favored region, the Lord in good time, found me. He showed me His wondrous grace, and called me to preach the everlasting Gospel of His son.[5]

That day, Smith's spirit began to rekindle. Nancy would be the one responsible for turning that small rekindling into a full-fledged flame.

After Smith moved back to Stockton's Valley, where he brought his young children to be cared for by family, neighbors

---

[1] *Ibid.* p. 111.
[2] *Ibid.*, p. 113.
[3] *Ibid.*, p. 114.
[4] *Ibid.*
[5] *Ibid.*, p. 115.

began to worry over Smith's downcast spirit and the gloom still very noticeable in his being. Smith therefore, was encouraged to take a preaching tour through the wealthier counties to seek an opportunity to marry rich. He was appalled by the latter part of this idea, for he never again wanted to seek after material wealth and worldly pride. Besides, before Smith left on this preaching tour, he had already chosen Nancy, a poor girl from Stockton's Valley. Before leaving, Smith had given no indication of his wedding plans except to Nancy, and she actually played along helping her neighbors speculate about the outcome of his tour, keeping the secret safe.[1] I think Nancy understood Smith's feelings and even this small sacrificial act of character helped John begin to heal.

Smith preached until he reached home on December 23, 1815, and on Christmas Day, John and Nancy were married.[2] Williams describes Nancy as having a "quiet temper," a "robust common sense" and "one of the kindest hearts in the world."[3] Smith would later find out that marrying Nancy was one of the smartest things he had ever done.[4]

In 1817, Smith was encouraged by Jeremiah Vardeman, a long-time friend and fellow preacher, to take over the preaching responsibilities in Montgomery County. While visiting this county, he was also encouraged to relocate there.[5] Smith said:

> I have made it a rule never to engage in any important work, nor commit myself by any promise, till I have first counseled with my wife; I never knew a man to lose any thing by taking counsel of his wife. I must go home, then,

---

[1] *Ibid.*
[2] *Ibid.*
[3] *Ibid.*, p. 120.
[4] Donaldson, *Raccoon John Smith: Frontiersman and Reformer.*
[5] Williams, *Life of Elder John Smith.*

without saying more to you then this; I will talk with Nancy, and then give you my answer.[1]

Nancy, one to always put her husband first, refused to give her opinion. Smith, one who respected the opinion of his cherished wife, decided that they would both make a trip to Montgomery County and then decide. Nancy loved the people and the land, so plans were set to relocate.[2]

Before the move and on Smith's way home from Montgomery County, he stopped in Lexington to preach. Here a silversmith asked Smith to let him have any silver in his pockets to make a set of teaspoons for his wife. Nancy was very proud of her teaspoons of pure silver made just for her. She loved to honor her guests with the teaspoons while serving tea; the special addition to her plain table gave her joy. However, the sisters of the congregation began to think Nancy's precious gift too uppity and at odds with their way of living, while the elders believed that the teaspoons gave the appearance of the preacher's wife being a bad influence. Therefore, to keep the peace and to keep her husband's good name untarnished, Nancy put away her spoons.[3] John Smith's biographer, John Augustus Williams, said Nancy was "patient almost to a fault." She used "sound judgment," and she was "artless and unobtrusive."[4] Sometimes preachers' wives need to follow Nancy's example of sacrifice, patience, and wisdom for the sake of their husbands.

In March of 1822, while Smith was preaching at Spencer's Creek urging sinners to repent of their sins or face damnation, he was struck by a thought. He realized that if the elect, those

---

[1] *Ibid.*, p. 132.
[2] *Ibid.*
[3] *Ibid.*
[4] *Ibid.*, p. 559.

predestined by God according to Calvinism, chose not to believe, they would not be damned, and accordingly his preaching would not be true.[1] Smith stopped in the middle of the sermon and said, "Brethren, something is wrong—I am in the dark—we are all in the dark; but how to lead you to the light, or to find the way myself, before God, I know not."[2] Smith then went straight home to talk to Nancy, who was "so often his strength in weakness and his comfort in trouble."[3] After spilling out all of his jumbled thoughts, the couple went before their Lord in prayer to ask Him to shed some light on their troubled thoughts. That night, Smith made a promise both to the Lord and to Nancy that he would take the Bible as his only guide by thoroughly examining the Word. He would follow the Bible alone wherever it would lead him, not the words of any man.[4]

Smith then began a disciplined, nightly study by candlelight, sometimes staying up all night long before going out to work again the next day. Nancy was probably attending to his every physical need while her husband studied. Smith realized that the spiritual death taught by the Calvinists could not line up with being a free moral agent with the freedom to choose. During this time of pondering, Smith began to read *The Christian Baptist*, a paper edited by Alexander Campbell. Still true to his pledge to stand on the Bible alone, he observed Campbell and his writings with a very critical eye.[5] He travelled 30 miles to Flemingsburg just to hear this Campbell, an educated man who claimed no affiliation with any denomination.[6] In later years, Campbell made

---

[1] *Ibid.*
[2] *Ibid.*, p. 145.
[3] *Ibid.*, p. 146.
[4] Donaldson, *Raccoon John Smith: Frontiersman and Reformer.*
[5] Williams, *Life of Elder John Smith.*
[6] Donaldson, *Raccoon John Smith: Frontiersman and Reformer.*

this comment about Smith, saying that "Raccoon Smith was the only man he ever saw that a college education would ruin."[1]

John Smith then began to read the Bible again as if he were a child and began to formulate in his head a way to present its truths to the churches in Kentucky. Upon this decision, he sat with Nancy by the fireside one evening, and together they counted off the sacrifices they would have to make including family, friends, land debts that his Baptist brethren promised to pay, and their reputations in the community.[2] Smith, at age 34, and Nancy, 25, were ready to climb tall mountains for the sake of their Lord.[3] Nancy and her husband committed themselves that night to shed the light of truth to as many as they possibly could. Nancy's sound judgment and unwavering character allowed her to step out for the truth and for her husband. In the years to come, while Smith was out trying to unite individuals through the simple truth of the gospel, Nancy was left to care for the children and the farm. This was her contribution to their newly found commitment.[4]

Nancy was married to a man of wit and humor. Scott Harp, webmaster of therestorationmovement.com, likes to tell this story about Raccoon John Smith: Once, when Smith was late to a preaching appointment, he rode in on horseback among his audience, grabbing a nearby limb of a tree. Hanging there, he shouted, "Take heed, take heed!" Then, letting go, he yelled, "Lest ye fall."[5] Not many preachers would use a sermon illustration like that one.

---

[1] Phillips, *A Medley of the Restoration*, p. 18.
[2] Williams, *Life of Elder John Smith*.
[3] Donaldson, *Raccoon John Smith: Frontiersman and Reformer*.
[4] *Ibid.*
[5] Scott Harp, personal communication, Sept. 2003.

Nancy was usually one to play right along with her husband's antics. While going over a new translation of the Scriptures that Campbell had endorsed, Smith found a certain section with which he didn't agree.

> "Nancy," he said, "This rendering is wrong, and I will not accept it. They have not been faithful to the Greek."
>
> Amused, Nancy asked, "What in the world do you know about Greek, Mr. Smith?"
>
> Smith replied, "I may be a barbarian, wife, but I know something of the mind of the spirit. Neither prophet, nor apostle when moved by the Holy Ghost ever spoke or wrote one word of nonsense."[1]
>
> One time when Smith was out on a preaching tour, he only had time to ride up to the gate of his home without dismounting to drop off his saddlebags. As he approached the gate he called, "Nancy, I have been immersing all the week. Will you take these clothes and bring me some clean ones right away? for I must hurry on."
>
> "Mr. Smith" she said, "Is it not time that you were having your washing done somewhere else? We have attended to it for you a long time!"
>
> "No, Nancy," was his reply. "I am much pleased with your way of doing things, and I don't wish to make any change."[2]

Another time some young travelling preachers stopped for a night's stay. They were not aware of whose house they were at, and Smith had Nancy play along while they discussed the day of

---

[1] Williams, *Life of Elder John Smith*, p. 177.
[2] *Ibid.*, p. 238.

Pentecost in the book of Acts. The guests did not think it possible to baptize 3000 in one day. Smith said that he saw a man baptize 41 in 45 minutes one day:

> "Nancy, what was that man's name that done the baptizing up yonder on Slate?"
>
> Nancy said, "It was Smith," but then she let out a laugh, and the guests knew that they were at the house of Raccoon John Smith. They admitted that Smith's "rustic" appearance really threw them.[1]

Raccoon John Smith displayed more direct antics when circumstances called for them. Once he grabbed a Methodist preacher against his will and dragged him towards the creek. When the preacher said it was not his will to be immersed, Smith told him, "Did you not but yesterday, baptize a helpless babe against its will, though it shrunk from your touch, and kicked against your baptism?"[2]

Another time Smith spoke to a man whose children he had just baptized and called him brother.

> The man said, "Don't call me brother, sir! I would rather claim kin with the devil himself!"
>
> Smith replied, "Go then, and honor thy father!"[3]

Another instance of Smith's direct wit may have called for patience on Nancy's part. It occurred when Nancy travelled with her husband to the North District Association meeting at Cane Spring in 1827. They had just buried one of their children, and

---

[1] *Ibid.*, pp. 518-520.
[2] *Ibid.*, p. 235.
[3] *Ibid.*, p. 224.

they were exhausted from seeing the child suffer for weeks. However, Smith knew that he had to attend this particular meeting, because the Baptist brethren were going to bring forward the points in which they disapproved of him and his non-Calvinistic tendencies.[1] To Nancy he said, "Many things will be said against me, and no one will be there to defend me, or to speak a word for the cause we love. I must then go. But, wife, I cannot leave you here alone in your bereavement; so I beg you to go along with me."[2] Smith's biographer, Williams, said, "Call it not weakness, if, in that dark hour, John Smith, forsaken by friends and afflicted of God, turned to his stricken wife for comfort and support."[3] Nancy had the character to support her husband despite her loss and the worry of having to leave the other five children (all aged 10 and under) in the care of her brother.[4]

At the meeting, there was much ill will towards her husband, and it made Nancy feel uncomfortable and fretful as charges of Smith's departure from traditional ways were brought before the Association. Beginning at this meeting, Smith made it a practice not to stay with friends overnight but to stay with the enemy, which in this case was Elder David Chenault, the moderator of the meeting. After dealing with ill feelings towards her husband all day I'm sure the last thing Nancy wanted to do was impose upon someone with those feelings to put them up for the night especially without an invitation.[5]

> "They [the Chenaults] do not want you to go, Mr. Smith," said Nancy.

---

[1] *Ibid.*
[2] *Ibid.*, p. 181.
[3] *Ibid.*
[4] *Ibid.*
[5] *Ibid.*

"I know it, Nancy," Smith replied, "and that is one reason why I want to go." "But, I have not been invited, and, of course, they will not expect me."[1]

Smith did not want to go against what Nancy thought to be proper, so he asked her if she would go if Brother Chenault invited her. Then he yelled across the crowd,

"Brother Chenault, I am going to your house, to-night; but my wife here says she is unwilling to go unless you invite her."

"Come along, sister; come along!" said he: "we have nothing against you."

"There, Nancy!" said Smith. "Brother Davy says you must come along. Now, let us go."[2]

Times like these Nancy may have had to use every ounce of her character and patience to be the wife of Raccoon John Smith. In years to come, Nancy would question her husband about his direct tactics against denominational creeds. He said, "Nancy, can I fill this tumbler with wine, till I have first emptied it of water? Neither can I get the truth into the minds and hearts of the people till I have first disabused them of error."[3] Smith grew strong in the face of opposition and used kindness as his best strategy, while Nancy used her character to support her husband in whatever way possible.[4]

The latter part of 1827 found Smith under probation from the district association and swimming in debt. Therefore, He

---

[1] *Ibid.*, p. 186.
[2] *Ibid.*
[3] *Ibid.*, p. 225.
[4] *Ibid.*

decided to stay home and try to get out from under this debt, but not without the help of his wife. Nancy used her frugalness and industriousness to work alongside him, saving on her own to help him. However, after the year came to an end Smith dropped his work apron at Nancy's feet and proclaimed to Nancy that he would not work anymore.

> Get whom you please to carry on the farm, but do not call on me! In all the land, there is not one soul to open his mouth in defense of the best cause under the sun! I am determined, from this time forth, to preach the Gospel and leave the consequences to God.[1]

In reference to Nancy, Williams writes, "Her zeal, henceforth, was no less than his; her sacrifices perhaps were as many and as great."[2] Nancy's character really came into play when Smith was away from home for so long. She helped to plan his preaching appointments that first week because she knew her husband would not be welcome in every home. Nancy found that from the moment her husband decided not to care about the association's probation, it was hard for him to get his mind off the Gospel. Even when she asked him to check on the fields, he sang "O tell me no more of this world's vain store, the time for such trifles with me now is o'er!"[3] Nancy happily accepted her new responsibilities of keeping the farm and family so her husband could devote himself to preaching, and being a woman of fortitude, she managed their farm with all her might. Once, when Nancy could not find hired help, she took the baby out to the fields alone and tended the scorching corn-rows, "nerved to her drudgery by the same spirit that was giving her husband voice

---

[1] *Ibid.*, p. 192.
[2] *Ibid.*, p 223.
[3] *Ibid.*, p. 239.

and power in the congregations."[1] Another time, Nancy was stirred from sleep by a stressful dream about her unharvested grain. A plentiful harvest was important with Smith being compensated very little for preaching. After kneeling by her bed and begging for strength from the Lord, she happened to look out on a field that was already harvested. Young Christians had answered her prayer and relief washed over her.[2]

Nancy was a trooper and pressed on without complaint. Even when Smith was home, his mind was in God's word; and at night he woke up, off and on, to study a word or text. Her husband was there physically, but mentally, he was often consumed by higher thoughts not of this world. When Smith looked back over that first year of bringing the simple Gospel message to the people of Kentucky, he thanked God and his wife for all their accomplishments, and after receiving his wife's consent, he continued to preach through 1829. At the end of 1829, Smith decided he needed to go back to work on the farm to be fair to his wife, but Nancy assured him she could handle the farm and was absolutely willing. Again in 1831, thanks to Nancy's *agape* love, Smith was able to continue his work through 1831 travelling around and checking on all the churches that had left their associations to stand on the Bible alone.[3]

In 1832, John Smith became a key figure in bringing together those who had been influenced by Alexander Campbell and those of Barton W. Stone. Both camps looked to the Bible as their only authority.[4] When speaking at the unity meeting between these two in Lexington, Smith concluded with these famous words:

---

[1] *Ibid.*
[2] *Ibid.*
[3] *Ibid.*
[4] *Ibid.*

> Let us, then, my brethren, be no longer Campbellites or Stoneites, New Lights or Old Lights, or any other kind of light, but let us come to the Bible, and to the Bible alone, as the only book in the world that can give us all the Light we need.[1]

The next three years, Smith travelled with John Rogers far and near to help unite the congregations.[2]

In June of 1833, John experienced a terrible battle with what some thought to be cholera. Nancy spent several fear-stricken months tending to her husband's sickness. She felt guilty for being hospitable to some travelers who were trying to get away from the cholera in their own towns and was afraid that she had exposed her family to the sickness, but John told her, "Nancy, you did exactly right, though we should all have to die for it. If we must die, let us die doing good."[3] Recovering from his time of sickness, Smith still spoke to people daily from his bed or within a few miles of the house, not letting anything slow him down. He also went into the water to baptize sinners almost twice a day.[4]

In 1839, Smith moved his family to Owingsville in Bath County and tended to his own crops, but he still preached for the same churches in Montgomery County to which he had been preaching for years. It was while living here that the Smiths lost their youngest son, Richard, who had fallen into a vat of boiling water during hog killing time. After receiving a message, Smith had hurried home with hope, only to collapse at the door upon hearing of the boy's death. The Smiths not only endured *this* event in their later years, they also went through a painful move

---

[1] *Ibid.*, p. 454.
[2] Shields, "Smith, 'Raccoon' John."
[3] Williams, *Life of Elder John Smith*, pp. 514-515.
[4] *Ibid.*

to Georgetown together. An unknown preacher arrived at Mt. Sterling and stirred up trouble with false accusations against John Smith. Withdrawing from the Mt. Sterling and Somerset churches was like saying goodbye to their own children. However, peace eventually returned, and Smith often went back to those churches to preach. Nancy used her character to support her husband through all of these hard times.[1]

Nancy Smith died on November 4th, 1861 in Georgetown. Despite little mention of her life, one can clearly see her keen sense in decision making, her vast amounts of kindness and patience, her quiet devotedness, her faithful sincerity, and purity of speech. She did nothing for show. She was hard working and a picture of neatness. She was the mother of eleven children, committed to her family and her God.[2] "It was through her heroic but unrecorded struggles with poverty and care, that he was at last known in the gates when he sat among the elders of the land." Nancy was definitely a "force of character."[3]

QUESTIONS

1. What is unique about Nancy's character? Does one descriptive word come to mind?
2. How are we like Nancy in regard to her use of the silver spoons? Would the use of the spoons be uppity or demonstrate a bad example?

---

[1] *Ibid.*
[2] *Ibid.*
[3] *Ibid.*, pp. 559-560.

3. Read Timothy 3:11. Do we as elders and deacons' wives follow different rules than our church sisters?
4. Do you think Nancy's more subtle humor helped her relationship with her husband, since John was so full of antics? Would you have the same character as Nancy in regard to her husband saying he would not work the farm?
5. Raccoon John Smith sacrificed a lot for the cause of Christ. Discuss a list of ways that Nancy sacrificed for Christ's cause and for her husband.

Nancy Smith's grave—Lexington Cemetery, Lexington, Kentucky (6/26/2024)

CHAPTER 4

Emily Harvey Thomas Tubman:
A Woman Who Gave
(1794-1885)

Emily Harvey Thomas Tubman lived from 1794-1885, a period when it was a challenge for a woman to be able to make financial decisions on giving. Nevertheless, Emily used the circumstances dealt her to bless the Church and many others in need. This remarkable woman gave from her heart. She was the type to give and give, and then turn around and look for more ways to give. She gave not only financially, but of her talents and her time. She was a Restoration woman to be remembered; she was a woman who gave.[1]

Emily was originally from Kentucky. She lost her father when she was around nine years old, and the great statesman,

---

[1] Nunnelly, *Emily Harvey Thomas Tubman: A Disciple Wonder Woman*

Henry Clay, became her legal guardian. Through the years, she grew into a young woman, and events started falling into place to lead this young woman to Georgia. One year while Emily and her family were vacationing in White Sulphur Springs, Virginia (now West Virginia) Emily met Mary Wares who became her dear friend.[1] In the fall of 1818, Emily desired to visit with Mary, so Nicholas Ware, Mary's uncle and adopted father, traveled to Kentucky to bring Emily back to Augusta for a visit. It was on this visit that Emily, 24, met and fell in love with Richard Tubman who was then a much older 52.[2]

Richard Tubman was an upstanding and well-known member of the community. He had come from Maryland in 1793 to Columbia County, Georgia to join his brother. The brothers bought their first tracts of land in 1802, and by 1833, Richard's sharp trading tactics had helped him to accumulate 2,250 acres in Columbia and Richmond Counties. His large plantation on the Savannah River consisted of fertile soil, excellent for growing rice, tobacco, cotton and indigo, and as a typical plantation owner in the South, Richard owned 65 slaves to work all of his land.[3]

With the Wares' blessing, the couple married within weeks of their first meeting. Soon after the wedding they planned a trip to Kentucky so that Emily's family could meet Richard. The decision was made to make this trip to Kentucky annually.[4] They could visit with Emily's family, but at the same time escape the mosquitoes and yellow fever during the height of humidity, typical of South Georgia summers.[5] As Richard grew older, the trip

---

[1] Ernst, "From Augusta to Africa, part 1: Journey to Freedom," *Augusta Chronicle*.
[2] Gifford, "Emily Tubman and the African Colonization Movement in Georgia," *Georgia Historical Quarterly*.
[3] Ernst, "From Augusta to Africa, part 1: Journey to Freedom."
[4] *Ibid.*
[5] Nunnelly, *Emily Harvey Thomas Tubman: A Disciple Wonder Woman*

also included detours to Warm Springs, Red Sulphur Springs, Mount Airy and other places of healing for Richard's asthmatic condition.[1]

In Augusta, the Tubmans were prominent members of society. The couple prospered through their plantation business, and Richard saw that he gave back to the community through projects like the Widows House Society.[2] Events hosted in the Tubman home were not to be missed. Emily was quite the hostess and entertained many important visitors, such as her guardian, Henry Clay. The event she was probably most proud of was the banquet she planned and hosted, put on by the city of Augusta in 1825 in honor of the Marquis de Lafayette.[3]

The Tubman plantation did not resemble the majority of plantations spread across the South. The people who worked on Tubman land were treated more like human beings and not as property. Emily once wrote that her and her husband wanted the slaves to work, "in their own time, for their own benefit."[4] She kept records of the slaves' cotton production and paid them together up to $1000 a year. Yet the Tubmans would do much more than this for their workers when everything was said and done, as we shall see.[5]

Emily was married to Richard Tubman for seventeen years before his death, which took place while on one of their annual trips home by horse and carriage, to Frankfort, Kentucky. Richard took sick, and Emily endured having to bury her husband on the side of the road. As Richard lay dying he requested that his wife promise two things: to continue making the yearly trip to

---

[1] Ernst, "From Augusta to Africa, part 1: Journey to Freedom."
[2] *Augusta Chronicle*, 2021.
[3] Ernst, "From Augusta to Africa, part 1: Journey to Freedom."
[4] *Ibid.*, p. 1.
[5] *Ibid.*

Kentucky and to free all their slaves. Emily agreed to both deathbed requests, but the latter may have seemed insurmountable.[1]

After Emily gathered her wits, she knew she had to make important decisions on how to go about keeping her promises to her dear husband. After finding herself the executor of her husband's estate, an incredible occurrence for a woman in 1836, she knew she needed to learn how to handle this new responsibility. Undaunted by adversity, she went to visit her brother, Landon Thomas, who worked as an attorney. From him, she learned business and law in a timely fashion. This intelligent woman who learned so quickly proceeded to do exactly what the man with five talents did in Jesus' parable. Emily expanded the plantation and the landholdings that her husband had left her, became a major stockholder in several banks, bought a railroad, and built a textile mill.[2]

Emily not only had to rely on her intelligence, but she also relied on her strong will to see things through, because it was quite a feat to free slaves in pre-Civil War Georgia. However, Richard Tubman had not doubted the abilities of his wife, giving this statement in his will:

> Now, in consideration of the unlimited confidence that I have in the discretion of my good wife, Emily H. Tubman, I do hereby constitute and appoint her my sole executrix of this my will with the full hope and belief that she will use every means in her power to carry every part of this will into complete effect.[3]

As instructed by her husband elsewhere in his will, Emily first went to the Georgia Legislature. She was to try and get a law

---

[1] Nunnelly, *Emily Harvey Thomas Tubman*
[2] *Ibid.*
[3] Ernst, "From Augusta to Africa, part 1: Journey to Freedom." p. 2.

passed in Georgia that would allow owners to free their slaves if they so decided. Emily was to take $10,000 and set it aside for this venture. Five thousand of it was to be used as an enticement to the state legislature. If the law was passed, then the remaining $5,000 would go to the University of Georgia. However, despite the University's need for the money, the bill was shot down.[1]

Having foreseen this turn of events, Richard had instructed Emily to take the entire $10,000 and use it to move their slaves to another part of the United States where they could be free. But here, Emily branched off from her instructions, knowing that true freedom anywhere in the U.S. would be hard to come by. Probably familiar with her former guardian's (Henry Clay's) involvement with the Colonization Movement, she began to educate herself on the whole process.[2]

The Colonization Movement was a push by a select group of Americans wanting to help African-Americans return to their homeland of Africa. Many believed that free slaves in the South would add unrest to the already troubled society at that time. It was not uncommon for others, especially slave owners struggling with their consciences, to speak out against slavery, yet still own slaves. This is why the Colonization movement appealed to Henry Clay, leading to his acceptance of the office of president of the movement.[3] He once said, "Can any humane man be happy and contented when he sees near thirty thousand of his fellow beings around him, deprived of all the rights which make human life desirable, transferred like cattle from the possession of one

---

[1] *Ibid.*
[2] *Ibid.*
[3] *Ibid.*

to another?"[1] However, it wasn't until his death that he freed his slaves.[2]

In 1820, President James Monroe obtained funds from Congress to establish the first American settlement in Africa, called Liberia. Monroe felt that the Colonization Movement would help to serve the law which required the slaves captured at sea to be confiscated from illegal traders. Liberia was chosen as a place to send them. Various states then started societies that organized trips to the 350 mile strip of the southwestern region of the African bulge. Emily demonstrated her wisdom in business by pitting two of the societies—the National and the Maryland—against each other to bring about the best possible situation for her slaves. Both societies were enticed by an owner being able to foot the whole bill and did their best to impress Emily. The National Society shipped people to Monrovia, named after James Monroe, but the Maryland Society shipped people to an area near Cape Palmas, which was a farming community. Emily wanted her freed slaves to have the best possible chance of success in their new life, so she put all the information about both societies before them and listened to their input. Some of the older slaves were partial to the Maryland Society due to their memories of Maryland, which was Richard's home state. Being sent to the area near Cape Palmas by the Maryland Society would also allow the slaves to continue farming, an occupation they were already familiar with. While the conditions in the unsettled area proved difficult for many, the Tubman people would be prepared to overcome. When the National Society moved too slowly for her taste after she gave them an ultimatum to meet her requests, it made

---

[1] *Ibid.*, p. 3.
[2] *Ibid.*

sense for Emily to go with the Maryland Society. She was a tough business woman.[1]

Once transportation arrangements were settled, Emily let her slaves decide between going to Liberia and returning to Tubman land to work for compensation. Forty-two of the sixty-five slaves fortified with pioneer spirit decided to go to Liberia and build a new life. Emily gave each man and woman two or three suits of clothes. Then she granted the whole group a shopping trip once they reached Baltimore. They spent $2,000 on mattresses, kettles, coffee pots, razors, tea, coffee, sugar, molasses and many other items needed for their journey and their start in the new land. The group named the town they founded Mount Tubman, after Emily and her late husband. The town prospered, and the Tubmans' freed slaves led the way for other groups that came to Liberia. They enjoyed the native resources of the land, plus they added their own cotton business. The Colonization Movement was pleased with the success story.[2]

Emily was ever concerned with the outcome of each of her former slaves. After living in Liberia for a while, one former slave decided he wanted to return to America, so Emily met him in New York and brought him back to Augusta.[3] Mindful of the future, Emily also put the remainder of the $10,000 into an account for her former slaves to use for any emergencies.[4]

History does not record Emily's feelings towards slavery. It is a hard truth that, although she carried out her husband's wishes to free their slaves, she continued to buy and sell other slaves after the deed was served. However, we can see that she was very kind to all her slaves, and changed the lives of all the Tubmans

---

[1] *Ibid.*
[2] *Ibid.*
[3] Nunnelly, *Emily Harvey Thomas Tubman.*
[4] Ernst, "From Augusta to Africa, part 1: Journey to Freedom."

of Liberia, thus changing the course of history.[1] In fact, one of the descendants of the group that she helped to send to Liberia—William Vaccanarat Shadrack (Tubman)—became Liberia's President and held office from 1944 to 1971.[2]

After fulfilling her promise to her husband, Emily turned her attention to religion. Emily had been reading Restoration leader Alexander Campbell's paper, the *Millennial Harbinger*, and she probably came in contact with P.S Fall and John T. Johnson in Frankfort, Kentucky. She was impressed with the New Testament Church they described. After studying her Bible, she decided to become a member of the Church in Augusta and quickly devoted herself to seeking ways to give. Emily gave money to Christian colleges and mission works. She provided the means to build numerous church buildings throughout Georgia. She also gave towards the preachers' salaries in many congregations. When the church building in Frankfort, Kentucky burned in 1872, she paid to rebuild it.[3]

A story has been passed down about another time when Emily was asked to donate money: Once, a preacher from a denomination came to Emily requesting her assistance with rebuilding a church building after a fire. Emily agreed to write this man a check if he "would honor only Christ in the name it should bear." In other words, she wanted this man to restore New Testament principles. The man was persistent in trying to convince Emily that "there is really nothing in a name." Emily finally handed the man a check. The man went straight way to the bank and handed the teller the check. Then he waited impatiently while the teller stared at the check. The teller said that he could not cash

---

[1] *Ibid.*
[2] NKAA, "Tubman, William V.S." in Notable Kentucky African-Americans Database.
[3] Nunnelly, *Emily Harvey Thomas Tubman.*

the check and that the bank was not familiar with the name on the check. The man didn't understand what the problem was. Mrs. Tubman was well known and dependable for her money. The man thought there must be some mistake. What Emily had done was she had one of her servants sign the check. The man straightway returned to Emily's doorstep and asked her why she did not sign her correct name. Emily simply looked at the man and said, "No, I have made no error. Did you not argue long and learnedly that there is nothing in a name? I only wished to convince you of the fallacy of your argument."[1]

After her husband died, Emily could have chosen to return to Kentucky, but instead, she chose to remain in Augusta and help her community there through her generous giving. Emily blessed the community with the first girls' public high school in Augusta. This school provided girls with the opportunity to take college-preparatory classes and not just domestic training courses. Tubman Middle School in Augusta bears her name still today representing the community's continuous pride in their benefactress. In addition to providing a school Emily had a number of houses built for widows and the elderly.[2] She created jobs for her community by founding the John P. King Manufacturing Company and continued to oversee the management of the Widows House Society founded by her husband.[3] During the hard years of the Civil War, Emily still helped all she could. She purchased Georgia's first ice machine for the benefit of the suffering soldiers, and she had housing built for Civil War widows. At the end of the war, Emily was there again for her community letting all

---

[1] Williams, *From Mounds to Megachurches: Georgia's Religious Heritage*, p. 46.
[2] Georgia Women of Achievement, 2016.
[3] *Augusta Chronicle*, 2021.

Confederate soldiers that needed transportation back home, ride for free on her railroad.[1]

Emily spread her charitable giving to Kentucky as well. She not only helped churches there, she founded a school for the under-privileged in Paris, and provided for those orphaned by Cholera by establishing the Midway Orphan School (eventually Midway College).[2] Emily continued "to bless mankind and to glorify God," through the charitable acts mentioned above and through many acts "of which she permitted no record to be made."[3]

Emily died at the age of 91 in the year 1885 and was buried in Frankfort, Kentucky. George Darsie, who personally knew Emily, mentions that she possessed a "sweet-spirited benevolence which filled her long life, even down to the very end."[4] Emily was always true to her community and in turn, her community did not forget her. In 1994, the city of Augusta commemorated a granite monument to Emily Tubman. This was the first historic monument in Augusta to be dedicated to a woman.[5] The community of Augusta continues to this day to be very proud of their historic benefactress and role model for young girls.

Emily possessed an unquenchable desire to give. When we think of Emily Tubman, we know we will probably never have the financial means to give as she did. Yet she reminds us to give what we have and to look around for more ways to give, to help those in need, to help the Lord's church and further the cause of spreading God's word to the lost. Emily is a Restoration woman

---

[1] Nunnelly, *Emily Harvey Thomas Tubman.*
[2] Morgan, *Emily Tubman: Christian, Emancipator, Humanitarian.*
[3] Darsie, "Mrs. Emily H. Tubman," in J.T. Brown (ed.) *Churches of Christ*, p. 443.
[4] *Ibid.*
[5] *Augusta Chronicle*, 2021.

to remember. Darsie would agree that her influence goes beyond the grave to future generations:

> The beauty of her giving lay in its cheerfulness and in the tender heart-gift that went with every contribution that she made. In consequence she found great joy and satisfaction in it. Again and again have I heard her say that it was the supreme happiness of her life. But the good she has done by her direct gifts, great as that is, seems to me to be even less than the good that she has done, and is still doing, by the unconscious influence of her great example. Being dead, she yet speaks to our whole generation, and proclaims the truth of Christ's great utterance, to which all human experience bears witness, that "it is more blessed to give than to receive."[1]

QUESTIONS

1. In today's world, Emily Tubman would have been called a tough business woman. Why was this description rare during her time?
2. Discuss ways in which Emily's strong will was evident. How was it demonstrated in burying her husband and carrying out his wishes?
3. Read 2 Corinthians 9:6-8. How does this passage of Scripture relate to Emily?

---

[1] Darsie, "Mrs. Emily H. Tubman," in J.T. Brown (ed.) *Churches of Christ*, p. 443.

4. How did Emily stress the importance of a name? Do you think there is importance in a name? Give an example from Scripture.
5. Discuss Scripture on giving. We may not be able to give in the same way or to the same extent that Emily gave, but how <u>can</u> we give to our church, our community, and beyond?

Grave of Emily Tubman Frankfort Cemetery/Frankfort, Kentucky (6/24/2024)

CHAPTER 5

MRS A CAMPBELL

*Truly Yours,
Mrs A Campbell*

Selina Campbell:
A Woman of Usefulness
(1802-1897)

Selina Huntington Bakewell was born in Litchfield, England, November 12, 1802. She was the only daughter among five brothers in the Bakewell family. In 1804, the Bakewells settled in Wellsburg, Virginia, a town where the famous Alexander Campbell eventually organized one of his early congregations patterned on the Bible alone. As a young lady, Selina attended this congregation and met Margaret Campbell, Alexander's first wife. Margaret suffered from tuberculosis and felt that her time on this earth would not be long. While setting her affairs in order, her thoughts pinpointed Selina as one worthy to take over as mother to her five daughters and wife to her beloved Alexander.[1] Selina must have stood out in Margaret's mind as a special young lady with a strong conviction to serve the Lord. That conviction was the source that fed Selina's life-long goal of leading a useful life. She whole-heartedly determined to be useful within all the spheres of influence in which she moved as sister, wife, homemaker, mother, grandmother, and writer.

Selina married later than most girls of her generation, perhaps due to her conviction to be useful within the married relationship to spouse and family. This in turn convinced her to search for the right Christian man. She had grown up witnessing strife between her own parents: Selina's father left the family to escape debtors' prison when she was about 14 years old.[2] Trying hard to hold out hope that her father would one-day return, Selina kept in touch, but, according to her father, he never seemed to have enough money to come home. Eventually Selina's mother began to develop a bitterness and indifference towards caring for her children. As a result, Selina took over the household and the care of her brothers at a young age. Through the years, Selina's letters to her father would come to no avail except to fuel Selina's conviction to lead a useful life for the Lord and not imitate that of her father.[3]

In her role as sister, Selina encouraged her brothers. Her brother Theron travelled with her father as he traipsed around from one city to the next. Selina worried especially about this brother during those years and would write to him of her concerns. Horatio, the second son, supported the family with his small glass making factory. Young Selina understood his burden

---

[1] Long, "Campbell, Selina Huntington Bakewell," *Encyclopedia of the Stone-Campbell Movement.*
[2] *Ibid.*
[3] Long, *The Life of Selina Campbell.*

and did her best to encourage his efforts. Through the years she also encouraged her other brothers in their education and life decisions. She also wanted to do everything she could to be useful to them as a sister.[1]

While attending the Wellsburg Church, Selina's conviction to live a useful life took another important step when she decided to be baptized. Alexander Campbell was the one who baptized her into Christ.[2] Selina became a sister in Christ so convicted towards the Lord and His mission for her that Margaret Campbell took notice. Margaret considered Selina a beloved friend and was comforted in those last days as Selina sang hymns by her bedside.[3] After her passing, Campbell recorded this epitaph of Margaret: "In truth a good wife, a tender mother, a faithful and affectionate friend. She lived the life of a Christian and died in the full hope of a blessed resurrection unto eternal life."[4]

There was no doubt in Selina's mind about what type of man she would marry. She wanted to lead a useful life for the Lord and not one hindered by a husband of unlike Christian goals and convictions. A few years before her marriage to Campbell, Selina was pursued by a man that did not meet her requirements. His faith did not come across as genuine, leaving Selina uninterested. Material wealth and social standing were not the keys to reaching this woman's heart.[5] Selina said, "I could not accept of his heart or his hand, because he was not a Christian."[6] Selina continued

---

[1] *Ibid.*
[2] Long, "Campbell, Selina Huntington Bakewell"
[3] Long, *The Life of Selina Campbell.*
[4] Phillips, *A Medley of the Restoration*, p. 51.
[5] S. Campbell, *Home Life and Reminisces of Alexander Campbell.*
[6] *Ibid.*, p. 327.

to wait for the right man, ignorant of her friend Margaret's request of Campbell to take her hand in marriage.[1]

In July 1828, Alexander Campbell and Selina Bakewell Huntington were married; they were 39 and 25, respectively.[2] According to Richardson, Campbell's biographer, Campbell chose Selina, "not only in deference to his first wife's earnest wish but in accordance with his own deliberate judgment, the wisdom which the future amply confirmed."[3] Selina was determined to be a useful helpmeet to her new husband, and she became his stronghold over the next forty years. She related to her readers in her book, *Home Life and Reminiscences of Alexander Campbell*, that the secret to wedded life was, "Never to become careless or indifferent to each other's happiness."[4] The couple communicated their love and appreciation for each other, and they looked out for each other's interest. Campbell would often convey his sense of loss while out on his preaching tours away from loved ones. In one letter he wrote:

> Amidst all the company which I have around me—and it is most acceptable and often greatly interesting—there is none that can fill the place of the mother of my dear children and partner of all my fortunes, good or evil. Strange relation! Wonderful Union! Certainly is a divine institution! God said it is not good for man to be alone. Alone in the midst of society I often am, merely because I am not all here. For the man is not without the woman, and the woman is not without the man in the Lord![5]

---

[1] Long, *The Life of Selina Campbell*.
[2] Harp, *Chronology of the life of Alexander Campbell, 1788-1866*. TheRestorationMovement.com.
[3] Richardson, *Memoirs of Alexander Campbell*, vol. 2 (1897), p. 243.
[4] S. Campbell, *Home Life and Reminisces of Alexander Campbell*, p. 333.
[5] Richardson, *Memoirs of Alexander Campbell* vol. 2, p. 458.

In another letter from Campbell to Selina on the 28th anniversary of his marriage to his first wife Margaret, he wrote words of reassurance to Selina expressing his deep affection for her and his gratitude for her support of his ministry: "You are my fellow soldier, my true yoke fellow, my partner in all my labors in the cause of religion and humanity."[1] Even in the small things, Campbell showed his love to Selina. Once, seeing her distress over a favorite tree being cut down, Campbell granted the tree a few more years of existence in order to please his beloved wife.[2]

Selina, in turn, was very proud of her husband and his work. She loved him and supported him in many ways both great and small. She would often be interrupted in the middle of her long list of household duties to listen to Campbell's readings.[3] Other times Campbell would give Selina a copy of each of his editorials for the *Millennial Harbinger* to read and comment upon.[4] Campbell respected her judgment, knowing that he could be sarcastic at times, and wished for her to soften or use a woman's delicate touch on any words that might offend anyone unnecessarily. He also respected her taste, for she was a lady of vast reading and culture.[5]

With great, unwavering faith in her husband's mission, Selina was the helpmeet that Campbell needed, both in the preaching field and in his teaching at Bethany College, a school that Campbell had established in 1840, in Bethany, VA (West Virginia). Selina was very proud of her and her husband's involvement in opening the school. The opportunity to teach the Lord

---

[1] *Ibid.*, pp. 460-461.
[2] S. Campbell, *Home Life and Reminisces of Alexander Campbell*, pp. 342-343.
[3] *Ibid.*
[4] West, "Selina Campbell: Keeper of the Home," in *Gospel Advocate*, July 2003.
[5] Richardson, *Memoirs of Alexander Campbell* vol. 2.

and His ways to so many young people was a great blessing. Seeking ways to be useful, she took on the job of sewing all the linens, and as the school years continued, she invited college students from Bethany to come to the Campbell home once a week for conversation and singing. She especially wanted the ones who were away from home for the first time to be comforted in her home. In 1857, Bethany College burned. Its burning was devastating to the Campbells, standing out in Selina's mind as one of the greatest difficulties she and her husband ever endured. The event challenged her to grow in ways she didn't know she could.[1] Usually Selina looked to her husband for support and admired his happy, cheerful, resigned peacefulness, while handling tragedies.[2] Nevertheless, when Campbell needed his wife's emotional support, Selina did her best to be there for him. The school survived the fire and the couple continued to bless students through their school.

Despite Selina's determination to be useful in all areas of her life, obstacles of life make it difficult to carry out goals at times. Selina often struggled with melancholy dips and might not have felt that she was the useful helpmeet that she aspired to be during these times. She especially needed her husband's gentle words of support after their greatest tragedy: of losing their ten-year old son, Wycliffe. Wycliffe, thought to be the one to follow in his father's footsteps, drowned while swimming in the Buffalo Creek near their house.[3] According to Richardson, Selina sunk into a devastating depression despite help from her friends:

---

[1] Long, *The Life of Selina Campbell*.
[2] S. Campbell, *Home Life and Reminisces of Alexander Campbell*, pp. 339-340.
[3] Richardson, *Memoirs of Alexander Campbell* vol. 2.

Overwhelmed with sorrow and unable to take any longer her accustomed interest in the household affairs, it was beautiful to see how gentle and subdued he (Campbell) was in his demeanor toward her, and how tenderly and encouragingly he addressed her. Seeking her always upon his return from college, he gave her as much of society as possible, and often, in the dusk of the evening, missing her from the family circle and suspecting that she had stolen away to weep at the grave, he would hasten to the cemetery to find her, and accosting her in the kindest accents, 'My dear,' he would say, 'my dearest Selina, the loved ones are not here they have passed beyond these earthly scenes to happier abodes;' and taking her arm with the most touching expression of sympathy and love, would lead her gently home. His affectionate condolence and the consolations of the word of God, which he constantly sought to impress upon her mind, together with the kindest expressions of sympathy from the brotherhood finally began to produce their appropriate effect upon Mrs. Campbell in imparting to her a greater degree of resignation.[1]

Selina made it through this valley in her life, but it didn't stop her from climbing the next hill with her single-minded determination to be useful.

From the start of her marriage Selina was committed to being a useful homemaker. As Richardson described, "It required no small degree of courage" to take over Alexander Campbell's extensive household.[2] Margaret Campbell had been raised in the country; Selina was a town girl. Therefore, she had to learn quickly, and that she did. She learned to cultivate a field and hire workers while coming across as a very decisive woman.

---

[1] *Ibid.*, p. 574.
[2] *Ibid.*, p. 295.

Campbell saw how very efficient she was at this, and never offered complaint.[1] Selina also stepped into the role of mother to four of Margaret's daughters, and later to six of her own children.[2] One of her first challenges was filling the role of nurse to the family. The first winter after her marriage, she had to deal with thirteen cases of measles within the household. Selina was more than happy to take on this responsibility, and many more, in order to help free Campbell's time so that he could fulfill his ministry.[3] Campbell began each day at 4:00 in the morning in his hexagonal shaped study built about 150 feet away from the Campbell home. Campbell was known to say that "all light, physical and spiritual, comes from above."[4] He wanted to employ "light from above," so the main source of light in the study came from a type of bell tower (minus the bell) with six window panes at the top of the roof. Later, Campbell had a fireplace and a side window added so that Selina could see him from their home.[5] Being able to see her dear husband fulfilling his ministry under the "light from above" probably encouraged her convictions to be useful in her own daily walk with the Lord.

Selina's homemaker responsibilities involved far more than her immediate family. She constantly came in contact with religious leaders, politicians and educators that would stay at their Bethany Mansion. James A. Garfield, Henry Clay, and Jefferson Davis were just a few of these guests. Bethany Mansion or the Brown/Campbell Mansion was built by John Brown, father of Campbell's first wife Margaret.[6] The home obtained additions through the years and one wing came to be known as "Stranger's

---

[1] *Ibid.*
[2] West, "Selina Campbell: Keeper of the Home."
[3] Richardson, *Memoirs of Alexander Campbell* vol. 2.
[4] Kenney, "Light from Above," in *Gospel Advocate,* March 2013, p. 39.
[5] *Ibid.*
[6] S. Campbell, *Home Life and Reminisces of Alexander Campbell.*

Hall" purposed for housing their frequent guests.[1] In those days a "strangers" length of stay at the Bethany Mansion could be as Selina described it, "protracted."[2] Nevertheless, Selina stepped up to the role of host without complaint. According to Selina, it was the desire of her and her husband to help their numerous visitors "enjoy a home feeling," and knowing the scriptural importance of "entertaining strangers" helped to lighten the load. Continuing this thought she wrote, "The idea with me was, while my dear good husband was feasting them intellectually and spiritually, it was my province to attend the wants of the body."[3] Entertaining well-known people in their spacious home also brought the responsibility of hosting dinner parties and sometimes big weddings. Once, just after a cook had resigned and her own children were sick, Selina still pulled off a successful dinner party.[4] A brother who owned a general store always came in handy, and I'm sure Theron was much appreciated by his sister when she was in a bind. In later years after the children were grown, Selina decided to travel more with Campbell and look after his health, but often the long trips would cause exhaustion. This brought on a battle against nerves and headaches while returning to a house commonly filled with visitors. Nevertheless, Selina would rise to the occasion and determinedly do what was needed to be useful in the Lord's work.[5]

To Campbell, home was a place of rest after traveling, but like the old saying goes, "A woman's work is never done." Selina's outlet was in talking with her friend Julia Barclay. Julia had been a missionary to Jerusalem with her husband James T.

---

[1] Long, *The Life of Selina* Campbell, p. 56.
[2] S. Campbell, *Home Life and Reminisces of Alexander Campbell*, p. 338.
[3] *Ibid.*, pp. 338-339.
[4] Richardson, *Memoirs of Alexander Campbell* vol. 2.
[5] Long, *The Life of Selina Campbell*.

Barclay.[1] Due to her husband's discovery of a gate on the interior, western wall of the temple, it is still today known as Barclay's Gate.[2] Another bit of history is the fact that Barclays were the first to own Monticello, after Thomas Jefferson's death. The couple kept the home a few years but sold it when their hearts began to tug at them to be missionaries. Selina and Julia not only shared their faith but had many close ties across their families. Selina's daughter Decima married J. Judson Barclay, one of Julia's sons, and Selina's niece married Julia's oldest son, Robert G. Barclay.[3] The close friendship between the two women fortified Selina, and she continued to strive to be the useful homemaker that would benefit her family and all who stepped foot into the Bethany Mansion for as long as she was able. She loved her home and cherished all the responsibility that went along with it.[4]

Selina also worked to be a mother and grandmother that God would deem useful on this earth. In turn, she imparted her goals of usefulness to her children and grandchildren. Campbell eventually lost all five of his daughters from his first marriage to tuberculosis (what they called consumption); it was the same disease that took their mother. Selina helped to raise four of these girls and suffered through the loss of these women in their young adulthood. To add to the list, Selina's first daughter, Margaret Campbell, was lost to consumption as well.[5] Of course as mentioned earlier the greatest emotional suffering that Selina encountered was that brought on by the loss of her precious Wycliffe. Selina was no stranger to death. In the light of the often short life spans of the times, Selina may have felt an urgency to teach her

---

[1] *Ibid.*
[2] Barclay, James, *City of the Great King*, 1882, pp. 489-490.
[3] S. Campbell, *Home Life and Reminisces of Alexander Campbell.*
[4] Long, *The Life of Selina Campbell.*
[5] *Ibid.*

children and grandchildren to live a life useful for the Lord. Campbell and Selina both had strong feelings about the spiritual education of their children. Campbell said, "Without this school (education) no system will ever meet the expectations of the world, the predictions of the prophets or qualify human beings for the high destiny spiritual and eternal which awaits them who walk in the paths of wisdom and virtue."[1] The Campbells' strong feelings about training up young people in the Lord resulted in many family devotions and many years of involvement with college students, but it also led them to take in a Native American boy from the Iowa tribe to educate and become part of their family.[2] Selina also took in her niece [Horatio's daughter], Emma Bakewell at age 10. She is the one who married Julia's oldest son, Robert. Emma named her daughter, Selina, after her dear aunt who influenced her towards the Lord.[3] Selina made herself useful in all of her motherly roles.

Campbell knew that women impart the earliest education and the important first impressions upon a child. In a letter to Selina in 1836, he wrote, "Remember, this is the great business of life, to transmit to those, and through those to whom you have given birth, the knowledge of God and of his Anointed for their sakes and for the good of theirs yet unborn."[4] We know that Selina took these words to heart and continued her efforts with her children even after they left the home, as is evident throughout the Campbell family letters. When Selina's first daughter left for college, Selina would write to her and encourage her to continue

---

[1] A. Campbell, "Schools and Education, No. II," in *Millennial Harbinger,* June 1839, p. 280.
[2] Richardson, *Memoirs of Alexander Campbell* vol. 2.
[3] Long, *The Life of Selina* Campbell, pp. 60-61.
[4] Richardson, *Memoirs of Alexander Campbell* vol. 2, p. 412.

in her "love of Truth" and in her "affectionate disposition."[1] She made it clear to Margaret that her character was far more important than her studies. We also learn from Selina's letters to her son William that she reminded him, "Without a moral cultivation, you have heard your father say; all learning in the world would be of no account."[2] Selina thought, "Many can be made worse by being what is called educated without having the heart and the affections rightly trained."[3] Selina tried to impart this wisdom to each of her children. However, because of individual freedom of choice her girls chose the Church and her boys did not.[4]

Selina continued to be a great example to her grandchildren. She especially spent a lot of time with her granddaughter Virgie, Decima's oldest daughter. Once when Virgie was a toddler, she ate poisonous cherries, but thanks to her well-read grandmother she was saved. Selina poured mustard, hot water, and diluted lobelia into the small child, and then later used mustard poultices. Another time, Selina was needed again at the home of Decima after her daughter became overly weak from childbirth. By that time, Virgie had developed a form of polio, and her loving grandmother patiently helped the young child with her braces while talking to her about God. Virgie was blessed to live long enough to attend Hamilton Female College, but she was especially blessed in those precious hours spent with her grandmother. Selina did her best to prove useful to all her grandchildren, and she did her best to educate them in being useful for the Lord.[5]

---

[1] S. Campbell, 1843, as cited in Long, *The Life of Selina* Campbell, pp. 129-130.
[2] S. Campbell, 1857, as cited in Long, *The Life of Selina* Campbell, p. 190.
[3] S. Campbell, 1858, as cited in Long, *The Life of Selina* Campbell, p. 190.
[4] Long, *The Life of Selina Campbell*.
[5] *Ibid.*

Alexander Campbell passed away on March 4th, 1866. The events of Campbell's last few days were preserved by Selina's daughter-in-law in her diary. During those days it was very hard to pull Selina away from Campbell's bedside. When she asked if he was in pain, he responded, "No, No only sorry for you, sorry for you." Keeping a cheerful attitude all the way to the end, Campbell said, "Why, mother I was just about to advertise you to find your whereabouts" when Selina had been out of the room for just a short while.[1] At the end, Selina said, "The blessed Savior will go with you through the valley of the shadow of death," and he said, "That he will, that he will."[2]

In her later years, Selina spent a lot of time going back and forth between her beloved Bethany Mansion and Decima's home in Alabama. Her dear friend Julia had gone to live with her children in Alabama during her twilight years, and the two would frequently sit on the front porch reading and quoting the Bible together as they sewed for their grandchildren.[3] However, Selina did not retire entirely to the rocking chair on that porch in Alabama. After Campbell's passing and after Selina had suffered through the worst part of her grieving, she determined to make her later years useful to the Lord in ways she may not have foreseen in her younger days. Selina decided to become a writer. She was convinced that, through the written word, she could reach others and touch their lives with the gospel message, and she believed that the story of her husband's life would accomplish this. She had never thrown away anything connected to her husband and she gave boxes and boxes of letters to Robert Richardson,

---

[1] Richardson, *Memoirs of Alexander Campbell* vol. 2, p. 677/
[2] S. Campbell, *Home Life and Reminisces of Alexander Campbell*, p. 502.
[3] Long, *The Life of Selina Campbell*.

whom she greatly aided in his two-volume work, *The Memoirs of Alexander Campbell.*[1]

Selina went on to write her own book entitled, *The Home Life and Reminisces of Alexander Campbell*, which included many personal insights into this great Restoration leader that the world may have never known without her. One example of this is a description of his table talk. When Campbell spoke at the dinner table, all would listen. According to Selina, "It was never wearisome or monotonous; all felt a kind of inspiration or fascination indescribable."[2] If a candle was accidently put out at the table, Campbell would speak about the value of light. Then he might discuss the eye and the importance of the eyelash, followed by a lecture on how the eye adapts to the light of the candle. No one would complain, but this is not to say that Campbell hoarded all the time at the table. After a while he would say, "Now, we will turn down the leaf and give place to the next generation."[3] Selina added personal descriptions of Campbell's patience, his love for children and his "proverbial kindness to animals." Sometimes it would surprise Campbell's visitors to see him taking out plates of food to a shepherd dog that frequented from a nearby house.[4] Selina also recorded excerpts that described Campbell's demeanor in his later years:

> On walking from bed to the fire some portion of Scripture or a hymn would be uttered, and while I would be engaged in bathing his feet he would exclaim, 'Only think my dear how many thousands of miles those feet have carried me, and I have never had a broken bone!' Then he would burst forth in expressions of gratitude and

---

[1] *Ibid.*
[2] S. Campbell, *Home Life and Reminisces...*, p. 338.
[3] *Ibid.*
[4] *Ibid.*, p. 329.

thankfulness for the Father of mercies for the manifold favors so long enjoyed from His gracious hand, so that his heart overflowed with love and gratitude.[1]

Selina wanted her writing to stand up against anything that did not represent the truth.[2] Deciding not to work through the different ladies' societies of the 1800's, she began to submit her writing to various journals. Selina really pushed for a stand on the Bible alone and its authority in 1880 when she wrote an article for the Christian Standard against women preaching. She wrote: "Can a 'thus saith the Lord' be adduced for the practice? If it can, where is it?"[3]

Selina also wrote to encourage. Of course, her favorite topic of writing was "The useful life." She felt that people of all ages wasted time that they could be using to improve themselves.[4] She wrote, "If we cannot do some great work, we can certainly find minor things to engage our hearts, and employ our hands in matters of usefulness for the Master's house, the church which is the pillar and support of the truth."[5] She liked to point out that the poor widow was "distinguished over the whole world" for her two mites, and she emphasized that women could sacrifice by setting money aside to donate for missions instead of saving it to spend on jewelry. Selina continued by writing, "Cannot we as Christian women deny ourselves something to have to give to the Lord?"[6]

Many editors respected Selina's writing. An editor of the *Memphis Appeal* said she was a woman who "employs all her

---

[1] *Ibid.*, pp. 339-340.
[2] *Ibid.*
[3] *Ibid.*, p. 402.
[4] Long, *The Life of Selina Campbell.*
[5] S. Campbell, "Woman's Work," *Christian Standard,* July 1878, p. 238.
[6] *Ibid.*

spare moments in doing good and setting an example of womanly endeavor in the cause of Christ."[1] The same editor shared that Selina's authority as an author came in part from her own hard work and not from the fact that she was Campbell's wife.[2] In his tribute to Alexander Campbell, E.K. Washington, once a tutor to the Campbell children, was surprised that in all the other tributes to this great man, there was not more mention of Selina. He said if Campbell could look down "from his glorious home in Heaven and look once more on the scenes of his labors he would say he could not have been what he was but for her."[3]

Selina stayed mentally sound, well into her 90's.[4] When she attended service at the Bethany church she sat on the second row supporting her elbow on the partition between the pews and holding her ear trumpet as she listened intently. The Bethany church knew to present their best when she was in attendance. This meant no instrument.[5] Selina also enjoyed visiting the college. She even had the opportunity to come on stage at one of her granddaughter's graduations to give her a hug, contributing to a very touching scene for all to see.[6] Selina was respected for the life she lived, and she did indeed achieve her convictions to be useful. In a letter addressed to her son, William, Selina made the comment that she was "happy to remember that I have valued the time allotted to me."[7] Selina felt that she had been useful while on her earthly journey. She was useful in all her spheres of

---

[1] "Mrs. Alexander Campbell," from the *Christian Standard*, June 1874, p. 187.
[2] Long, *The Life of Selina* Campbell, pp. 165-166.
[3] Washington, "In Memory of Alexander Campbell," *Millennial Harbinger*, December 1866, p. 530.
[4] Long, *The Life of Selina Campbell*.
[5] Scott Harp, personal correspondence.
[6] Long, *The Life of Selina Campbell*.
[7] S. Campbell, 1892, as cited by Long, *The Life of Selina* Campbell, p. 185.

influence, as sister, wife, homemaker, mother, grandmother and writer. Let's all strive to feel the way Selina did when it is time for the Master to call us home, and may He say, "Well done, good and faithful servant" (Matthew. 25:21).

QUESTIONS

1. If Campbell's first wife, Margaret, had not been such a selfless person, do you think Selina's and Alexander's lives would have been different?
2. Selina's mother was bitter about her own marriage relationship. Why do you think Selina was not bitter about relationships?
3. What did Selina say was the secret to wedded life?
4. Selina was determined to be useful. What proof do we have that she succeeded?
5. Why do you think Selina felt such a great urgency to teach her children and grandchildren to live a useful life for the Lord?

Grave of Margaret Campbell, God's Acre Cemetery/Bethany, WV (6/28/2024)

Selina's pew with armrest at Bethany Church of Christ

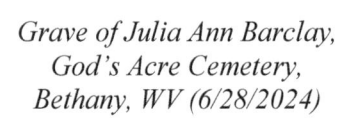

Grave of Julia Ann Barclay, God's Acre Cemetery, Bethany, WV (6/28/2024)

Grave of Decima Campbell Barclay, God's Acre Cemetery, Bethany, WV (6/28/2024)

Grave of Selina Campbell, God's Acre Cemetery, Bethany, WV (6/28/2024)

*Grave of Virgie Barclay, God's Acre Cemetery, Bethany, WV
(6/28/2024)*

Chapter 6

**Charlotte Fall Fanning:
A Woman Who Loved to Teach
(1809-1896)**

The historian Earl West asserts, "Unquestionably the most influential preacher in the Southland before the War Between the States was Tolbert Fanning."[1] He was a man whose custom it was to decide slowly what was right and then to throw everything he had into what he believed.[2] All this and more could be said about his wife, Charlotte Fanning. James Scobey, a biographer of Charlotte Fanning, said, "He could preach, she could sing; he could

---

[1] West, *Search for the Ancient Order*, vol. 1, p. 108.
[2] *Ibid.*

argue, she could persuade."[1] Emma Page Larimore, a student of Mrs. Fanning's said, "...her Christian character—her sweetness of manner, her firmness, her unfailing charity toward the failings of others, her earnest desire to help every soul with whom she came in contact to attain to lofty motives and upright life. I am glad to aid in any way in perpetuating the influence of such a life as hers."[2] In personal study, Charlotte Fanning has influenced me more than any other woman from the Restoration. She was truly a woman who taught for the Lord and a teacher who loved to teach. As a fellow teacher I feel compelled to share her significant influence with you.

Teaching was in Charlotte Fanning's blood. Born near London, England on April 10, 1809, Charlotte travelled with her family over the Atlantic to Kentucky later in her childhood.[3] Soon after arriving, her mother died after the birth of her eleventh child, and her father's death soon followed. At age 19 the oldest son, Philip S. Fall, found himself responsible for his large family. Acting as executor of his father's will this young man took responsibility for two sisters, one of which was Charlotte, and four of his brothers.[4] He also made the decision to support his siblings by teaching. In 1818, he established an academy near Louisville, Kentucky, and also began to prepare to preach. From 1821-1824 he preached for a church in Louisville. After examining the scriptures and comparing Campbell's debates and publications to his study of God's truths, he and the Louisville church decided to stand on Restoration principles.[5] Philip S. Fall eventually became

---

[1] Larimore, *The Life Work of Charlotte Fanning*, p. 2.
[2] *Ibid.*, p. 2.
[3] *Ibid.*; and Jenkins, "The Legacy of Charlotte Fanning," *Gospel Advocate*, July 2003.
[4] Jenkins, "The Legacy of Charlotte Fanning"; and Doran, "Phillip Slater Fall," *World Evangelist*, Sept. 1991.
[5] West, *Search for the Ancient Order* vol. 1.

one of the most loved preachers in the South, sometimes convincing whole churches to follow Restoration principles.[1]

In 1825, Fall was invited to move to Nashville and teach at the Nashville Female Academy.[2] Under the tutelage of her brother, Charlotte prepared to become a teacher as well. Quite the student, Charlotte learned Greek, Hebrew, Latin, French and German.[3] Her first experiences teaching began at a very young age in private homes near Nashville. These experiences were followed by the opportunity to join her brother in teaching at the Nashville Female Academy. Here Charlotte found her calling and her reputation began to spread as a fine teacher of girls.[4] While teaching at the school, Charlotte met Tolbert Fanning, a talented and zealous young preacher. He was a widower who had lost his wife shortly after the marriage had begun.[5] Nevertheless, the year 1836 brought two great events in this young man's life: First, he had the opportunity to travel to New England with the illustrious Alexander Campbell. Dennis Loyd, an editor of the *Gospel Advocate*, said this about the relationship that developed between these two men on this trip: "Their tie must have been somewhat like that of Paul the apostle and his young protégé Timothy."[6] Second, Scobey describes an even greater event upon the young preacher's return from his trip:

> … and with her whole heart, she placed her trembling hand in his, and thus they pledged their troth,[7] each other's to be, until them death would part. During the

---

[1] *Ibid.*
[2] *Ibid.*
[3] Jenkins, "The Legacy of Charlotte Fanning."
[4] Scobey, *Franklin College and Its Influences.*
[5] *Ibid.*
[6] Loyd, "The Beginning of the Gospel Advocate," *Gospel Advocate*, July 2012, p. 24.
[7] Commitment, faithfulness, and loyalty in marriage.—*Editor.*

> Christmas holidays of 1836, when each, perhaps, were free, from pressing former engagements, Tolbert Fanning and Charlotte Fall entered into holy bonds of wedlock and commenced the journey of life together.[1]

The union between Tolbert Fanning and Charlotte began a great endeavor in education.[2] Together the Fannings were involved in seven educational institutions.[3] Within a month after the wedding day, the couple opened a school in Franklin, TN, the Eclectic Institute for Young Ladies. "They were poor financially, but rich in faith and strong in courage, willing and anxious to labor for the good of humanity."[4] Here they taught for three years, becoming quite the power couple of teaching. They taught during the week and then travelled around the area for Fanning to hold meetings on Sundays.[5]

Upon leaving Franklin, the Fannings bought a farm at Elm Craig, east of Nashville. Here they started another school for girls followed by an additional school for boys. The Fannings had been tossing around the idea of a manual labor school, and a working farm was vital to this method. A half day's work on the farm was required for each young man, and it was the wish of Charlotte to teach and labor with her girls in all good works around the home. "It was the cherished belief of both that manual training should form part of the education of every boy and girl whether rich or poor."[6] Fanning believed in a holistic approach which provides opportunities for pupils with a wide range of aptitude. In like mind, Charlotte's belief, as described by her sister-

---

[1] Scoby, *Franklin College...*, p. 49.
[2] Larimore, *Life Work of Charlotte Fanning*
[3] Anderson, "Tolbert Fanning: A Spiritual Giant," *Gospel Advocate*, July 2003.
[4] Scobey, *Franklin College...*, p. 149.
[5] *Ibid.*
[6] Larimore, *Life Work of Charlotte Fanning*, p. 4.

in-law, Eleanor R. Fanning, was that "education embraces the whole man or woman; that it is the leading out, the developing, of all the faculties of mind, heart, and soul. The physical, as well as the intellectual and moral powers, were to be called forth and trained for usefulness."[1]

Tolbert Fanning led the way for his boys in demonstrating a holistic education.[2] E.G. Sewell described Fanning this way: "He was a man of positive character in everything he touched. As an agriculturalist and stock grower, he had but few superiors, and was of much service to the society in these regards. Indeed, he was well posted in everything pertaining to practical life."[3] Fanning also expanded his students' knowledge outside the classroom by taking students on trips to the Appalachian Mountains or Mammoth Cave, camping in tents and cooking over open fires. All the while, Fanning was teaching the Bible through every subject and letting God's word develop a stronghold within each pupil.[4] E. Claude Gardner, former president of Freed-Hardeman University, once wrote, "Great preachers have a well-rounded education like Fanning."[5]

Eventually, the Fannings' educational beliefs and their successful work with young people at Elm Craig led to the establishment of Franklin College.[6] This school opened in January of 1845 with a new building holding 200 students, a chapel, recitation rooms and two society rooms.[7] (Jenkins, 2003). "Franklin College soon became the leading school in the South among the

---

[1] *Ibid.*, p. 7.
[2] Tidwell, "Building a Heritage of Faith," *Gospel Advocate*, July 2012.
[3] Sewell, "Brother T. Fanning," *Gospel Advocate*, May 1874, p. 493.
[4] Tidwell, "Building a Heritage…"
[5] Gardner, "Tolbert Fanning: The Successor to Alexander Campbell," *Gospel Advocate*, July 2004.
[6] Larimore, *Life Work of Charlotte Fanning*.
[7] Jenkins, "The Legacy of Charlotte Fanning."

disciples. Young men who expected to make preaching their life's work were offered all the benefits of the institution free, and many prominent preachers of the Church of Christ were educated there."[1] "David Lipscomb, who graduated in 1849, said that after 50 years of experience with schools, he had never seen a college that did better work."[2] Charlotte's "pleasant" schoolroom was attached to their home and was also a part of Franklin College, yet remained a separate institution.[3] The two schools only joined together in the morning for chapel and in singing at the end of dinner.[4] Fanning's agricultural ideals for the school came to a halt after three years due to a lack of teachers in sympathy with his half-day work program. However, the school prospered until 1861 and the beginning of the Civil War, when the school closed its doors after many students became soldiers.[5] During the war years, the Fanning home was burned by the Union army after Fanning's conscience held him back from taking an oath of allegiance. The couple also struggled to even have enough to eat during those years, but they persevered. Franklin College was reopened in 1865, but soon closed forever due to an accidental fire which burned the main school building a few months later.[6]

The Fannings were not stopped in their educational dreams, however; they opened a new school just 300 yards away by purchasing Minerva College. They renamed it Hope Institute and

---

[1] Larimore, *Life Work of Charlotte Fanning*, p. 3
[2] Jenkins, "Franklin College: The Shadow of a Great Man," *Gospel Advocate*, July 2013, p. 18.
[3] Larimore, *Life Work of Charlotte Fanning*, p. 3.
[4] Jenkins, "Franklin College: The Shadow of a Great Man," *Gospel Advocate*, July 2013.
[5] Larimore, *Life Work of Charlotte Fanning*.
[6] Jenkins, "The Legacy of Charlotte Fanning."

started the new school for girls in 1866.[1] This school continued until 1874, closing after the death of Tolbert Fanning. After ten years of silence in the halls of Hope Institute, Charlotte made the decision to donate all of her and her husband's holdings to start an orphan home for girls. Under the condition of funds being raised to match the value of the property, she deeded 160 acres and the buildings of Elm Craig to a board of 13 trustees, one of whom was David Lipscomb. She only asked that she could reside in two rooms in the old Hope Institute building until her days were through. The girls of the Fanning Orphan Home were taught in accordance with Fanning philosophy just like all of Charlotte's girls before them. They were taught to work hard at domestic endeavors and study well. They also enjoyed Bible classes taught by Charlotte for as long as she was able.[2] Charlotte Fanning dedicated her whole life to educating young people in one way or another. Let's take a closer look at Charlotte Fanning the teacher.

Charlotte was a teacher who was passionately devoted to the welfare of her students.[3] Charlotte never bore any children of her own, but she possessed great wisdom that aided many young people dear to her, teaching and training them for the duties of life. Charlotte's sister-in-law, Mrs. Eleanor R. Fanning, said, "I have never known a teacher more conscientious and faithful in the discharge of duty, or more unselfish and devoted in her efforts to bring out all that was noblest and best in those committed to her care and training."[4] Charlotte taught her students that it was God's will for them to use their bodies as His temple with the Holy Spirit guiding their souls to be useful in serving their purposes here on Earth. She taught that mind, heart, and soul should

---

[1] Scobey, *Franklin College...*
[2] Jenkins, "The Legacy of Charlotte Fanning."
[3] Scobey, *Franklin College...*
[4] Larimore, *Life Work of Charlotte Fanning*, p. 6.

all be put to good use. When visiting the sick, her students were taught to not sit there and pass on local gossip to the ill one, but to lead them to the "source of all help."[1] Charlotte wrote this about Christian character: "It has been said, 'The Bible is God's revelation to Christians, and Christians are God's revelation to the world.' The world does not read the Bible, but it does read the lives of Christians. The noble character of true disciples of Christ lead the world to value him whose influence produces such characters."[2]

Charlotte looked out for the welfare of her students through her belief in manual labor. She taught her girls a strong work ethic, especially through her own example. She could teach all day and keep the home and garden at night, all the time with a happy disposition.[3] She taught her students the "dignity" of work; she said, "It is an honor to do things, and to do them well."[4]

Demonstrating her care for the welfare of her girls at times also included strong reprimands for quick glances, flirtatious smiles and handkerchief waving at boys. This did seem harsh to her students. Emma Page Larimore thought at first that Mrs. Fanning did not like boys, but as time progressed, she learned it was all done out of her teacher's care for their future. Charlotte once stated, "I like boys, notwithstanding I seldom write to them. If they are good, I have a special regard for them. Good boys generally make good men, and good men are a blessing to the world. If they are bad, I am truly sorry, knowing that, if they do not change, they will make bad men, and bad men are shall I say a curse to the world."[5]

---

[1] *Ibid.*, p. 7.
[2] *Ibid.*
[3] Scobey, *Franklin College...*
[4] Larimore, *Life Work of Charlotte Fanning*, p. 6.
[5] *Ibid.*, p. 11.

Despite her strict views, the boys of Franklin College did have the utmost respect for Mrs. Fanning. Scobey stated, "Her motherly, womanly ways in her actions towards them elicited their admiration and secured their hearty cooperation in every endeavor she made to secure and foster the welfare of both the students of her own school and those of the college."[1] Occasionally Charlotte would arrange a meeting between a boy and a girl of good standing, but her eyes were always watching. Any who transgressed her expectations were given a private lecture.[2]

Beginning at the school at Elm Craig, Charlotte's classroom became known as "Aunt Charlotte's room." First, the students would gather here in the evenings to have a devotional together. This would be followed by an evening snack of fruit that Charlotte kept on hand for them.[3] Charlotte was never too busy for her girls. When they were ill or troubled, she comforted them. Though "severely precise and prim," as Emma Page Larimore described her, she would often sing and play guitar with her students, enjoying life.[4] Charlotte was such a talented teacher that she could teach anything from guitar to Hebrew, Greek, Latin, German and French. Charlotte Fanning loved being a teacher. She genuinely loved all her students with agape love no matter the color of their skin or their financial background; it was a love that helped to prepare them for their future.[5] T.B. Larimore said this about Charlotte Fanning:

> Though, never a mother, she was ever motherly, and she impressed upon her pupils the essential elements and principles of the sweetest, purest, truest, and best

---

[1] Scobey, *Franklin College...*, p. 154.
[2] *Ibid.*
[3] Jenkins, "The Legacy of Charlotte Fanning."
[4] Larimore, *Life Work of Charlotte Fanning*, p. 6.
[5] Phillips, *A Medley of the Restoration*.

Christian womanhood so as to perfectly prepare them to properly fill the highest and most important positions to which providence might ever appoint them. Her labor of love has blessed, brightened and made happy many a home, and is destined to bless generations yet unborn.[1]

Charlotte Fanning also showed her devotion to young people through her articles and letters. She wrote often for the *Historian* in addition to personal letters sent to those in need. She said, "If I can in the least, assist them to look more frequently, more lovingly, to the Father above, to their Elder Brother who gave his life for them, I shall not have written in vain."[2] Addressing articles to both young boys and girls, she wrote on subjects like: "How to be a comfort to parents," "How good boys can grow up to be good men," "How young girls can grow up to be loving wives" and "How to train your children."[3] She included many wonderful insights into how to make a happy home and a happy marriage. She also warned young people of the evils of intoxicating liquor. Other articles included: The history of the English Bible, the story of redemption, prayer, the Sabbath and the Lord's Day. One theme that occurs throughout her writings and one that she really pushed young people to understand is the importance of not letting time be wasted. Charlotte encouraged, "If we could only appreciate the importance of doing right at the present moment, it would prevent many vain regrets."[4] She advised: "One who rises in the morning without a definite plan as to how he shall spend the day is far more apt to waste than to improve it."[5] She advised, "Many do not realize how important it is to do right

---

[1] Larimore, *Life Work of Charlotte Fanning*, p. 8.
[2] *Ibid.*, p. 16.
[3] *Ibid.*
[4] *Ibid.*, p. 16
[5] *Ibid.*, p. 12.

now."[1] She warned, "O, that Christian girls would consider their words and actions and remember they assist in leading others to the bliss of heaven or to the torture that never ends!"[2]

Charlotte Fanning not only imparted God's wisdom through her teachings; she lived it. This was why her students dearly loved her. E.G. Sewell said, "Sister Fanning's life is measured not so much by what she said or what she wrote, but what she actually did."[3] David Lipscomb wrote:

> She was of a gentle disposition, kind and sympathetic in spirit, deeply religious in character, a faithful and constant student of the Bible, and she earnestly sought to practice the teaching of the Bible in all walks of life. I will say further (and it is not saying she was perfect, for, I believe, perfect people do not live upon earth), as a good, earnest, sincere Christian, molding the character of all with whom she came in contact, I have never known her superior.[4]

Charlotte lived God's teachings in her relationship with others. At the Fanning Orphan Home she was not only a mentor, but a "helpful friend of all superintendents and matrons… never dictating or demanding but always kindly sympathizing and gently counseling."[5] David Lipscomb, Jr., a superintendent of the Fanning Orphan Home, said:

> Mrs. Fanning, with all the wisdom of her years and long life spent in the classroom was never critical, but always helpful and during a residence of more than eleven years in the school never so far as I know, offered one word of

---

[1] *Ibid.*, p. 11.
[2] Scobey, *Franklin College…*, p. 163.
[3] Larimore, *Life Work of Charlotte Fanning*, p. 7.
[4] *Ibid.*
[5] *Ibid.*, p. 4.

complaint or interfered in the slightest degree with the management that her clear eyes must have seen was often faulty. This fact I regard as the highest test of self-denial. Many have given away property for public use, but few like to relinquish all voice in its after management.[1]

Another example of Charlotte living out what she taught was her love to those in need. When given a cake, she would seek permission to take it to another sister in need. Giving all she had to the needy, she would give of her time by visiting the homes in her neighborhood and cheering those who were suffering from illness. Sometimes Charlotte would almost literally give her all to the needy. After her first stroke, loved ones discovered that she didn't even have enough clothing left to meet her own needs. She had given them to a woman in need.[2]

After Charlotte's stroke in 1895, she was confined to bed for about a year before her death. She always had plenty of friends and students to look after her needs. She often wanted her favorite passage, Psalm 86:1-6, read to her, and when the words, "I am holy," were read, she would point to herself and shake her head.[3] Charlotte Fanning died on August 15, 1896, and was buried next to her husband in front of the Fanning Orphan Home building in "the circle." Later, in 1943, both bodies were moved to the Olivet Cemetery when the school was sold to the Nashville Airport Authority.[4] Charlotte's students had cherished their time with their precious teacher. They might have remembered "her quaint little figure, clad in silver gray wearing heelless shoes and the old fashioned hoop skirts, without which she never appeared in public, with a neat little bow of ribbon at her throat and soft gray curls

---

[1] *Ibid.*
[2] *Ibid.*
[3] Jenkins, "The Legacy of Charlotte Fanning," p. 17.
[4] *Ibid.*

about her ears."[1] However, more importantly, they remembered and held in their hearts the teachings that she lived. During Emma Page's school days, "the circle" was her and her schoolmates' playground at the Hope Institute. When Emma found out that the Fannings' graves would be located there, at first she was saddened. Her happy childhood play place would be brought down with the "gloom of the grave."[2] However, Emma soon found out that "the circle" was still a cherished, happy place for the girls at the Fanning Orphan home. They came there to read or to talk and sing with each other. Emma said:

> Mrs. Fanning loved girls—loved to see them bright and happy—and it seems meet that her body should rest where the orphan girls for whom she has done much to provide Christian care and training should often go to make merry, as she loved to see them do. Her influence still speaks to them there, for those who gather about her tomb may read a sweet lesson of the beauty of their daily service and self-sacrifice in the inscription written at the request of her neighbors, on the slab above her grave: "I was sick and you visited me."[3]

Charlotte's girls went on to be wonderful wives, mothers and women in the workplace. Their precious teacher's legacy has been passed down for generations. Scobey said at the closing exercises of the Fanning Orphan School, May 25, 1904, "Gentle in spirit, kind and considerate, always abounding in good works, she reached and molded the heart force of her pupils, giving them some of her spirit and some of her love."[4] Alexander Campbell

---

[1] Larimore, *Life Work of Charlotte Fanning*, p. 6.
[2] *Ibid.*, p. 5.
[3] *Ibid.*
[4] Scobey, *Franklin College...*, p. 344.

once called Charlotte, "Tolbert's accomplished lady."[1] In my opinion, if the *Life Works of Charlotte Fanning,* a book written by Emma Page Larimore, was republished today as a ladies' class book, today's women would benefit from her teachings just as much as her students did in the 1800's. She was a remarkable teacher. May we all benefit from her wisdom and follow in her footsteps. The following is a quote from Charlotte aimed towards future teachers. If you are a teacher or aspire to be one, take these words to heart:

> Some of you expect to become teachers. In that case you will have strong influence. Pray that it may be such as will lead your pupils upward to a higher, nobler life, and exert all your energies to that purpose. Let the Bible have its influence in our everyday life. Lay up the precepts of God's word in your hearts, and let it mold your characters. Teach its truths with earnestness and simplicity. The life of women should be earnest. They are capable of doing good that others cannot affect. Will you not walk thoughtfully, remembering that your influence may lead others to the Savior whom you have elected to follow, or may render them careless of the things that concern their peace?[2]

---

[1] Phillips, *A Medley of the Restoration*, p. 53.
[2] Larimore, *Life Works of Charlotte Fanning*, p. 10.

QUESTIONS

1. What Bible verses come to mind on the subject of teaching?
2. In what ways did Charlotte make an impact on her students?
3. Do you think Charlotte would be described as too strict? Why or why not?
4. Describe how Charlotte gave until it hurt.
5. At Franklin College, the Fannings used the holistic approach. Define holistic. Do you think this approach works today?

*Grave of Charlotte Fall Fanning,
Mount Olivet Cemetery, Nashville, TN (3/30/2024)*

Chapter 7

Nancy Larimore: A Woman of Motherly Love (1813-1902)

  Imagine a mother that looks down at her newborn and feels a psalm of thanksgiving seeping into her heart. Imagine a mother that feels an overwhelming sense of responsibility to mold and shape her precious love with the Lord's help into a worker in His vineyard. Imagine a mother that sacrifices for her child despite life's many hurdles. Many mothers of the Restoration probably felt these feelings, as many mothers do today, but one mother stands above all others, at least in the eyes of the beloved Restoration teacher and evangelist, T.B. Larimore. In his writings, he spoke so lovingly of his dear mother and her sacrifices. Throughout his lifetime he held her love and teachings close to his heart, and he held her memory so dear. T.B. Larimore would want you to remember his mother, Nancy Larimore, a great woman of motherly love.

L.L. Brigance once wrote in an article in the *Christian Leader*, "There is no doubt but that Brother Larimore is by far the best and most favorably-known preacher in our ranks…"[1] Due to his great humility, the great evangelist and beloved teacher of Mars Hill College in Alabama would never commend himself for his accomplishments. However, he would give credit to his Lord and to his mother. He once said this of his mother: "I had never realized before that I owe to her my life and whatever good may be in me—whatever good I may have done or may ever be able to do."[2] Nancy Larimore gave birth to Theophilus B. Larimore in 1843. Raising her son near Dunlap, Tennessee, in the Sequatchie Valley, Nancy's tender care could be seen even in the midst of tragedy.[3] From the few times that Larimore ever spoke of his childhood we learn the following:

> The very best blood, both maternal and paternal, is blended in my veins. I was born in a humble hovel, right where two royal roads of ruined wealth and shattered fortunes met in the shadow of security debts and midnight of the reign of the intoxicating bowl. In other words, my ancestors on both sides were rich, intellectual, influential, successful and popular. Just as the converging lines came together, some immense security debts had to be paid. There was no shirking. Every dollar was paid; but took everything… Result—nothing, absolutely nothing left but poverty and honor. Just then, I was born-just when the shadows were deepest. Men, hurled from such heights to such depths, turned from these troubles to worse—to

---

[1] As quoted in West, *Search for the Ancient Order*, vol. 3, p. 261.
[2] Larimore, "What I Owe My Mother," *Gospel Advocate*, Dec. 1915, p. 1204.
[3] West, *Search for the Ancient Order*, vol. 3.

strong drink; then the gloom of the darkest night began to gather round my cradle. I can well remember when the yell of the drunken one coming home in the otherwise still hours of night, would start all of us from the hut to the woods... We would slip, like little partridges after a scare, back to the gloomy nest... Debt and drunkenness have depressed me and cause me to be dejected all my life.[1]

It was very hard for Larimore to speak of his past and very little can be pinpointed about his father, especially in regards to the children taking their mother's maiden name. According to Srygley, we do know that the father was not there for the family, because Larimore did write, "I never knew what it was to have the advice, protection, and support of a father."[2] Nevertheless, when Larimore spoke or wrote about his mother, his words were beyond appreciative, especially of her devotion and sacrifice during his tender years.

Through motherly love, Nancy did all she could to support her little family through what Larimore referred to as "the deepest depths of poverty."[3] She took on as many sewing jobs and other odd jobs that she could find in the area. Still, as poor as they were, Nancy would never turn anyone in need away.[4] She did get to the point where she had to put young Larimore to work on a neighboring farm belonging to the McDonoughs. Throughout the week, Larimore worked alongside "Old Granny a little, old, shabby, bay pony," plowing fields sometimes to the point of passing out from nosebleeds.[5] He slept in the loft with McDonough's two boys. Then each Saturday night, her young

---

[1] Srygley, *Larimore and His Boys*, p. 58.
[2] *Ibid.*, p. 53.
[3] *Ibid.*
[4] *Ibid.*
[5] *Ibid.*

son would travel home through a dark patch in the ravine, between the river and the hills of the Cumberland, to meet his mother. Nancy worked hard all week as well and anxiously awaited this weekly reunion with her beloved son. Feeling a little nervous and scared, like her son, she would call, "Is that you, my son?"[1] Then both would walk home feeling happy and secure together. Larimore imagined that going home to heaven would be a similar scenario when he would meet his mother once more.[2] Through her motherly love, Nancy taught her son to persevere and to find happiness in times of despair.

Through motherly love, Nancy used gentle but effective discipline. Probably as a result of her husband's alcoholic raids, Nancy approached discipline quietly. Larimore said, "Late in life she told me she never whipped me, never scolded me—never once in all her life—and still she so controlled me that I really never realized it was possible for me to disobey her."[3] Some days I think of Nancy when I am searching for the sense of calm needed to discipline my children without flying off the handle.

Through motherly love, Nancy modeled and taught a strong work ethic to her children. Every New Year's Day, starting very early in the day, Nancy would prepare the best breakfast of the year. Then she and the children would squeeze in as much decent work as they could possibly squeeze into the day. The rest of the year they would strive to meet or surpass that first day of work. The next year they would try to set a new record.[4] Larimore said once in later years, "True to that teaching, I was ready for business before the sun rose this morning, and deem it my duty to be busy till the best day's work I can do today has been done as

---

[1] Larimore, *Life, Letters, and Sermons of T.B. Larimore*, p. 48.
[2] *Ibid.*
[3] *Ibid.*, p. 56.
[4] *Ibid.*

wisely and well as I can do it."[1] Larimore also reflected upon his mother's care and wisdom: "Never a strong child, and frequently hovering between life and death, but for her tender care and good judgment I could scarcely have passed through the period of boyhood; but during all that trying period, she never, as she and others have told me, lost hope that I might become a strong useful man."[2]

Through motherly love, Nancy made sure that Larimore believed in himself. Larimore described this incident:

> Once Larimore had saved money and purchased a red calf, and then wanted another to go with it. A wealthy neighbor had several cattle with a red calf among them, and Larimore offered to work for him to buy it. The man smiled and said, 'In four years that calf will be worth forty dollars, but you'll never be worth that much.' His mother saw that the remark crushed her child, and she reassured him, "Yes you will, my son. That poor old man doesn't know what he is talking about.[3]

How many times have we had to lovingly assure our children that the mean, awful words they heard at school are far from the truth? Another time a teacher told T.B. that he would never learn to write. Nancy decided not to leave her child's education up to an individual who did not believe in her son, and she took it upon herself to teach Larimore.[4] She taught her son to believe in himself, and she oversaw his education when it was needed.

Young Larimore internalized his mother's encouragement. In his teenage years his drive for an education helped him to excel

---

[1] *Ibid.*, pp. 48-49.
[2] *Ibid.*, p. 55.
[3] As cited in West, *Search for the ...*, vol. 3, p. 80.
[4] *Ibid.*

beyond other students in his part of the country, even while studying at home and attending school only a few months a year. Eventually, a path was paved for him to attend Mossy Creek College, which is today Carson-Newman University.[1] Ever thinking of his mother, Larimore described his departure to college:

> I walked that forty miles between two nights, without fear or discouraging fatigue. The shadow of sorrow hung over me all the way, however, for I was leaving behind me my mother whom I loved devotedly, and every step lengthened the distance between us. The assurance that it would grieve her for me to turn back kept me from doing so.[2]

While Larimore was away at college, Nancy and Larimore's sister had the opportunity to hear a Gospel preacher by the name of Madison Love who was preaching through the Sequatchie Valley. Meanwhile being surrounded by influences at the Mossy Creek College, Larimore was struggling with the subject of unconditional election. Similar to Raccoon John Smith's experience, Larimore tried in vain to "get religion" or to experience something that would guarantee that he was part of the elect.[3] Emma Page, Larimore's second wife and biographer, said:

> He could find no relief, and in the shadow of the doctrine of 'unconditional foreordination and election,' he suffered for months the agony of believing himself to be one of the 'non-elect.' It was a terrible ordeal for a sensitive soul; but, according to God's great law of compensation, he brought out of that harrowing experience the ability to

---

[1] Larimore, *Life, Letters, and Sermons...*
[2] *Ibid.*, p. 10.
[3] *Ibid.*

combat in later years, with telling power and effect, that unscriptural doctrine.[1]

Through motherly love, Nancy shared the Good News with her son. When Larimore returned home from school she met him at the door and told him that she and his sister had been baptized. "'When did you get religion?' he inquired, and she replied, 'You don't have to get religion. You practice it,' and she then and there told him some things he had never heard about the gospel plan of salvation."[2] Larimore then decided that he would faithfully read his Bible and pray. Even though Larimore did not obey the Gospel until after the Civil War, what a joy it is for a mother to be given the opportunity to share the Good News with her child. In later years, Larimore reflected that, to him, his mother was the height of all Christians. He said, "My mother's religion was Christianity pure and simple and in her convictions with truth for her stay she was immovable as the mountains, steadfast as the everlasting hills. Her faith never faltered, her hope never wavered, her love never failed."[3]

As T.B. Larimore grew into the great man who inspired so many young boys and who brought so many people to Christ, his mother's qualities could clearly be seen in her son. Historian Earl West describes it this way: "His mother had taken special care to weave all her good qualities in the fabric of her son."[4] Therefore one could say Nancy's influence spread to all who entered the grounds of Mars Hill. West wrote, "Larimore's personality was impressed upon everything and he was loved by all and as a result his gentle humility, kindly disposition and refinement of manners

---

[1] *Ibid.*, p. 11.
[2] *Ibid.*
[3] *Ibid.*, p. 62.
[4] West, *Search for the Ancient Order* vol. 3, p. 80.

were reflected in the teachers and pupils and in all others within the range of the school's influence."[1] One could also say that Nancy's influence touched thousands of lives through Larimore's evangelistic work. One listener said, "There was an indescribable pathos in his voice, and his general appearance that melted audiences to tears, and moved hearts long hardened by sin to repentance at the appeal of the gospel."[2] Audiences were drawn to Larimore's gentle personality. West states, "Larimore's power, however, lay more in the man than in his pulpit supremacy. He was loved because he was good, pure and God-like. His life was a thing of beauty."[3] Motherly love and influence could definitely be seen in this great man.

Nancy Larimore spent her final years mainly in Henderson, Tennessee, at the home of her daughter, Mrs. R.P. Meeks. She died September 2, 1902.[4] R.P. Meeks, head of the Bible Department at West Tennessee Christian College, said this of his mother-in-law:

> Mother was an ardent admirer of flowers; loved the Lord devotedly; and was ever in sympathy with the poor, afflicted and distressed. She was the soul of honor; the embodiment of politeness; and an angel of mercy, mixing and mingling with the human race to relieve pain, to wipe away tears of sorrow and to cheer the broken-hearted.[5]

In his later years Larimore looked forward to seeing his mother in the hereafter, and he reflected upon his dear mother as a blessing:

---

[1] *Ibid.*, p. 86.
[2] As cited in Phillips, *Medley of the Restoration*, p. 61.
[3] West, *Search for the Ancient Order* vol. 3, p. 93.
[4] *Ibid.*
[5] Meeks, "Grandmamma Larimore," *Gospel Advocate*, Jan. 1903, p. 27.

> My brave little mother, who knew not the meaning of the feeling called 'fear,' was to me a treasure sublime and almost divine. She loved me as only a mother can love to the end of her pilgrimage here, and she lived in this beautiful world nearly ninety years. Who can tell, with tongue or pen, the worth of that priceless treasure, a mother's love? I was rich.[1]

In the summer of 2018, Tom Childers of Henderson, Tennessee, took my husband and me to visit the grave of Nancy Larimore. I often reflect upon that day and upon the gentle evangelist's sweet mother. I think about Nancy Larimore when I think of my own sweet mother who has always modeled the Lord's will and has faithfully encouraged me through the years. I also think about Nancy Larimore when I need to remember what's important while raising the two children with which God has blessed me and to remind me of my important mission in passing down our Lord's teachings. Nancy Larimore is a mother to be remembered. If it were a perfect world, all children would revere their mothers as T.B. Larimore revered his, and all mothers would persevere in using their powers of motherly love to influence their children towards the Lord.

---

[1] Larimore, *Life, Letters, and Sermons...*, p. 8.

QUESTIONS

1. On Saturday nights when Nancy journeyed to meet her son she would say, "Is that you, my son?" When we are walking through the darkness of our lives, do we say, "Is that you, Lord?" Do you feel happy and secure knowing He is there—even if your trouble is still there?
2. Nancy had a great work ethic. Who in the Bible had a similar work ethic?
3. Nancy used gentle but effective discipline. Why did her gentle discipline work?
4. Discuss three important lessons Nancy taught her son.
5. T.B. Larimore was a great evangelist and beloved teacher at Mars Hill College. Who did he credit for his accomplishments and why?

Gravestone of Nancy Larimore
Clear Creek Church of Christ Cemetery, Stantonville, TN
(6/30/2018)

CHAPTER 8

Margaret Lipscomb:
A Woman of Invention
(1842-1926)

Margaret Lipscomb, or "Aunt Mag," as she was affectionately called, was a woman of invention. She was the type to shed a positive outlook on any situation she encountered and then use her many talents to make a situation better. Whether her tendency to reframe her outlook resulted in a physical invention or just an optimistic disposition, this ability made her a woman to be admired. She used her inventiveness to effectively take care of her husband, the many children that they called their own and the Lord's Church. She was always willing to help all within her reach with her positive and humble attitude. Margaret's husband, David Lipscomb, was a long-time editor of the *Gospel Advocate* and a preacher known for approaching the Scriptures with total honesty.[1] Robert E. Hooper, biographer of David Lipscomb,

---

[1] West, *The Life and Times of David Lipscomb*.

related Aunt Mag's explanation of her inventiveness as follows: "Often when complimented on her inventiveness or her intelligence, she would modestly answer, 'I could not have lived with Mr. Lipscomb as long as I did without catching some of it.'"[1] Let's take a look at this unique woman of invention.

Margaret Ophelia Zellner was born at her home in Maury County, Tennessee on June 2, 1842. Her family was made up of fervent Baptists.[2] However, her mother, Martha, was the only one who had accepted religion officially. Margaret had two sisters. One died in infancy, but the other sister, Lucy, she grew up with, and the two were especially close. Margaret and Lucy attended Columbia Atheneum together until Lucy died unexpectedly in her last term. Margaret had planned to put off one year of her education so that she could graduate with her sister, but it was not to be. This loss was probably on the minds of both Margaret and her father, Henry Zellner, when they both responded to the gospel call at a meeting by R.B. Trimble on Knob Creek in 1860. Father and daughter walked down separate aisles of the meeting that Sunday night, not knowing the other's intention. They were eventually joined by Margaret's mother, and the family became members of the Philippi congregation on Knob Creek.[3]

David Lipscomb was at the R.B. Trimble meeting that Saturday night before Margaret's and her father's response.[4] When he saw young, 18-year-old Margaret for the first time, he supposedly leaned over to Trimble and said, "Brother Trimble, there goes my future wife."[5] Margaret recalled that she was wearing a

---

[1] Hooper, *Crying in the Wilderness: A Biography of David Lipscomb,* p. 322.
[2] Stroop, "The Pioneer Spirit of Aunt Mag Lipscomb," *Gospel Advocate,* July 2003.
[3] Hooper, *Crying in the Wilderness.*
[4] *Ibid.*
[5] *Ibid.*, p. 78.

hand-made dress and a hat that she had constructed from corn shucks that night.[1] This was just one example of Margaret's inventiveness.

According to David Lipscomb, Margaret's father, Henry Zellner, was "a model of promptness" and "one who never turned out a shoddy piece of work."[2] To know the characteristics of the father is to know the daughter. Henry was of German descent. He was mechanically talented, patenting several machines, including a hemp break, a clover huller and a hay baler. He installed the water works for the town of Columbia.[3] He constructed almost every pre-Civil War bridge in Maury County, and he submitted scientific farming articles to the *Gospel Advocate* as well.[4] Keeping all of Mr. Zellner's accomplishments in mind, it has been said in reference to Margaret that she was one "whose mechanical talents rivaled her father's."[5]

Margaret's father was not impressed with David Lipscomb's first visit to their home. Lipscomb drove up in an old, dusty buggy without a top, and his appearance was very similar to his unkempt, cocklebur infested horse.[6] This sight was not pleasing to Mr. Zellner as a father or as an admirer of fine horses.[7] Aside from his appearance, Lipscomb also had a regular awkwardness, with a nearly six-foot, large boned frame and a large head.[8] One of Henry and Martha's granddaughters remembers Mr. Zellner asking his daughter, "Mag, what in the world do you see in that

---

[1] *Ibid.*
[2] *Ibid.*, p. 80.
[3] West, *Life and Times of David Lipscomb.*
[4] Hooper, *Crying in the Wilderness.*
[5] *Ibid.*, p. 80.
[6] *Ibid.*
[7] Stroop, "The Pioneer Spirit of Aunt Mag Lipscomb."
[8] Hooper, *Crying in the Wilderness.*

man to admire?"[1] Whatever wheels were turning in Margaret's head, they were ones of an inventive, positive nature. According to historian Earl West, "Margaret saw that with a woman's polish and care, David would go far in life."[2]

At age 20, Margaret married David Lipscomb, who was eleven years her senior. After their wedding on July 23, 1862, she went straight to work using her ingenuity to improve her new husband's personal grooming. Margaret was a pretty, black-headed young woman who was as particular about her personal appearance as her husband was impassive about his. Lipscomb did keep a closely shaven beard, which was not the fashion of the times, but Margaret's preference: According to their arrangement, Lipscomb would keep his mustache shaven off in exchange for her removing her dress trails which he continually tripped over. Lipscomb's preference for comfortable clothes was one of the main causes of his unkempt appearance, especially in his later years. Margaret decided early on to make all of her husband's clothes, since it was hard to purchase clothes that would fit his frame. She knitted his socks and lovingly made him presentable; she even combed his hair before he went out the door.[3]

Setting up housekeeping in Lawrenceburg, Tennessee, during the Civil War years also called for an inventive and positive disposition on Margaret's part. Starting off without a cook stove, she tried her best to make Lipscomb's favorite cornbread over an open fire.[4] Her great niece said, "She learned how to prepare meals with a burned face, burned shins and burned food."[5] Thankfully a local blacksmith rebuilt an old stove that he had

---

[1] As cited in Hooper, *Crying in the Wilderness*, p. 81.
[2] West, *Life and Times of David Lipscomb*, p. 80.
[3] Hooper, *Crying in the Wilderness*.
[4] Stroop, "Pioneer Spirit of Aunt Mag Lipscomb"
[5] *Ibid.*, p. 12.

salvaged from the Duck River and made young Margaret a proud owner of her first stove.[1] Later in life she commented on her cooking saying that she learned, "through trials, tribulations, and burns."[2] Margaret was positive and never gave up. Through the years this was proven by the fact that those that sat at her table highly praised her cooking abilities.[3]

The war years were hard on the Lipscombs and their neighbors. Losing two-thirds of everything they owned, the Lipscombs, like so many others in Tennessee, were near starvation the last two years of the war. Lipscomb remembers visiting the Fannings when little bread was available.[4] He reflected later, "We have visited other families that were near to us, in which we felt that every mouth full of food we ate was taken from women and children who must suffer for the want of it."[5] During these times Margaret was a trooper. Just as she was positive about her cooking situation, she was also inventive with the meager supplies available. Once, Margaret even made a pair of shoes out of an old felt hat to place upon her own feet.[6]

After Lipscomb taught for a year in Lawrenceburg, Margaret and David moved to a cabin on a farm in Bell's Bend.[7] Margaret mentioned in a letter to a friend that the farm "had enough rattlesnakes to fence the yard and enough chiggers to chink the cracks."[8] However, it did have a lot of timber that could be sold for firewood to military-controlled Nashville. It was here at

---

[1] Hooper, *Crying in the Wilderness.*
[2] *Ibid.*, p. 272.
[3] *Ibid.*
[4] *Ibid.*
[5] Lipscomb, "A Word To Our Southern Brethren," *Gospel Advocate*, November 1866, p. 758.
[6] Hooper, *Crying in the Wilderness.*
[7] Stroop, "Pioneer Spirit of Aunt Mag Lipscomb"
[8] *Ibid.*, p. 12.

Bell's Bend, on September 23, 1863, that Margaret gave birth to their only child, Zellner Lipscomb, a child not long for this earth. Zellner passed away that next spring, probably due to dehydration from teething.[1] Margaret had a coffin made from a cedar tree and, with a neighbor's help, sewed a cotton gown for little Zellner. At four in the morning, the Lipscombs rode past Federal and Confederate picket lines to bury their son in Maury County at the home of Margaret's father. War times made the couple unsure about burying their child anywhere near Bell's Bend and Nashville.[2] If this tragedy had not happened during war times a doctor may have been on hand to save her son. Nevertheless, Margaret stayed strong and took it upon herself to console her husband, although she found this a hard task.[3] As the couple left their farm with the coffin on their lap, Lipscomb said, "We have no baby, and when we get back, we may have nothing here."[4] The neighbor who had helped to make the burial gown, Mrs. Moore, later said that she "had never witnessed such nerve, such resignation as Margaret Lipscomb exhibited throughout the entire ordeal of the sickness and death of Zellner."[5] Thirty years later John S. Sweeney was preaching a sermon at the College St. congregation. His topic was King David's grief over the loss of Absalom. Sweeney advised those who had lost a child to try and forget. Lipscomb, then an elder of that congregation, bowed his head and a deep sob was heard throughout the silenced meeting house.[6] The death of their only child required probably the most difficult effort submitted by Margaret to be positive and to keep her husband positive, but God had a plan for the Lipscombs.

---

[1] Hooper, *Crying in the Wilderness.*
[2] West, *Life and Times of David Lipscomb.*
[3] Stroop, "Pioneer Spirit of Aunt Mag Lipscomb"
[4] Hooper, *Crying in the Wilderness*, p. 84.
[5] *Ibid.*
[6] *Ibid.*

Although they never had any more children of their own, the Lipscombs were hardly ever without children. The first two children taken in and raised by the Lipscombs were Horace Greeley Lipscomb, David's half-brother, and Margaret's sister, Henrie Zellner. These two eventually married each other. David Lipscomb, Jr. came to live with the Lipscombs in 1870. He was the son of David's older brother William and came to the Lipscombs five years before his mother Anna passed away. Margaret and David affectionately called him "Our Davy." The remainder of Anna and William Lipscomb's children came under the care of David and Margaret after Anna's death.[1] That same year, the loving couple also took in thirteen-month-old Margaret Callender, the daughter of Margaret's younger sister Mary Jane.[2] Margaret's positive disposition helped her through the loss of her own child until God made a way to bless her with many more.[3]

In order to care for such a large household, Margaret tapped into her talent of invention. She was a very progressive homemaker. Through the years, Aunt Mag designed two homes on the road that is today's Granny White Pike, in Nashville. The first "Avalon" home, as they called it, had a dairy built over an underground spring. Aunt Mag designed a room over the spring with a staircase, and in this room Margaret put in a pump and a sink. She also had shelves to store all canned goods and vegetables. The spring ran over a huge flat rock where she placed milk and butter. At the second "Avalon" home, Aunt Mag had a cistern dug under the kitchen and outside the bathroom so that she could have water piped into the house. A zinc washtub and spigot were connected to a tank which collected water from the roof. The used water was drained through tile pipes which led to a septic

---

[1] *Ibid.*
[2] Stroop, "Pioneer Spirit of Aunt Mag Lipscomb"
[3] Hooper, *Crying in the Wilderness.*

tank. Every couple of years she would climb into the cisterns and clean them herself.[1] A home with innovations like these in the early 1890's was a sight to see.

Zelma Stroop wrote this about her great aunt: "Aunt Mag was as modern as the day. She availed the house of every modern convenience as soon as it was obtainable."[2] She had a bathtub installed, complete with a pump that brought in water from the cistern. Later, she added a toilet that used a pump to flush it and also used the tile pipes to drain it to the septic tank. Margaret used a gasoline cook stove as well as her wood stove in the kitchen. She used a coal oil stove to heat the bathroom. At the second Avalon, the Lipscombs had the house wired for electricity and installed a hand-powered washing machine followed by a telephone.[3] Margaret also had a Leonard refrigerator by that time. According to Zelma, Aunt Mag "believed in lightening household chores, if at all possible, creating more time for other things."[4] And, yes, she believed in chores being done quickly, but she was still a very thorough cleaner. Zelma even admitted this about Aunt Mag: "If she received a dirty bill, she would wash it before putting it into her purse."[5]

Aunt Mag furnished her house with her inventive and creative spirit, making her home very pleasing. She did not believe in draping her windows. She wanted to see the view and let in the bright sunshine. Her walls were adorned with her own paintings, and she made her own quilts for the beds and scatter rugs for the floors.[6] She embroidered and crocheted her own cushions,

---

[1] Stroop, "Pioneer Spirit of Aunt Mag Lipscomb"
[2] *Ibid.*, p. 13.
[3] *Ibid.*
[4] *Ibid.*
[5] *Ibid.*
[6] Hooper, *Crying in the Wilderness.*

afghans and dollies. Once, she even made a stool out of tin cans. If she had a piece of furniture that was too tedious to dust, she would trim it down and refinish it. She also made toys for the children. Zelma recalled her great aunt, somewhere around the age of 82 making a play pen, complete with rollers, out of a table while refusing any help.[1]

Providing for her family by using her inventive, positive spirit to garden, Margaret would study the *Southern Agriculturist* and experiment with a large variety of fruits and vegetables. Then she would inform her neighbors about which grew the best.[2] Among many other crops, she grew oranges, bananas, grapefruit, berries and even peanuts, with which she made her own peanut-butter.[3] When she grew grapes, she pinned little paper bags to the branches to scare away birds.[4]

Aunt Mag was also known for her fresh wheat bread which was made from her own crop of wheat and milled with her own hand mill attached to a window sill. Lipscomb was so proud of his wife for all that she did.[5] Once, when John T. Lewis was invited to supper, Uncle Dave proudly bragged, "Brother Lewis, Mag ground the flour these biscuits are made of."[6] J.C. McQuiddy would often say, "Brother Lipscomb thinks his wife is the greatest woman in the world."[7]

Lipscomb thought so much of Margaret's abilities that he eventually transferred the management of the farm to his wife so he could spend more time preaching and editing the *Gospel*

---

[1] Stroop, "Pioneer Spirit of Aunt Mag Lipscomb"
[2] *Ibid.*
[3] Hooper, *Crying in the Wilderness.*
[4] Stroop, "Pioneer Spirit of Aunt Mag Lipscomb"
[5] Hooper, *Crying in the Wilderness.*
[6] Lewis, "A True Helpmate," *Gospel Advocate*, April 1926, p. 377.
[7] Hooper, *Crying in the Wilderness*, p. 308.

Advocate. Margaret used her positive attitude and continued to be thrifty even in the years after the war. She completely understood her husband's commitments, and she assumed the responsibility of running the farm efficiently.[1]

Margaret Lipscomb had a positive mindset when it came to helping the poor. David Lipscomb believed in the Christian's pledge to follow Christ's example and help those in need. During the summer of 1873, a cholera epidemic swept through Nashville. African Americans were affected the most. An already sickly David Lipscomb went into homes, not concerned with differences in skin color or economic status and nursed many to health; he cleaned their homes and cooked their food; he took the lead among the young men of the Church by going into areas where others feared to go. When Catholic sisters needed transportation while nursing the sick, it was Lipscomb who personally escorted them in his buggy into the poorer sections of Nashville.[2] Margaret Lipscomb's positive mindset and giving heart matched that of her husband's. Her great niece Zelma said that she gave away a lot of her "fancy work."[3] She even gave away a walnut bedroom set to help her servant's family after a house fire. Zelma said, "In fact, she gave away everything they didn't need because she never hoarded anything."[4] Poor neighbors were welcome to pick berries on their Bell's Bend farm. Margaret would also bring her fresh bread, canned goods, butter, eggs and flowers to the sick. She would say, "Don't try to repay me. Just do it for someone else when there's opportunity."[5]

---

[1] *Ibid.*
[2] *Ibid.*
[3] Stroop, "Pioneer Spirit of Aunt Mag Lipscomb" p. 14.
[4] *Ibid.*
[5] Hooper, *Crying in the Wilderness*, p. 177.

Margaret was a positive helpmeet for her husband through trying times. "The Lipscombs were builders. They did not understand quitting or failure for lack of trying."[1] We see this in David Lipscomb as he struggled to keep the *Gospel Advocate* and the Nashville Bible School alive, as he helped Southerners after the Civil War and as he stood between extremes in the religious world, often taking abuse from both sides. He did all this while pleading for all to "remember the old paths."[2] (Through all the hard times, David Lipscomb "believed the world was truly getting better because of the spreading umbrella of Christianity. It never entered Lipscomb's mind that the Restoration Movement might fail..."[3] Hooper attributes Lipscomb's hopefulness to Margaret, saying, "Possibly the greatest immediate cause of optimism was his home life where Margaret Zellner Lipscomb was the very embodiment of the godly wife as described in Proverbs chapter thirty-one."[4] Margaret's inventiveness and cheerfulness lifted her husband throughout their married life. A.B. Lipscomb witnessed this Godly relationship between his aunt and uncle and reflected upon it:

> There they were, two wonderful souls praying together as they faced the sunset, but in the spiritual sense the twain had become one—one in their respect and reverence for the word of God, one in their unfailing trust in all his promises, one in their love for the church and God's children, one in their sympathy for all mankind, one in their hope of eternal life.[5]

---

[1] *Ibid.*, p. 305.
[2] *Ibid.*, p. 12.
[3] *Ibid.*, p. 172,
[4] *Ibid.*
[5] Lipscomb, "Thank Her and Thank God," *Gospel Advocate*, April 1926, p. 364.

A positive, inventive attitude is always needed to help the Church. Margaret was willing to work in her Lord's vineyard. While living at Bell's Bend early on, Lipscomb built a one-room building across the road from their farm.[1] According to Zelma, settlers called "melangerers," a mixture of Spanish, Indian and French origin, came together to worship there.[2] When Lipscomb was on the road preaching, Aunt Mag prepared the communion, taught Bible classes and made sure that the worship was carried out.[3] The Sunday school that Margaret established encouraged many in the Bend to attend the little Church.[4] Hooper says, "If anyone should be given credit for keeping the church in Bell's Bend functioning then Margaret Lipscomb deserves the plaudits."[5] Together the Lipscombs were also involved in establishing the South College Street Church in 1887, and later in their marriage whenever Lipscomb was away Aunt Mag helped a small church by the name of Compton's Chapel. When a male song leader was not present, she led the singing from her seat. Once, when Aunt Mag's nephew Horace S. Lipscomb was attending, she "ordered him to participate."[6] In Margaret's later years, when she was about 74 years old, she still taught a Sunday morning Bible class to the senior girls in her home. Then she would walk with them to Chapel Hall for worship on the Nashville Bible School campus.[7]

Margaret's optimism and inventive spirit also helped her husband through many sick days. Though Margaret showed love to all, Hooper asserts, "The greatest love and concern of the

---

[1] Stroop, "Pioneer Spirit of Aunt Mag Lipscomb"
[2] *Ibid.*, p. 13.
[3] *Ibid.*
[4] Hooper, *Crying in the Wilderness.*
[5] *Ibid.*, p. 178.
[6] *Ibid.*, p. 266.
[7] *Ibid.*

'virtuous woman' was poured out upon her husband who was often ill, occasionally unto death."[1] David Lipscomb suffered from asthma and hemorrhaging of the lungs. Margaret was there to nurse him back to health, and she often used her inventive prowess to help in the situation at hand. Once, she sawed off a portion of the legs on his favorite easy chair so he could rise from the seat. Another time, after 85-year-old Lipscomb got to the point where he couldn't sleep lying down or leaning back in a chair, Margaret made a chair with a pillow attached to a board that allowed him to lean forward and rest.[2]

On November 11, 1917, as Lipscomb passed from this life, Margaret bowed her head and said, "Lord Jesus, receive his spirit."[3] The Lipscombs had worked side by side for 55 years. Margaret, ever determined, continued on her earthly journey with a positive spirit. She stayed close to her home on the campus of David Lipscomb College her last nine years, but she stayed busy. Administration would ask her for advice because she knew the mind of her husband so well; students did likewise. Rooms were rented in the upstairs of her home to students, and the senior college girls would attend a Bible class taught by Aunt Mag in the early 20's. By 1923, Zelma came to live with Margaret, but she found her great aunt as self-reliant as ever, not willing to share much of the housework. Down time for Margaret was spent writing to missionaries, particularly Sarah Andrews, a missionary in Japan.[4] She wished so much that she could do more to help Ms. Andrews. Whether it was missionaries abroad or local students, Margaret Lipscomb continued serving everyone that her life touched with a positive spirit.

---

[1] *Ibid.*, p. 181.
[2] *Ibid.*
[3] West, *Life and Times of David Lipscomb*, p. 286.
[4] Hooper, *Crying in the Wilderness.*

Zelma shared this with us: "One time I heard Aunt Mag tell sister E.A. Elam that she did not know why the Lord had let her live on [after Uncle Dave's death], but she was sure he had some purpose, and she hoped to fulfill it."[1] Aunt Mag was just being Aunt Mag, serving others and patiently waiting for her time to rejoin her husband in heaven. However, this unassuming woman would never realize just how much she served His purpose, day in and day out even in her later years. Sister Elam said this about Margaret:

> This was characteristic of her life. It was always loving and serving in such a quiet, unostentatious way that only those closest to her really knew what she did. In life's perplexities and trials she possessed the gift of knowing what to say to every one to make the road a little smoother, the hope a little brighter, and the burden a little lighter.[2]

May God bless us with such an inventive, positive light to carry us through hard, lean, discouraging times and to spread that light to all those around us in the same way Margaret Zellner Lipscomb did. Margaret passed away into eternity kneeling beside her bed, her positive spirit likely prompting her to get out of bed one last time to talk to her Lord before meeting Him face to face.[3]

---

[1] Stroop, "Pioneer Spirit of Aunt Mag Lipscomb" p. 14.
[2] Elam, "Association with Sister Lipscomb," *Gospel Advocate*, April 1926, p. 363.
[3] Hooper, *Crying in the Wilderness*.

QUESTIONS

1. What do you admire most about Margaret Lipscomb and why? Describe some of her inventions.
2. What did Aunt Mag believe about cleaning house?
3. What was David's and Margaret's attitude toward the poor?
4. Margaret Lipscomb certainly had a very positive attitude towards everyone and everything. Do you feel that we need to adjust our attitudes? Discuss Scripture verses that encourage a positive attitude.
5. The woman of Proverbs 31 and Margaret Lipscomb did not have the modern conveniences we have today, but they seemed to find time for every task. Have we forgotten how to be inventive and use the minds God gave us? Are we prioritizing our time for His purpose?

Grave of Margaret Lipscomb,
Mount Olivet Cemetery, Nashville, TN (3/30/2024)

CHAPTER 9

Julia Esther Larimore:
A Woman with a Song in her Heart
(1845-1907)

The following are quotes about the beloved preacher, teacher and founder of the Mars Hill Bible College: "The world is better and happier because T.B. Larimore lived in it."[1] "Larimore had the mind of a philosopher, the heart of a woman and the innocence of a little child."[2] "He was loved because he was good, pure, and God-like… He loved the good and the beautiful wherever he found it. Women had confidence in the purity of his heart and loved him with sincere tenderness. Children, especially little girls, clung to him like a father."[3] As evidenced by these quotes, T.B. Larimore may have been the gentlest, humblest and

---

[1] Boles, *Biographical Sketches of Gospel Preachers*, p. 336.
[2] T.W. Caskey, quoted in Phillips, *Medley of the Restoration*, p. 61.
[3] West, *Search for the Ancient Order*, vol. 3, pp. 93-94.

kindest spirit to ever grace the pages of Restoration history. Besides his maker, whom does the world owe for such a man as this? F.D. Srygley, biographer of T.B. Larimore, said, "It takes two great women to make a great man; the one is usually his mother and the other should always be his wife."[1] A previous chapter has already been devoted to Nancy Larimore, his dear mother whom he held so close to his heart. The second sweet woman to share Larimore's life was his first wife Julia Gresham Larimore, a woman with a heart full of song. She was the woman that married this gentle giant and helped him to serve the cause of the Restoration Movement in Northern Alabama and across the U.S.

Julia Esther Gresham was born July 11, 1845, to Phileman and Delilla Files Gresham. Esther's father died when she was only five years old, leaving her mother to manage the small Gresham farm and tend to a large family. The Gresham land was obtained by Esther's grandfather, Thomas Gresham, who was among the first settlers to enter the Native American land that became Lauderdale County. Thomas fought in the American Revolution, and in 1816 received a land grant of 160 acres in Lexington, Alabama.[2]

Esther Gresham grew up on the farm, learning to be "industrious," "economical" and "business-like." From her widowed mother, she inherited a "well-balanced intellect," a "courageous and affectionate heart" and a strong stature. Esther stood 5 foot ten ¼ inches.[3] According to Emma Page she possessed a "never-

---

[1] Srygley, *Larimore and His Boys*, p. 219.
[2] McDonald, *The Gentle Lady of Mars Hill*.
[3] Srygley, *Larimore and His Boys*, p. 220.

failing hopefulness that enabled her to surmount difficulties that might have overwhelmed a weaker spirit."[1]

All of these qualities were useful during the hardships of the Civil War years. Esther's schooling was cut short due to the war, and she found herself having to grow up fast. When speaking of the war, Srygley mentioned that even the most pampered women rose to the occasion during war time. He said:

> Women are women, and whether you find them in the frozen regions of the North or fanned by the balmy breeze of the South; facing wild beasts in the jungles of Africa or gracing parlors in the most refined society in American cities; wherever they are found, they are ready to make any sacrifice or submit to any hardships which fidelity to the object of their love may require.[2]

With no manufacturers in the South, women used what they had before the war or resorted to making substitutes. Thorns were used instead of pins. Combs were made from cow horns, and buttons from leather. They had to make their own furniture, hats and clothes. Sewing needles that were still around were kept busy day and night.[3]

Food was scarce and hard to keep in supply. Women near the Tennessee River Valley, where both armies swarmed trying to cut off the other's supply lines, had to put up with robbers appearing from nowhere. Food had to be hidden in various locations to keep it from being confiscated. Women had to find substitutes for needed staples: Instead of coffee, tea was made from corn, acorns, okra, meal or rye. Sometimes water was even drained

---

[1] Page, "Julia Esther Gresham Larimore," *Gospel Advocate*, July 1907, p. 451.
[2] Srygley, *Larimore and His Boys*, p. 84.
[3] *Ibid.*

through the dirt of smoke-houses (like the process of getting lye from ashes) to obtain a tiny amount of black salt.[1] Larimore added to Srygley's description of the times in a letter to him:

> Women and children worked as slaves and lived in constant dread of robbers, murderers, the knife and the torch—anxious for news, but always afraid to hear it. Women who had spent all their antebellum days in ease, affluence and luxury, followed the plow, fed hogs, hid their bread and meat in cellar, loft and field, spun and wove shucks and straw, made coffee of corn bran, carried corn to the mill, hid their horses in the bushes—in short sun burnt and hard handed, lived labored, and looked like squaws of the forest—dragged down by cruel war, but bravely battling against hard times, loving God, serving their generation and giving their lives for those they loved.[2]

Esther recounted some of these hard times to her husband. She remembered that she and her sisters did everything during those times except for using the reap hook or the sickle.[3] "They plowed, grubbed, made, gathered and hid the crops, made rails (handled ax, maul and wedge) built fence etc."[4] To hide their meat, they dug a hole in their smokehouse floor and carried off the excess dirt so no one could tell of the hole's presence. Then, deep into the night when fierce hunger pains struck, some would stand guard while others dug up the box, obtained what they needed and then covered the hole with dirt. Esther said that they did all this expecting the whole time to turn around and see their house go up in flames,.[5] Larimore wrote, "We laud the

---

[1] *Ibid.*
[2] *Ibid.*, pp. 88-89.
[3] *Ibid.*
[4] *Ibid.*, p. 89.
[5] *Ibid.*

Carthaginian women, who ages ago gave the hair of their heads to make bow-strings for their soldiers; but neither Greece nor Rome, nor Carthage, nor Jerusalem, nor this wide world, has ever developed sublime specimens of true, genuine heroism, than 'Hard Times in Dixie'"[1]

Esther endured these hard times for four years, living on the north bank of the Tennessee River. Larimore stated, "The four years of our Civil War began just as she entered hopeful, responsible girlhood; and the experiences of that time that tried the souls of men and women, boys and girls, developed as probably nothing else could have developed some of the fine, strong traits of her character."[2] Srygley described this young woman trained by the cruelty of war as he knew her in the years afterward:

> She rarely becomes excited and always makes the most of what is in sight—the best of the situation. If her house were in flames, she would first see that every member of the family was safe and then, if she could save nothing but a wash bowl or a dish rag, she would save that and go right along to work singing, as if no loss had been suffered.[3]

Despite living through four long years of war, Esther was a young woman with a song in her heart.

At war's end, Esther met a young Confederate veteran and evangelist from East Tennessee by the name of T.B. Larimore. They met at the Hopewell meeting house when Larimore was on his way to teach at the Mountain Home Academy near Florence in 1868. Larimore had been preaching in the mountains of

---

[1] *Ibid.*
[2] Larimore and Page, *Letters and Sermons of T.B. Larimore, vol. 3*, p. 131.
[3] Srygley, *Larimore and His Boys*, p. 221.

Northern Alabama during his vacation from school.[1] At the age of 23, Esther married Larimore on Sunday, August 30, 1868.[2] Upon their marriage, Esther's mother deeded the young couple 28 acres of land. Land went for ten dollars an acre then, but Larimore said the land deeded to them was worth more because of its beauty and location. The hills around were covered with great oaks and bubbling springs. Larimore dubbed their new home "Mars Hill."[3]

It was Mars Hill and the Great Commission that called to Larimore and Esther. By 1870 the Mountain Home School had failed, and after taking two short-term teaching jobs in Tennessee, Larimore was struck with the idea to build a school for boys and girls on their own beautiful land.[4] This school would bring great change to the Reconstruction era of the Muscle Shoals area.[5] War-torn and poverty-stricken mountains had already beckoned Larimore to come evangelize, and Larimore answered. Larimore had never forgotten the struggles of poverty in his childhood, but usually preferred not to mention them.[6] Once, he spoke sadly to his own children for laughing at the poor and said, "Don't laugh about that, little darlings you do not know what it is to be cold and hungry and homeless."[7] With their own school and Larimore's gentle but dynamic Gospel preaching, Larimore and Esther could make a real difference for the Lord in their area.

When Larimore was struck with an idea, it was usually big. He didn't think small. When he bought a bell for Mars Hill

---

[1] McDonald, *The gentle Lady of Mars Hill*; West, *Search for the Ancient Order* vol. 3.
[2] McDonald, *The Gentle Lady of Mars Hill*.
[3] Larimore, *Life, Letters, and Sermons of T.B. Larimore*, p. 107.
[4] Larimore, *Life Letters, and Sermons...*; Srygley, *Larimore and His Boys*.
[5] McDonald, *The Gently Lady of Mars Hill*.
[6] Srygley, *Larimore and His Boys*.
[7] *Ibid.*, p. 61.

College, he bought the largest bell and finest bell that could be made, weighing 1800 pounds and sounding up to eight miles out. When he bought a barnyard gate, he put the posts in five feet deep and they loomed 14 feet above ground. When he began publishing a paper, he paid for 20,000 copies out of pocket before having the first subscribers.[1] Failure was not in his vocabulary.[2] Therefore, Larimore still young and short on money, needed the business sense of his new bride to borrow money for the school. Syrgley submitted the following about Esther: "In formulating and carrying out practical business plans, she is an invaluable assistant of her distinguished husband. In this line she is peculiarly well adapted, both by natural gifts and early training."[3] Larimore said:

> I have never had reason to regret having followed her advice; but often have I deeply regretted going contrary to it. Such has been my experience in this respect, that now, I always deem it safe to do as her judgement dictates, and unsafe to do otherwise, even when I see the case in an entirely different light. In everything, little and great, she has been a safe adviser for me for 20 years; but often I have gone contrary to her advice and as often found, when it was too late that she was correct.[4]

Esther worked alongside her husband, sharing his big dream. Together, they built a three-story building that served as a home, dormitory, and school on top of Mars Hill with twelve rooms and three halls.[5] Larimore described Esther as "bright and beautiful

---

[1] Srygley, *Larimore and His Boys.*
[2] Larimore, *Life, Letters, and Sermons...*
[3] Srygley, *Larimore and His Boys*, p. 221.
[4] *Ibid.*
[5] McDonald, *The Gentle Lady...*; West, *Search for the Ancient Order* vol. 3, p. 85.

and as good as she could be. Withal she was an incessant worker."[1] The school was finished within 12 months of Larimore's idea and was marked with success.[2] Then another decision had to be made: At the foot of Mars Hill lay more beautiful land with a playful creek, a beautiful grove of trees and a foundry. This land was owned by Germans that were determined to turn the old foundry into a brewery. Esther and Larimore discussed this one day while on a walk through the beautiful grove. The couple's sad thoughts about the land turned to hope when the idea hit them to buy the 700 acres of land themselves. The couple knew it meant more debt, but according to Larimore, "We lived hard and worked hard, practicing the principles of self-denial and strictest economy till the estate of seven hundred acres was free."[3] Esther worked from day one and continuously throughout the years of the school, and she was a big part of its success.[4] She took on each day only as she knew how: meeting each day with a song.

Each school day was a lot of work for Esther in and of itself. Larimore woke the students every morning at 4:00 a.m. and kept them busy until lights out at 9:00 p.m.[5] When reflecting upon the role that Esther played, Srygley said:

> She does more hard work, or did in the days when I was at Mars Hill, than any other woman I have ever known. She never complains, and she knows how to get work out of her children too. She seems actually to love work and she has not patience with worthlessness or idleness.[6]

---

[1] Larimore, *Life, Letters, and Sermons...*, p. 107.
[2] *Ibid.*
[3] *Ibis.*, pp. 108-109.
[4] Larimore and Page, *Letters and Sermons...* vol. 3.
[5] Srygley, *Larimore and His Boys.*
[6] *Ibid.*, p 222.

Srygley labeled Esther as having the "fortitude of a martyr."[1] She led those around her by the example of her work ethic and inspired them not to be idle. She sacrificed for the school and its students by doing most of the household work herself and supervising the rest. Nevertheless, with all her work, Esther still found time to practice and study her music with small babes in arms.[2] She worked at Mars Hill with that song in her heart. She sang while she was cooking. She sang while attending her babies. She sang while she sewed. She sang while preparing the dining room. She sang while gardening. Esther Larimore sang everywhere she went.[3] Syrgley especially remembered her great love for the "hymns of faith."[4]. Esther's favorite hymn was "Softly and Tenderly, Jesus is Calling" (Christian Hymns No. 34). Later in life, Larimore reflected upon Esther's favor for this song. He said, "How often I have stood in silence at the close of the last song before preaching and looked at her till she softly and sweetly said, 'Thirty-four!'"[5]

The students would sing before breakfast and then, after all their studies and recitations, they would meet each afternoon for an hour of singing practice. Sometimes people from Florence would come to the school to hear them. Larimore wanted all to sing. He even printed "Let all the people sing" on his order of worship cards that he used in his meetings. Larimore sat in as a student during those singing sessions and sang with all his heart, but often missed the pitch when it changed. Once, a young man at the school became so discouraged with himself that he felt he should flee the singing session. The other students felt sorry for

---

[1] *Ibid.*, p. 221.
[2] McDonald, *The Gentle Lady...*
[3] Srygley, *Larimore and His Boys.*
[4] McDonald, *The Gentle Lady...*
[5] Larimore, *Life Works of Mrs. Charlotte Fanning*, p. 451.

him, but Larimore knew just what to do. In addressing the young man he said, "Do not be discouraged, you can learn to sing. These boys and girls used to laugh at my blunders when I first began to sing, and see what a great singer I have made."[1] The whole student body exploded in laughter, including the young man. One might assume Esther was in these sessions as well; but, supper did follow the singing session. However, if Esther was in the kitchen, I'm sure she was singing over the cook stove or singing while setting the table, right along with the students.

Esther touched so many at Mars Hill with the song in her heart. This song especially touched her husband. Larimore could enter melancholy moods at times, as evidenced by some of his gloomy reflections on his childhood, but Esther was always dignified and calm. Srygley said that Esther was:

> quick to read his feelings in his face when he is despondent, and, stopping her song for a moment she will rally him, with a laugh and a 'see here my boy, that'll never do. We're all alive, and able to work. If we do our best God will provide a way out of all our difficulties. Just think how much worse it might be.'"[2]

What a blessing this song of Esther's was to Larimore.

Esther used her song to help herself manage through difficult times as well. She sang to keep herself going when Larimore was called away on preaching tours during vacations from school. Esther handled the business, the home and the farm matters out of that same love in her heart evident in her song.[3] If only we all had that same song.

---

[1] Srygley, *Larimore and His Boys*, p. 135.
[2] *Ibid.*, p. 222.
[3] *Ibid.*

Esther used her song to teach all of her children. The Larimores had seven children: Dedie, Granville, Theophilus (Toppie), Herschell, Julia Esther (Ettie) and Virgil. Minnie Bell made seven, but she did not live very long.[1] As the couple taught their family and their students, their objective was to make Christians. Larimore taught that life was the time to prepare for our heavenly home. Srygley remembered, "Many a time have I heard him say in the presence of the school that he would rather see his own children grow up in ignorance of even the English alphabet and be Christians, than to graduate with highest honors from Yale or Harvard and live without Christ.[2] With Larimore away preaching a lot, much of their own children's training fell on Esther's shoulders. She loved her children and helped to train them in the ways of work and Christian duty.[3] Both Larimore and Esther taught by their examples by being the good people that they were. Like Larimore, Esther did not have to drive her children but just led by her goodness, and her children followed her example.[4] The children at the school were equally blessed. Larimore said, "We loved one another and love ruled the school."[5] Esther was a big part of that love with her song.

Esther also used her song towards animals that made their home around Mars Hill, and her eminent kindness played a big part in her song. Emma Page spoke of Esther's kindness in an article for the *Gospel Advocate*. She wrote:

> Kindness—loving kindness—characterized her all the days of her life—kindness, not only to loved ones near and dear to her, but kindness to every creature about her.

---

[1] Larimore, *Life, Letters, and Sermons*...
[2] Srygley, *Larimore and His Boys*, pp. 138-139.
[3] Larimore and Page, *Letters and Sermons*... vol. 3.
[4] Srygley, *Larimore and His Boys*.
[5] Larimore, *Life, Letters, and Sermons*... p. 111.

The animals on the farm; Tony, the little dog that died of grief because of separation from her; the pet squirrels she loved and played with as if they had been children, were won to her by the sweetness of her voice, the tenderness of her touch, the constancy of her care.[1]

Esther especially felt sorry for work animals. Once, after she witnessed through her window a man beating his team mercilessly, she struggled to the door, barely able to walk, to confront him.[2] She convinced the man to stop and quoted the following: "A righteous man regardeth the life of his beast" (Proverbs 12:10).[3]

Esther's song spread through her influence on the school and the motherly love she expressed toward "Larimore's Boys." By 1877, the school started to experience changes. Some of the academic departments gradually withered away since the school was only open six months a year to allow for evangelistic work the other half of the year. Eventually Mars Hill College condensed down to just the Bible department.[4] Nevertheless, this was the part of the school that resided in Larimore's heart. Srygley quotes Larimore as saying, "The design of the school was to build up the church, and the object of education was to make Christians."[5] Larimore and his boys accomplished this task by setting out from Mars Hill on foot and on horseback, planting churches and bringing sound gospel preaching in gentleness and love throughout Northern Alabama. They were a great blessing to the Muscle Shoals area. The last graduation and the closure of the school came sooner than one may have thought: the school only ran from

---

[1] Page, "Julia Esther Gresham Larimore," p 451.
[2] *Ibid.*
[3] *Ibid.*
[4] Srygley, *Larimore and His Boys.*
[5] *Ibid.*, p. 138.

1871 to 1887 (17 years).[1] Larimore just felt more needed in the pulpit.[2] Larimore's boys (his students), like F.B. Srygley, J.C. McQuiddy, E.A. Elam, and F.D. Srygley, were just a few that took the good news all across America.[3] This was the legacy of Mars Hill, of which Esther's song was a part. Esther was the "Gentle First Lady of Mars Hill."[4]

So where did Esther's heart song come from? What song could carry Esther through the years without her father, four years of cruel war, lean years of paying off debts on their school, lonely days of managing responsibilities alone while her husband brought the gospel to others and through a debilitating disease in her last years? Her song began when she took on Christ in baptism on October 21, 1859. Esther had a "deeply pious nature."[5] She was kind, and she honored Christ with an affectionate and courageous heart as a mother, wife and Christian. Esther loved to take an active part in the cause for Christ, and she would have never been persuaded to leave His cause. She attended services faithfully, and her heart sang when sinners were converted to Christ. This was the song that Esther sang to Larimore, to her children, to the young students at Mars Hill and to all she influenced.

Larimore had accomplished so much by the year 1907, and this giant of a man was loved by all, but Srygley asked this question:

> Who has thought to consider the magnitude of her part in his labors, or sound abroad her praise for her labors of love and prayers of faith in furthering his good works? I

---

[1] West, *Search for the Ancient Order*, vol. 3.
[2] Larimore and Page, *Letters and Sermons...* vol. 3.
[3] Srygley, *Larimore and His Boys*.
[4] McDonald, *The Gentle Lady of Mars Hill*.
[5] Srygley, *Larimore and His Boys*, p. 220.

would not take from his crown a single star to ornament hers; but I beseech you brethren, in common justice, to remember always to make the one crown of his praise encircle both their brows; for are not the twain one flesh?[1]

Julia Esther Gresham Larimore had a song in her heart that reached far and wide. However, her sweet song was cut short because she was called home early (on March 4, 1907). Despite her disapproval, Larimore cancelled his preaching tour to be with her and to help take care of her through the last year of her debilitating disease. Most of her children were there as well to take care of her. Toppie was called from this earth a few years before his mother's death.[2] As her time approached, "She gave directions for her funeral as quietly as she had been accustomed to give directions about household affairs."[3] Larimore wrote this just before her journey home:

> She wishes some of our "boys"—our pupils—to say whatsoever may be said at her funeral—the first funeral from our new Mars' Hill meetinghouse—"a memorial of love, liberality and loyalty to the Lord," as well as a reminder to many of the labors, sacrifices, self-denial and sufferings of the mistress of Mars' Hill—the mother—whom so many boys and girls loved so tenderly and truly when they were pupils here—whom all our blessed boys and girls now living love so truly and tenderly yet. We'd have all of them with us at the burial of their mother, if we could; but we recognize that as an absolute impossibility, of course.[4]

---

[1] *Ibid*, p. 223.
[2] Larimore and Page, *Letters and Sermons...* vol. 3.
[3] Powell, *The Man From Mars Hill: The Life and Times of T.B. Larimore*, p. 56.
[4] Larimore and Page, *Letters and Sermons...* vol. 3, pp. 136-137.

Larimore said of his sweet wife, "Few have sung in a lifetime, more than she has sung....She has sung her last song here, but she'll sing forever over there."[1]

Esther Gresham Larimore was a remarkable woman. When we read her epitaph, may we all remember this courageous woman with such an influential song in her heart.

> **Esther Gresham Larimore**
>
> First wife of T.B. Larimore
>
> A dutiful daughter; an affectionate sister; a faithful friend; a loyal, helpful, hopeful wife; model mother; a sweet singer; a truly conscientious consistent Christian, always consecrated, loyal and true to Christ and his cause, she was perfectly prepared for that sweet home where sorrows and sad expressions are unknown— where life is stern and a treasure sublime
>
> 'Farewell, sweet wife—by faith divine, we'll meet you over there.'
>
> Your lonely husband.[2]

---

[1] Larimore, *Life Work of Charlotte Fanning*, p. 451.
[2] Phillips, *Medley of the Restoration*, p. 35.

QUESTIONS

1. In Larimore's description what is meant by "the heart of a woman"?
2. Compare Civil War era women to women of today. Do we have "Southern Grit"? (You don't have to be from the South to answer)
3. Define Esther's song. Was it just words that she sang? How did her song help not only herself but those around her?
4. Esther loved animals and was an advocate for their well-being. How was she being a good steward?
5. If the object of education today was to make Christians, how would the world look?

*Grave of Esther Larimore,
Gresham Cemetery, Florence, AL (3/31/2024)*

CHAPTER 10

**Mattie Carr:
A Woman on a Mission
(1846-1907)**

Mattie Carr knew from a very young age the mission that would consume her entire life. Mattie's childhood days were filled with loss, from the deaths of her mother and two of her sisters to the departure of her dear older brother, Joe, whom she so much wanted to emulate, when he left to open a school in Lancaster, KY. This loss left a young child alone in a big house in Stanford, KY, save the love of her father and her nurse. The nurse pondered over what to do with this child who at one time was not thought strong enough to live past infanthood. What should she do with a child so quiet, reserved and touched by death? Mattie's father struggled over what to do with one whose mind was always so full of deep thoughts, who preferred to befriend older companions and who loved to listen to theological discussions. Father and nurse could only ponder, but Mattie knew her mission. When her brother Joe opened his school, Mattie opened her school. For Mattie, her mission began with her school for dolls, but one day her mission would come to fruition with her school for young ladies, a place on a hill overlooking Sherman, Texas, by the name of Carr-Burdett College.[1]

Mattie began her mission at eight years old by convincing her father to send her to her brother's school. Eight years old was unusually young to be at boarding school, but Joe looked after his young sister and her dolls. Mattie enjoyed her years at Lancaster and her close relationship with her brother. Often in the evenings, Joe would play the flute for Mattie, and as the young child sat listening, it is likely that she was dreaming of her mission to teach. Always very serious about her education, she absorbed all the learning that she could possibly squeeze into each and every day. She was positive that her mission on this earth was to be a teacher.[2]

At age 12, Mattie was ready for the next step. She travelled to Harrodsburg, KY, to attend Daughters College.[3] Daughters College had a reputation for being very thorough and for being the best women's college in the area at that time.[4] Here she met a teacher who became a mentor, exemplifying all she hoped to be, John Augustus Williams. Williams was the President of Daughters College and the author of the biography on Raccoon John Smith. He taught that the natural vocation of women is teaching. Mattie admired Mr. Williams greatly. Often, he would read his biography of John Smith and have his class parse each

---

[1] Ellis, *The Story of a Life*.
[2] *Ibid.*
[3] *Ibid.*
[4] Brown, *Churches of Christ*.

sentence.[1] He taught in a way that touched Mattie's soul and she absorbed every word when he said things like:

> You have an infallible criteria by which you may determine the success of your own and your teacher's labors. If you feel in your heart a greater susceptibility to truth, a livelier appreciation of the purely beautiful, a profounder regard for virtue, a warmer affection for good and a sublime devotion, esteem your labors as eminently successful; but if your attainments varied and extensive as they may be, are to render you less amiable in disposition, or less pure in thought—less charitable to your fellow, or less devoted to God, then we have labored in vain and your learning, also has been in vain.[2]

Mattie determined that she wanted to instill the love of learning in young girls and help them achieve a higher view of life, just as Mr. Williams had instilled in her.

Mattie also purposed herself to be an instrument of God to spread His gospel. As a small child, she had been held on the knees of Barton W. Stone and John Smith. She had seen Alexander Campbell and Walter Scott. She knew the plea for all to unite under the simple gospel, and she knew numerous scriptures and arguments from listening to religious discussions.[3] Mattie was on a mission for God and was determined to carry it out. The following evidence of Mattie's determination was found in one of her school notebooks amidst lines of poetry from Elizabeth Barrett Browning (her favorite) and classroom notes: "God, grant that I may never find enjoyment in the foolish pleasures of the

---

[1] Ellis, *Story of a Life.*
[2] *Ibid*, p. 12.
[3] *Ibid.*

world; but that my soul may soar far above its ephemeral joys unto the unsearchable riches of Christ Jesus my Lord."[1]

Though Mattie was a determined young lady, set-backs remained a constant battle in her life. At times she let her unquenchable thirst for knowledge out-run her physical ability to keep up with it. While attending Daughters College from ages 12-16, Mattie was described as a young girl entirely too thin, in a modest plain dress with a serious look. She put everything she had into every class, and this took a toll on her body. As she attended church at Main Street, where she often heard sermons by Robert Milligan, Robert Graham and Robert Richardson, her spiritual convictions were deepening, but her constitution was waning. After church, her mind was not on the young men from Bacon College like the other girls. Mattie spent every break she had on her school studies. Growing thinner and paler, she studied until fever broke out. When she became too weak to carry on at Daughters College, Brother Joe, who understood his sister, brought her home to recuperate. However, unable to hold her heart's desire down for long, Joe arranged for Mattie to attend St. Catherine de Sienna's Convent, hoping that the atmosphere would be less stressful and give Mattie time to heal.[2] Here she finished her senior year with the top grades of her class. Mattie then returned to Daughters College and finished the senior courses there.[3]

During the summer breaks from school, Mattie went to stay in the home of her married sister, Mrs. Kate O' Bannon. It was here, and not at Herrodsburg where Daughters College and Bacon College were located, that Mattie met her future husband,

---

[1] *Ibid.*, p. 65.
[2] *Ibid.*
[3] Brown, *Churches of Christ*

Oliver Anderson Carr.[1] Oliver returned to his home land on summer vacations from Bacon College to preach gospel meetings and fulfill his heart's desire of bringing the gospel to others. While still a student, he brought around 500 people to Christ in Northeast Kentucky.[2]

Oliver had grown up in Mayslick, Kentucky, the town of retirement for the well-known Restoration preacher, Walter Scott. The great preacher took an interest in the children and spoke at Oliver's school when he was a young boy. All felt the need to put forth their best when in the presence of Mr. Scott, even the grown-ups. Aside from Oliver's encounters with Walter Scott and one attempt to visit the local Sunday school, he did not set his mind towards becoming a Christian until the local blacksmith Eneas Myall encouraged the young man by asking, "Ollie, isn't it about time you became a Christian?" Oliver did decide to become a Christian, and that same blacksmith determined to pay Oliver's way through college at Kentucky University.[3] Oliver did his best to prove himself worthy of his gifted tuition even though he struggled extensively with his studies in Latin and Greek. He also struggled with money. Looters from the Civil War were hard on his family, and a couple of times professors would slip money to Oliver to try and help his situation. In addition to these struggles, Oliver constantly struggled with his health, much like Mattie, and he was advised to go home from school and rest. With the possibility of consumption looming before him, he drank mineral water for three months. Nevertheless, Oliver pushed his way past his hardships, determined to finish his studies. His quest to spread the gospel began during his so-called time of rest, and

---

[1] Ellis, *Story of a Life*.
[2] Brown, *Churches of Christ*.
[3] Hagger, "Biographical Sketch on the Life of O.A. Carr" in *Heralds of Christian Unity*, boyhood section, para. 3.

he would not be held back from preaching through the mountain trails and the little towns in the hills of his home land. It was at Mount Carmel, the church of Mattie's sister where Oliver was invited to preach, that he met a young lady with a heart on fire for the Lord to match his own.[1]

After Mattie and her sister, Mrs. O'Bannan, heard Oliver's sermon, the intriguing youth was invited to Mrs. O'Bannan's home, where Mattie and Oliver talked for the first time. Both found it awkward to carry on a conversation with each other except when they talked about religion. Finding this topic one that brought them together, Oliver soon started to make trips to Daughters College to sit and talk more with Mattie. Mr. John Augustus Williams, of course, was there to chaperone in the parlor while the two enjoyed this happy time.[2]

Even though the winds of change began to blow, Oliver and Mattie found ways to nourish their relationship. Oliver's school, Bacon College, had originally started in Georgetown with Walter Scott as president. Eventually it was brought to Harrodsburg by J.B. Bowman and became Kentucky University in 1858. Harrodsburg was the location of Daughters College as well, so the couple was in close proximity. However, when Robert Milligan moved the school at Harrodsburg to Lexington due to a fire, he merged the school with Transylvania University. This meant that Oliver had to go to Lexington as well, and the couple would be separated. During this time many letters were exchanged between the two. Oliver would mail a debate that he had been working on in return for a copy of a lecture given by John Augustus Williams from Mattie. In his letters, he asked Mattie to try and share the gospel with his sister Mary and to pray that his parents would

---

[1] Ellis, *Story of a Life.*
[2] *Ibid.*

respond to the gospel. If either slacked in their duty to write each other, there was always the understanding that the opportunity to hear Brother Moses Lard, or someone else who held their admiration, was an excuse of great importance. When opportunities arose for Oliver to visit with his studious young love, he would bring her gifts such as McGarvey's commentary, knowing that she would appreciate it like none other.[1]

Mattie had found her match, yet her mission was never put on the backburner. Soon after graduation, Mattie opened a school of her own in Lancaster, Kentucky, named Franklin College, having already secured the positions of owner and president.[2] Meanwhile, Oliver had been presented with the opportunity to work in the mission field of Australia. G.L. Surber had written to Brother McGarvey about the need for preachers there, and McGarvey presented Oliver with the opportunity.[3] Not wanting to leave his love behind, Oliver presented the situation to Mattie, who found herself torn. Mattie had just finished one term with her new school and was finally the teacher she had always wanted to be. Was she now to up and leave her new school? Of course, her admired teacher, Mr. Williams, wanted to see her excel at her "natural vocation."[4] Then there was her brother Joe, who would not hear of her moving. According to Ellis, he would play songs like "Old Kentucky Home" and "Home Sweet Home" on his flute in Mattie's presence to persuade her to stay.[5] Oliver was ever persistent though. He knew that he had the support of his beloved Bible teacher, Brother McGarvey, who approved of the young couple marrying and making the trip. McGarvey said, "Come

---

[1] *Ibid.*
[2] *Ibid.*; Brown, *Churches of Christ.*
[3] Hagger, *Heralds of Gospel Unity*
[4] Ellis, *Story of a Life,* p. 136.
[5] *Ibid.*

Ollie, it is just as near heaven from that country as from Kentucky."[1] At last Mattie said yes, knowing that she could teach in Australia just as well as in America. The couple tried to sneak away on the stage coach, only to be stopped in the road by Joe, but Mattie would not be stopped for long.[2] She was still in pursuit of her mission. She just hadn't known at first that it would involve travelling to the other side of the world.

Oliver and Mattie were married on March 26, 1868, at five o'clock in the morning. Many friends and family attended, including the blacksmith who had paid for Oliver's tuition. Several receptions were given, including one at the former home of Henry Clay, and then the couple travelled to Mayslick. Oliver's mother travelled on with them from there to Maysville, where she responded to the gospel (his father had been baptized a short time before). What a blessing that event was for the couple before their departure! From Maysville they travelled to New York, then to England for two weeks of sightseeing and then ventured out on a long, three-month journey to Australia. Oliver and Mattie had never been out of Kentucky before this trip.[3]

In Melbourne, Australia, the couple was welcomed with "Tea on the Tables at Half Past Six."[4] Tea and goodies lined four tables beautifully decorated with fresh flowers (tradition there granted the flowers to the guests of honor). This fellowship was followed by a meeting of several speakers. Even at this first meeting with their Australian brethren, a school of girls for Mattie was discussed. Another tradition that the Carrs learned quickly was that the evangelist spoke on Sunday night and not Sunday morning. Communion and talks from the lay people made up the

---

[1] Hagger, *Heralds of Gospel Unity*, "Off to Australia" section, para. 1.
[2] Ellis, *Story of a Life*.
[3] *Ibid.*
[4] *Ibid.*, p. 171.

Sunday morning service. One also had to get used to the backwards seasons on the other side of the world, but the Carrs made adjustment and went right to work.[1] The couple proved to be excellent missionaries. Oliver preached almost every night, and during the day he taught young boys in his home using his material from Kentucky University. Mattie started her school with about 20 students and made a lasting impression on them. Both were very busy and happy doing the Lord's work in Melbourne where they resided for three years (Ellis, 1910). Once, Oliver demonstrated his wisdom during a disagreement of church members on what material to use in constructing a new church building in Collinswood. Oliver preferred brick, but he said, "Let the majority decide. If the majority says a wooden chapel, a wooden one it will be."[2]

Many letters from family, friends and the couple's mentors went back and forth over the seas. Mattie wrote to John Augustus Williams about coming back to the states to raise money for a college in Australia, but Williams was not encouraging towards the idea in light of unsuccessful past endeavors. Mattie continued to hold onto her dreams, which would begin to unfold upon her return home to the states in 1872 for health reasons. Before returning, however, the Carrs spent one year in Tasmania, where they started a church; the couple also took a trip down the Nile and visited the Bible lands.[3] Mattie had gained much experience, more than the average young lady from Kentucky, but she was still on a mission.

Intending to return to Australia, but also feeling the need to stay in the states, the Carrs searched for the proper place to reside.

---

[1] *Ibid.*
[2] Hagger, *Heralds of Gospel Unity.*
[3] Ellis, *Story of a Life.*

Oliver was happy preaching around to whoever needed him. However, Mattie was on her mission to find the school where her talents would have the greatest impact on her pupils. She stayed at Hocker College under President Robert Graham for one year, but it was not what she was looking for. She had her own set of ideas on how to run a college. Again directed by her beloved teacher John Augustus Williams, Mattie decided that Missouri held great opportunity for her; therefore, the couple moved to St. Louis. Oliver preached while Mattie committed herself to study and travel until she was able to establish Floral Hill College for girls in Fulton, Missouri. Mattie was happy to be in a position where she could use her wisdom to bring the college to her set of expectations. However, Floral Hill could never attain this height with Christian College in Columbia nearby. By the end of its second year, it was decided that Floral Hill would be consumed by Christian College. Mattie would be an associate principal, but again her ideas of education and conduct were different than those in leadership.[1]

In 1879, on reputation alone, Mattie was asked to come to the University of Missouri, where she would spend the next ten years. Here she was a professor of English and Dean of the Young Ladies Department.[2] According to Ellis, as "Lady Principal," she came in contact with both boys and girls and strove to bring them to a "higher spiritual plane of life."[3] She also taught her students the importance of keeping one's body physically fit. However, Mattie still pushed herself beyond her limits to bring her educational ideals to their potential. She gave lectures and corresponded with prospective students. She met with state representatives to discuss bills being brought up in Jefferson City

---

[1] *Ibid.*
[2] *Ibid.*
[3] *Ibid.*, p. 327.

and met with Dr. Laws often to discuss the state of the University. She even corresponded with Miss A.M. Longfellow, the daughter of the famous poet; Miss Longfellow held a similar position to Mattie's at Harvard. Despite all of her other duties, Mattie always insisted on teaching. Mattie was a busy lady, and she had accomplished a great deal by this point in her life, but her heart was still searching for her mission formulated so long ago.[1]

McGarvey had kept up with the Carrs, and he mentioned to Oliver that he wished Mattie could find work "directly in the interests of Christianity."[2] Oliver wanted this for Mattie as well, "A college whose foundation stone should be the word of God."[3] Therefore, Mattie decided to resign from the University of Missouri and reside in Springfield where she would "rest" and make plans for her future college, the height of her mission. She did not rest in the normal sense of the word, but compared to her previous six years, those in Springfield were a bit more relaxed.[4] In 1884, Oliver had been appointed state evangelist for Missouri, keeping him constantly busy and away from home.[5] Often he would write to Mattie and tell her to take a vacation. However, Mattie's idea of a vacation was to take a shorthand class on the phonograph or working in missions and in the Women's Christian Temperance Union. She also helped in the campaign of John A. Brooks for governor and helped her husband write a book on J.K. Rogers.[6]

Oliver and many of Mattie's friends continued to look for the perfect place for Mattie's dream school. After much deliberation and many setbacks, Sherman, Texas, was the decided place.

---

[1] *Ibid.*
[2] Ellis, *Story of a Life*, p. 349.
[3] *Ibid.*, p. 346.
[4] *Ibid.*
[5] Hagger, *Heralds of Christian Unity.*
[6] Ellis, *Story of a Life.*

Mattie's long-sought-after mission was starting to become a reality. Thinking back to a time in Springfield when Mattie cut off her finger, picked up the appendage and held it there until help arrived, one can't help but admire Mattie's toughness. That toughness is what Carr-Burdett College was founded upon. Mattie was quite the business woman, and she used her skills to get business people on board with her plan. She had the local business men visualize all of the business that a college of girls would bring to their town: bulk loads of groceries from the grocer, more patients for the doctors and druggists and clothes, books and music supplies to be purchased from other merchants. Then she pointed out that the building of the college would help those in carpentry and hardware. It would help the local furniture and carpet stores, and it would also benefit the coal industry. Mattie persuaded many to donate to their school. Then she appealed to the pride of Sherman's educational and religious interests. For the next two grueling years, the Carrs sold lots to help the private college become a reality.[1] After selling 250 land lots for $200 each, Mattie said, "We struck out the word 'fail' and all its derivatives from our vocabulary, and addressed ourselves to the task."[2] Oliver continued to travel and preach, trying to sell more. Finally, the building that Mattie had designed was under construction. Mattie was the one who guided the plow at the ground breaking, and a cornerstone ceremony was conducted at the building's completion. At this event Mattie spoke about her long-sought-after mission and its achievement thus far.[3]

At Carr-Burdett College, a mission became a reality. The school opened its doors in September of 1894.[4] Mattie was able

---

[1] *Ibid.*
[2] Lane, *History of Education in Texas*, p. 101.
[3] Ellis, *Story of a Life.*
[4] *Ibid.*

to impart the cultural type of education to girls so long formulated in her mind. "Her education was that of the typical 'female seminary' of that day with its emphasis English Literature, French Conversation, 'the accomplishments,' music and art, lady-like conduct and the social graces with a sort of subdued recognition of the expectation that the young lady would someday be the mother of a household."[1] The girls expected the head mistress to be somewhat peculiar, and Mattie proved to be so with her seriousness. She was quite the disciplinarian and her students either loved her or feared and despised her discipline.[2] Girls were taught that "study is not play, any more than play is study," and those who didn't view school in this way were sent home.[3] One must remember that to Mattie, education was "serious" and "lifelong." She saw education as a development of mind and heart to be a blessing from the Lord upon the world. It was an important part of everyone's character.[4] Carr-Burdette College gave Mattie the opportunity to teach her girls that, through a Godly education, they were called to action to "give love a voice" to those around them and to God.[5]

Mattie continued to teach at Carr-Burdett almost fourteen years. Oliver joined his wife and the staff in teaching and was a great asset as a scholar of so many subjects. The couple spent their last years together enjoying the fruit of Mattie's mission. However, in October of 1908, Mattie died. Oliver carried out the duties of President of the school until his death in 1913, and the school closed in 1929 due to a lack of funding and students.[6]

---

[1] Harp, *Oliver Anderson Carr 1845-1912,* Notes from *History of Texas Christian University.* TheRestorationMovement.com.
[2] Ellis, *Story of a Life.*
[3] *Ibid.*, p. 433.
[4] *Ibid.*
[5] *Ibid.*, p. 201.
[6] Harp, *Oliver Anderson Carr 1845-1912,* TheRestorationMovement.com.

Mattie had believed that her school would "redound more to the interests of the church" in Texas than anywhere else in the United States. She also "as originally intended, deeded the grounds and buildings to the Christian Church of Texas."[1] However, upon examination of the deed after the deaths of Mattie and Oliver, it was clear that if there was more than one Christian Church, the trust would be spread equally. At that time division had occurred in Sherman, and as more and more Christian Church officers were added to the Board of Trustees the school fell into the hands of what is today known as the Christian Church.[2]

Oliver Carr said this in a *Gospel Advocate* article that he wrote in his sweet wife's memory: "She gave the last thirteen years of her life to the college. I feel that she literally sacrificed her life itself to the accomplishment of her high purpose; for I know that she toiled with mind and body beyond her strength, forgetful of self."[3]

Mattie Myers Carr was a woman on a mission. Carr-Burdette was that mission, her ideal that she strove to obtain her whole life. Mattie's whole life was a mission for the Lord. Beginning with her small school of dolls, to her work in Australia, to her impact on her students in all of the schools where she taught—how many lives had she touched while teaching? How deep was her impact on the Restoration Movement? We may never fully realize. Mattie's grave-stone reads:

---

[1] Lane, *History of Education in Texas,* p. 101.
[2] Harp, *Oliver Anderson Carr...*
[3] Carr, "In Memory of Mrs. O.A. Carr," *Gospel Advocate*, November 1907, p. 762.

> 1846—Mrs. O.A. Carr—1907
> Carr-Burdette College Is Her Own Monument
> Founder, Built And Donated By Her.
> From Youth A Christian with High Ideal.
> She Devoted All To Uplift And Save.
> For 42 Years A Teacher In Australia,
> Kentucky, Missouri, Texas
> "She Opened Her Mouth With Wisdom And
> In Her Tongue Was The Law Of Kindness.
> A Woman That Feared The Lord, She Shall Be
> Praised. Let Her Own Works Praise Her."[1]

Grave of Mattie Carr, West Hill Cemetery—Sherman, Texas

---

[1] Mattie F. Myers Carr 1846-1907—FindAGrave.com

QUESTIONS

1. Mattie knew at a young age what her mission was in life. Did you have a mission in mind at so young an age? Did you fulfill that goal?
2. Mattie's mission was to be a teacher. She never wavered from her mission. Do we let obstacles or even just life in general, stand in our way or keep us from completing our goal?
3. Both Oliver and Mattie had health issues, but this did not stop them from the Lord's work. Do we let little things stop us?
4. Who influenced Mattie spiritually? Who influenced you?
5. Mattie's whole life was a mission for the Lord. How can we evaluate our goals and dreams at different points in our lives to see if our mission puts the Lord first?

CHAPTER 11

Influential Mothers of the Restoration

There were many women that contributed to the Restoration Movement. However, due to circumstances during and surrounding the Civil War era, there is very little written record of these women. This chapter and those that follow are designed to shed light on women that just received maybe a line or a paragraph here and there amongst the many paragraphs about their sons and husbands. Even a small glimpse of these women can pull them out of the shadows so we can glean from their lives. You've already read about the motherly love shown by Nancy Larimore. Let's take a look at more of our Restoration mothers. Our first mother is Mary J. Potter (1842-1936), a mother that influenced the building of a school and an orphan home.

MARY J. DUNN POTTER

Mary J. Dunn Potter had a character of consistency. As a young girl, she wanted for little on a large plantation that her father owned in Warren County, Kentucky.[1] Ben F. Taylor, author of *The History of Potter Orphan Home* said, "Mary J. Potter was reared in the aristocracy and refinement of the 'Old South' and her years did not separate her from them."[2] Mary never altered the appearance of her home or her dress even though she was surrounded by the changes that the South undertook following the war. "Sister Potter was a noble representative of the refined culture, the serene dignity, and the lady Queenliness of a departed South. She was the 'last leaf upon the tree,' and all stepped up to obey her "authoritative dignity"[3]

Mary was also consistent in living her life for the Lord. She was sixteen years old when she was baptized on March 9, 1859.[4] She was immersed by a brother in the church by the name of Smith at Pleasant Hill. It is believed that this man was Edward H. Smith from the Horse Cave Kentucky area. Mary served in the Lord's church for 77 years, and her impact was left on the churches of Pleasant Hill, Bowling Green and Rich Pond.[5]

B.F. Rogers was largely responsible for bringing the simple Gospel truth to the community of Rich Pond, Kentucky. He relocated here to establish a school, having based his decision to begin this work on a prayer sent up in indecision over two offers for his services. Feeling that God wanted him at Rich Pond, he began to preach in the community's school building once a month.[6] Taylor said, "Brother Rogers exerted an influence which became the lasting warp and woof of the moral and spiritual life of the Rich Pond community."[7] B.F. Rogers struggled with his

---

[1] Taylor, *History of Potter Orphan Home.*
[2] *Ibid.*, p. 46.
[3] *Ibid.*, p. 47.
[4] *Ibid.*
[5] *Ibid.*
[6] West, *Search for the Ancient Order,* vol. 3.
[7] Taylor, *History of Potter Orphan Home.*

work in this community at first: no church in that area patterned itself after the New Testament or followed the Bible alone. According to Taylor, Mary J. Potter was the only member of the church around those parts. However, after a lot of fortitude and with the help of E.G. Sewell, who came to do a debate and a two-week meeting, many started to obey the gospel. Mary had influenced her husband, C.C. Potter, to attend this meeting, and he was baptized by E.G. Sewell in 1874.[1] Mary must have also had a strong influence on many of the Potter relatives—there were several Potter families in the growing congregation at Rich Pond.[2]

Mary had been married previously to C.C. Potter's brother Albert, and in 1866 this couple had a son. However, the infant died at birth, and Mary carried this sorrow underneath her "Old Southern" dignity, barely speaking of this child throughout her years. Nevertheless, on June 19th of 1871, she was blessed with the son of her heart, Eldon S. Potter.[3] When Eldon was only two years old, his father Albert died. Clinton (C.C. Potter) stepped into a father's role to Eldon and six years later married Mary.[4]

Mary's son Eldon was a special boy. He was baptized in 1889 on the same day as his good friend, Clarence H. Rogers, son of B.F. Rogers. He grew up in a wealthy home on the Potter's vast land holdings.[5] According to James A. Harding, Eldon received his inheritance of an estate worth around $60,000.[6] The *Bowling Green Daily Times* described Eldon as "Possessing wealth not exceeded by more than one young man in the county,

---

[1] *Ibid.*; West, *Search for the Ancient Order* vol. 3.
[2] Taylor, *history of Potter Orphan Home.*
[3] *Ibid.*, pp. 47-48.
[4] *Ibid.*
[5] West, *Search for the Ancient Order* vol. 3.
[6] As cited in Young, *A History of Colleges Established and Controlled by Members of the Churches of Christ*, p. 111.

he was as unpretentious and plain in his walk as if oblivious of the fact that he had an abundance of this world's goods."[1] In the summer of 1899, the Rich Pond congregation was working on raising money to construct a church building to house the 12th St. Church of Christ. Eldon donated about a third of the total contribution.[2] Mary was very proud of her young Christian man with such a giving heart for the Lord's work, and Eldon surely would have given more and more in years to come. However, according to Klingman, his life was cut short consequential of the Spanish American War, and Eldon died in 1899.[3] He was only 28 years old.[4] According to Harding, Eldon was the one who indicated that his estate be used upon his death for "some Christian service."[5] This is just another demonstration of a special young man with a giving heart towards the Lord's work.

The apple didn't fall too far from the tree. Eldon came by his giving heart honestly. Taylor stated, "The history of the lives of Clint and Mollie as each called the other, is that of two hearts and two lives welded together."[6] Throughout their 55 years of marriage one story after another portrays C.C. Potter discussing with Mary their course of actions in financial decisions concerning the work of the church or just helping out a neighbor. When donating money, C.C. would say, "Of this amount I will give two thirds of the amount and my wife will give one third.[7]" Sure enough, there would be two checks signed by C.C. and one signed by Mary. The Potters used this same teamwork to put their heads together about what to do with Eldon's estate and honoring his request to

---

[1] "Eldon S. Potter," *Gospel Advocate*, Nov. 1899.
[2] Taylor, *History of Potter Orphan Home*.
[3] As cited in West, *Search for the Ancient Order* vol. 3, p. 263.
[4] *Eldon S. Potter 1871-1899*, FindAGrave.com
[5] As cited in Young, *History of Colleges Established...*
[6] Taylor, *History of Potter Orphan Home, p. 63.*
[7] *Ibid.*, p. 63.

use it in Christian service.[1] Taylor said, "One haunting dread stood out in the heart of Sister Potter. Nursing her broken heart, she wondered if her beloved son would become forgotten and unknown by future generations."[2] Wanting so desperately to honor their son and give hope to others, the Potters together convinced James A. Harding, a teacher at the Nashville Bible College, and his son-in-law, J.N. Armstrong, to help them start Potters Bible College. It would be located in Bowling Green on the Potter's farm with Harding serving as President.[3] In 1901, the school started with a strong faculty, and "its influence was far-reaching. Numerous gifted preachers were educated within her walls while others went to mission fields, particularly Japan."[4] Harding reported in the *Gospel Advocate* that the teachers and students of Potter Bible College had led 652 people to the Lord in the 1907 school year.[5] As the years went by, students at Potters Bible College began to enjoy the classes more than graduating, and the school began to dwindle away. The school closed its doors in 1913, soon after Harding's term as president ended in 1912.[6] The Potters had turned the school over to the Twelfth Street Church of Christ in 1901, but after the Bible College closed, the Potters again stepped in to help the school with its transition into an orphan home in 1914.[7] Eldon Potter's legacy and Mary's influence lives on in the Potter's Children's Home that remains to this day, offering young children the hope that the Potters saw in their precious son. Mary, out of love for the work

---

[1] *Ibid.*
[2] *Ibid.*, p. 119.
[3] West, *Search for the Ancient Order*, vol. 3.
[4] *Ibid.*, p. 269.
[5] McQuiddy & Harding, "Potter Bible College," *Gospel Advocate*, Dec. 1909.
[6] West, *Search for the Ancient Order*, vol. 3.
[7] Taylor, *History of Potter Orphan Home.*

of the church and a mother's love for a son taken too soon, has influenced more than she could ever imagine.

MARGARET LINGOW ELAM

Other Restoration mothers may not have had the financial means to influence the start of a school, but some have spread their influence by just being an encourager and a prayerful mother. E.A. Elam's mother, Margaret Lingow Elam (1835-1907), was one of these mothers.[1]

Elam's father was taught the gospel by Tolbert Fanning and raised his family on a small farm in Fosterville, Tennessee. Mrs. Elam was a great Christian helpmeet to her husband and carefully trained her children in religion.[2] She had a great mind and was "cultured above the average" despite little education;[3] most of Margaret's education she pursued on her own by teaching herself at home.

Margaret was especially gifted at being an encourager. She was known by her neighbors for her encouraging words and her kindness, but she was especially an encourager to her church. According to J.D. Floyd, Margaret "was the real founder of the Church of Christ at Fosterville, and up until her death was one of its strongest pillars." In reference to Margaret and her struggle to help establish this congregation, Floyd said, "The struggle was a long one, and a less tenacious person would have given up in despair. A union house had been built there and the first meeting for prayer that was ever held there was held at her earnest request."[4]

---

[1] *Margaret Lingow Elam 1835-1907*, FindAGrave.com.
[2] Srygley, *Biographies and Sermons*.
[3] Floyd, "A Noble Woman Gone to Rest," *Gospel Advocate*, March 1907, p. 166.
[4] *Ibid.*, p. 166.

Margaret was also a great encouragement to her children. As her husband's second wife, she sewed a cord of family love between his three children from the previous marriage and the five children she bore to him. J.D. Floyd wrote, "She so impressed herself upon these children that they all seemed to be of one family. The older children have frequently told me that they knew no difference between her and their own mother."[1]

Margaret sought God in prayer just a few minutes after her son, E.A. Elam, was born. She prayed and offered her first-born's life to the Lord much like Hannah did with Samuel. She prayed for God to help her train and guide this new life for His service.[2] After writing an article on Motherhood in a 1907 *Gospel Advocate*, Selina Holman included Margaret's response letter where she described this prayer:

> I have just read "Motherhood." It brought so vividly to my mind my varied thoughts and feelings when 34 years ago, my first babe, a dear, blue-eyed boy was placed in my bosom. I think I have never prayed a more solemnly earnest prayer than I prayed while my first babe was for the first time clasped to my heart.[3]

Selina Holman then continued, saying that she never looked into E.A. Elam's "grave, earnest, kindly blue eyes" without thinking of his mother's prayer. She said that, "the example of such a mother becomes a beacon of light to help other mothers to a fuller life, to a stronger feeling of the duties and responsibilities and the glorious privileges and recompenses of motherhood."[4]

---

[1] *Ibid.*
[2] Srygley, *Biographies and Sermons.*
[3] Holman, "A Good Mother," *Gospel Advocate*, April 1907, p. 210.
[4] *Ibid.*

Margaret taught her son to read and helped him with his studies. She was there for him all through childhood. E.A. Elam was baptized at 16, and prayed his first prayer in front of the congregation at Fosterville in one of its early meetings.[1]

Upon E.A. Elam's departure for boarding school, Margaret gave him a Bible in which she had marked all the passages he would need to read when faced with temptation. Once when some young men were trying their best to get E.A. Elam to drink with them, he resisted by remembering the sacrifices that his parents had made to send him to school. He continued his schooling with diligence, attending Franklin College, Burritt College and Mars Hill. In between school terms he worked on launching his preaching career.[2] In addition to preaching, Elam went on to bless the world with his writings. He spent nearly 50 years writing for the *Gospel Advocate*. He wrote Sunday school literature and a number of books. He also served on the board of the Nashville Bible School.[3] It all started with a mother's prayer; and through her encouragement of her son, it continued on in her son and the many others that her life touched.

J.D. Floyd was one of these people whose life Margaret influenced. After his first year of working with the church at Fosterville, Floyd had reached a point where he was completely discouraged. He said:

> More from the earnest entreaty of Sister Elam than anything else, I agreed to continue another year. That year I baptized twenty-one persons. This gave strength and encouragement, and the struggle has not been so great since.

---

[1] Floyd, "A Noble Woman..."; Srygley, *Biographies and Sermons*.
[2] Srygley, *Biographies and Sermons*.
[3] Boles, *Biographical Sketches of Gospel Preachers*.

The success was the result of the labors, prayers, and tears of Sister Elam and the faithful few who stood by her.[1]

May we as mothers to our own children, or as mothers to the children in our congregation, remember to use the power of an encouraging word and the power of prayer like Margaret Elam.

MARY LUMPKIN BARNES (MISS. POLLY)

Other mothers of the Restoration influenced their children by being great students of God's word. J.M. Barnes' mother, Mary Lumpkin Barnes (1811-1891), was one of these mothers and a great example to all through her knowledge of God's word. Mary's father, Thomas Lumpkin, moved his family from a South Carolina plantation to the pioneer wilderness of Alabama when Mary was 14. In 1830, at age 19, she married Elkanah Barnes, a planter and businessman 14 years her senior. Barnes was a co-owner of the mercantile, a surveyor, land agent and business contractor, and thus a prominent figure in the early days of Montgomery County.[2]

Two years previous, at age 17, Mary was baptized by William McGauhy. McGauhy was a preacher from Georgia who had left the Methodist Creed behind and desired to follow the Bible alone. He had come out of the southeastern movement spread by the churches influenced by James O'Kelly in North Carolina. The southeastern movement traveled through Georgia and into Alabama. It is important to point out that these "Bible Christians," as they were called, influenced Alabama before Stone and Campbell. Mary's conversion and the first church of Christ in Montgomery County originated with this movement. Mary had been

---

[1] Floyd, "A Noble Woman..." p. 166.
[2] Kimbrough, *Miss Polly: The Life of Mary Lumpkin Barnes*.

studying her Bible and seeking truth early in her teenage years.[1] She knew when "she heard the plea for a 'thus saith the Lord,' she accepted it, and for years she was the foremost defender of the truth in her section."[2] She was even called "One of the best Biblical Scholars of her day" by secular historians.[3] Mary loved truth, and she loved to learn. She kept many books and periodicals around her log cabin home. She even wanted to name the community they lived in "Strabo" after the Greek philosopher, but through postal misinterpretation the name ended up being Strata.[4]

Whether it was at her cabin home or later at her plantation home Mary or "Miss Polly" as many affectionately called her, was quite the host. She always found time to make her home as engaging as her personality. Earl Kimbrough quotes Mary's grandson, E.R. Barnes, as saying, "…she made [her home] so inviting and its spirit so hospitable that cultured people were glad to visit in it." It "reflected her own nobility of thought and appreciation of culture and progress."[5] Many preachers and famous politicians were entertained in her home. Once, she tried to show Judge Bibb of Montgomery County the way more perfectly from the Bible. The judge attempted to quote scripture back and failed in his application and quotation of the text. Mary gently said, "Ah, judge I see you know more about politics then about the word of God." The judge thereafter liked to tell the story of how Mrs. Barnes "got the best of him" in arguing religion.[6]

---

[1] *Ibid.*
[2] Srygley, *Biographies and Sermons*, p. 398.
[3] Kimbrough, *Miss Polly*, p. 5.
[4] *Ibid.*
[5] As cited in Kimbrough, *Miss Polly*, p. 6.
[6] Srygley, *Biographies and Sermons*, pp. 399-400.

Mary put all her heart into training her children in the Lord's ways. She taught Justus MacDuffie, or J.M., to not look down on others or to offend them. Once when J.M. was ten years old he spoke in an offensive way and ordered a free African American off their land for interrupting their work. This young lady was visiting her husband on the Barnes' Pre-Civil War plantation. This deeply saddened Mary, but she did not speak to her son about it right away. J.M. could not bear to play as he was worried about his mother's mood. Finally, he fell into her embrace crying uncontrollably until she explained that he had taken authority that wasn't his and spoken to a person impolitely. J.M. never forgot this lesson.[1] Mary also demonstrated correct love and respect further by exposing all of her husband's slaves to the gospel, and starting the first Black congregation of Christians in Montgomery County. Mary's teachings about respect for others seemed to stay with her son all of his life and are evident in his teachings.[2]

Srygley stated, "…it was the joy of her life and the climax of her ambition when her only son became a Christian and determined to be a preacher."[3] Mary struggled with tears when her son left for Bethany College. She gave him a paper with words of advice and encouragement which J.M. Barnes attached to his trunk. He kept that paper on his trunk until 1883, when it was destroyed in a fire.[4] The words he remembered were:

> Be your own self; never affect to be what you are not. Be kind and courteous to everyone. Be polite and respectful to those older than yourself. Treat others as you would

---

[1] *Ibid.*
[2] Kimbrough, *Miss Polly.*
[3] Syrgley, *Biographies and Sermons*, p. 399.
[4] *Ibid.*

have them treat you. Trust God and serve him, and he will take care of you.[1]

J.M. Barnes went on to be a great preacher, teacher and writer. "He never made a sacrifice or endured a hardship for the love of truth as a preacher while his mother lived that she did not stand bravely by him with gentle, loving words of praise, comfort and encouragement."[2] His mother's influence was probably what drove Barnes to teach underprivileged boys and girls while losing money from his own pocket and to start a school in Strata that eventually became Highland Home College.[3] John T. Poe, who worked with Barnes at a Montgomery meeting in 1911, thought that he was the best "drillmaster of young people" that he had ever seen.[4] Barnes would often enthusiastically encourage young and old alike to sing at his meetings and to learn through his stories. H. Leo Boles said that "he could tell Bible stories to children in an interesting, attractive way, and at the same time instruct older people."[5] Some of these unique qualities may have come from his experience as a teacher, but I suspect that some started taking root from the teachings of his mother. Barnes also wrote columns for the *Gospel Advocate* and other papers. For the *Advocate*, he wrote a column called "Away Up in Tennessee" about his experiences there. He submitted other stories under the pen name "The Little Man."[6]

Historian Earl West stated, "No name would stand higher in the history of the Restoration Movement in Alabama than that of

---

[1] *Ibid.*
[2] *Ibid.*
[3] Kimbrough, *Miss Polly*; West, *Search for the Ancient Order*, vol. 3.
[4] West, *Search for the Ancient Order*, vol. 3, p. 165.
[5] Boles, *Biographical Sketches of Gospel Preachers*, p. 278.
[6] West, *Search for the Ancient Order*, vol. 3.

Justus McDuff Barnes."[1] Miss Polly instilled in J.M. Barnes the qualities that made this great man. She was definitely a mother of influence.

LUCY JANE B. McCALEB

Some mothers of the Restoration left an imprint by being strong in the face of trials. These were mothers who taught their children to look down on no one and to love all. John Moody McCaleb's mother was one of these. Her name was Lucy Jane Beasley McCaleb (1829-1882).[2] Lucy was the daughter of John Pitts Beasley, and her family came from North Carolina to settle at Mill Creek in Hickman County, Tennessee. She was married to John McCaleb and bore six children.[3] Two of them she named John because she thought that her husband was such a good man that he deserved two sons named after him. John Moody was the

---

[1] *Ibid.*, p. 164.
[2] *Lucy Jane Beasley McCaleb 1832-1882*, FindAGrave.com. Sources give her birth year as 1829 (as seen on the website in question), but her tombstone says 1832.—*Editor.*
[3] Srygley, *Biographies and Sermons.*

youngest of the six sons. A girl was born in 1861 but did not live long.[1]

J.M. McCaleb's great nephew believes that Lucy's husband was killed when John Moody was still in the womb.[2] One day when Mr. McCaleb was out and about, a Civil War soldier commanded Mr. McCaleb to halt, but due to the noise from a nearby stream the order went unheard and John Moody's father was shot through the heart. When no one would help Lucy bring her husband's body home on the muddy roads and in bad weather, Lucy and her oldest son started out alone before, finally, two neighbors decided to help. Lucy was left a widow with six children during the cold years of the Civil War.[3] She had to gird herself with an inner toughness that all single moms must find and look to her Lord for His help. Nevertheless, at this time in this strong woman's life, her sorrow seems more for her husband and her children. Once, when little John McCaleb found his mother crying in the stairway, Lucy gently took the boy into her arms and said, "I am weeping for your poor dead father."[4]

Lucy was a multi-tasker. She taught her children from the seat of her loom while she kept her family clothed. McCaleb went barefoot throughout his childhood and did not own a suit purchased from a store until he was grown.[5] Lucy kept her family busy on the farm, teaching her children to do just about anything and everything around the house. She even educated them in the skill of carpentry work.[6] McCaleb thought highly of his mother, and she held a special place in his heart. Her teachings were

---

[1] McCaleb, *John Moody McCaleb*, email correspondence with a descendant.
[2] *Ibid.*
[3] Srygley, *Biographies and Sermons.*
[4] As cited in West, *Search for the Ancient Order*, vol. 3, p. 272.
[5] *Ibid.*
[6] Srygley, *Biographies and Sermons.*

especially treasured. She taught her little McCaleb his ABC's from the Bible. When McCaleb was grown, he would fondly remember his mother's teaching about honesty by her turn of phrase, "It was as bad to steal a pin as to steal a horse."[1] Srygley said, "She was a good woman; she loved everybody, but she was not blind to the faults of anybody. She often criticized severely those whom she loved dearly."[2] She loved the poor and reprimanded her children if they were impolite to them. She had no patience for aristocratic attitudes that looked down on others. She was always at church services, which met two miles from her cabin, and kept her children reined in by keeping them busy with lessons or going to meetings.[3] Lucy did marry again. Five years after her first husband's death, she married J.N. Puckett, a member of the Church of Christ.[4] Puckett must have been a great influence on Lucy and her sons because they were eventually baptized and became New Testament Christians.[5] J.M. McCaleb was baptized when he was about 14 years old by J.M. Morton in Dunlap, Tennessee, after responding to the gospel call at a meeting conducted by J.M. Barnes. According to historian Earl West, Lucy McCaleb "threw her arms around her son and pressed her cheek to his."[6] What a glorious day for any mom when her child is born again into Christ!

McCaleb attended several schools growing up, including William Anderson's Carter Creek Academy.[7] As the years

---

[1] Colley, "John Moody McCaleb," *Glory to God: Freed-Hardeman University Lectures 1989*, p. 62.
[2] Srygley, *Biographies and Sermons*, p. 290.
[3] *Ibid.*
[4] Colley, "John McCaleb Moody."
[5] Olbricht, "Where Sin Has Gone Must Go His Grace: John Moody McCaleb," *Gospel Advocate*, July 2019.
[6] West, *Search for the Ancient Order*, vol. 3, p. 228.
[7] *Ibid.*

passed, he began to teach school and to preach. He also took a Bible course through the mail put out by Ashley S. Johnson.[1] In 1888 he decided that he would enter Kentucky University, where he had the opportunity to hear many missionary speakers.[2] During and immediately following his time at the university in Lexington, he travelled about Kentucky and Tennessee preaching until March of 1892 when he journeyed to Japan, and preached for almost 50 years of his life.[3] He always said that Christians in the New Testament "went everywhere preaching the word," so to Japan John McCaleb went.[4] McCaleb burned with a deep passion for saving lost souls, and in fulfilling this passion, he serves as one of the greatest role models to missionaries still today.[5]

Later in his life, J.M. McCaleb penned that beloved song in our hymnals, "The Gospel Is for All." Sadly, his mother died when he was at the young age of 20.[6] How proud Lucy McCaleb would have been to hear "The Gospel is for All" sung! This great song represents a mother's precious teaching to her son—to look down on no one and to love everyone. "Receive ye freely, freely give, from every land they call, For why should we be blest alone? The Gospel is for all." J.M. McCaleb was blessed with a strong Christian mother who influenced him to be strong in taking the gospel to others even as far away as Japan.

---

[1] Srygley, *Biographies and Sermons*.
[2] West, *Search for the Ancient Order*, vol. 3.
[3] Srygley, *Biographies and Sermons*; West, *Search for the Ancient Order*, vol. 3.
[4] Srygley, *Biographies and Sermons*, p. 295.
[5] West, *Search for the Ancient Order*, vol. 3.
[6] Srygley, *Biographies and Sermons*.

ELIZA BALLOU GARFIELD

Many mothers of the Restoration were mothers of men who gained fame as great preachers or debaters. However, one mother of the Restoration was a mother who influenced a very famous Christian, the 20th President of the United States, James A. Garfield. Her name was Eliza Ballou Garfield (1801-1888). F.M. Green wrote this about Eliza:

> Whatever Mrs. Garfield did for her son in other directions nothing is clearer than that her influence was great in keeping his mind and heart in the direction of the moral and the spiritual. His whole life was religiously influenced by the seed which was planted by his mother's hand, while he lived with her in the little log-cabin in the wilderness.[1]

Both of Garfield's parents moved from New England and settled in Cuyahoga County, Ohio. Garfield's father, Abram, had worked on the Ohio Canal as a young man but followed his

---

[1] Green, *A Royal Life: or, the Eventful History of James A. Garfield, Twentieth President of the United States*, p. 152.

childhood playmate Eliza to settle in the Ohio area soon after her family moved west. When Eliza was eighteen, she and Abram married and made a home in a small cabin about 15 miles southeast of Cleveland. Eliza kept house and bore three children while Abram farmed. In 1826, the family moved to New Philadelphia in Tuscarawas County where their fourth child was born. However, in 1830, this child died and the family moved to Orange Township back in Cuyahoga County, where they built a new cabin with the help of Abram's half-brother. The cabin was located in the middle of the woods and was small and crude. The older children slept on straw in the attic, and the younger ones slept on a trundle bed near their parents.[1] It was in this cabin that James Abram Garfield was born in 1831, taking the name of the fourth baby that the Garfields had lost.[2]

Garfield grew up playing around his family cabin with his cousins, the children of Abram's half-brother and Eliza's sister.[3] As an older man he cherished memories of sleeping in the small attic of the cabin with his elder brother, Tom. Once, when Garfield was a soldier, he was lying on the ground asleep next to a military officer, and he mumbled the words, "Thomas, cover me up."[4] His own words startled him and brought back memories of childhood and his mother's "tenderness." Then the grown man wept.[5]

Orange Township, part of the Western Reserve, was where Abram and Eliza were influenced by the Restoration Movement and both were baptized.[6] In her later years, Eliza described to

---

[1] Hosterman, *Life and Times of James Abram Garfield.*
[2] Peskin, Garfield: A Biography.
[3] *Ibid.*
[4] Green, *A Royal Life*, p. 53.
[5] Hosterman, *Life and Times of James Abram Garfield*, p. 38.
[6] Wasson, *James A. Garfield: His Religion and Education.*

Garfield in a letter how she and her husband had "resolved to live a different life" after their fourth son died. Moving west had broken their religious ties with family in the East and now they could "find the right way" through the preaching of Adamson Bentley, a convert of Campbell's.[1]

Disaster struck when James Garfield was just about two years old. Abram died of a cold and exhaustion after fighting a forest fire. Eliza, left to raise her family on her own, managed to get along by selling some of their land and by using her God-given courage. She often did without to keep her family going. There was a time when Eliza had to measure out the corn for the children and go without dinner and supper for herself.[2] Garfield never forgot the determination he witnessed in his mother's endless efforts to support their poverty-stricken family. His respect for her clearly "caught the admiration of the nation" in Garfield's later years.[3]

Eliza was just as determined to guide her children's walk with the Lord as she was to keep them clothed and fed. Eliza would march her children three miles to the meeting house for service every Sunday.[4] Hosterman, an early biographer of Garfield, described their family life in the cabin as follows:

> If Christianity ever meant anything to a mother, it certainly did to Eliza Garfield. No sacrifice or duty was too arduous to perform, and with such a mother's influence, the children grew up to youth, and then to manhood and womanhood. A short, cheerful prayer each morning, no matter how early she and the children rose; a word of thankfulness at the beginning of every meal, no matter

---

[1] *Ibid.*, pp. 11-12.
[2] Hosterman, *Life and Times of...*
[3] West, *Search for the Ancient Order*, vol. 2, p. 199.
[4] Peskin, *Garfield: A Biography.*

how meager, and a thoughtful Bible-reading and prayer at night, formed part of that cabin life.[1]

Eliza taught herself to manage the farm and the children learned life lessons about hard work. She also gave herself book knowledge by mastering every book she could get her hands on, in turn sharing her learning with her children. She worked very hard to see that Garfield followed the best educational path possible. At one point, when she felt that her children were travelling too far to the school, she donated a piece of her land and gained support from neighbors to build a log cabin school that was much more convenient.[2] Hosterman stated, "If there was not another luxury or privilege her children could have, there was one they should enjoy, and that was a good education."[3] Then more importantly and in accordance with her strong belief in her children's spiritual education, Eliza encouraged a Church based on the Bible alone be organized in this same school building. According to Rushford, "…this became the focal point for many religious activities of the Garfield family."[4]

Eliza was especially disappointed when Garfield left home at age 16 with the dream of becoming a sailor on the Great Lakes. After ending up as a driver of horses that pulled a barge up and down the Erie and Ohio canals, he soon returned home, battling a case of malaria but undaunted in his dream. Eliza strategically suggested that Garfield be educated for a teaching position so he would have a job in the winters when the canal was closed. Garfield soon entered Geauga Seminary. Before he left, Eliza asked her son to remember her when the sun was going down each night

---

[1] Hosterman, *Life and Times of…* pp. 33-34.
[2] *Ibid.*
[3] *Ibid.*, p. 34.
[4] Rushford, *Political Disciple: The Relationship Between James A. Garfield and the Disciples of Christ*, p. 10.

because this was the time she read her Bible. Garfield made it a habit the rest of his life to read his Bible at this time, just as if he were reading with his mother.[1] Garfield was baptized in 1849 at age 18 by William A. Lillie and soon forgot about his nautical dreams.[2] After Geauga Seminary, he entered the Western Reserve Eclectic Institute under A.S. Hayden. In 1854 he transferred to Williams College, and upon graduation returned to the Eclectic Institute to teach and serve as the school's president until he entered the political world. In 1858, he married a young girl he had met while attending Geauga Seminary, Lucretia Rudolph.[3]

During these years of schooling and teaching, Garfield began to preach and to debate and grew to be very good at both. When he accepted his first nomination to political office, the brethren were concerned that he would lose his character, but upon seeking his mother's opinion, she gave him her prayers and blessings despite her wish for him to be a preacher.[4] Garfield was greatly influenced by his mother's teachings. While serving in the military during the Civil War, Garfield did not forget what his mother had taught him and attended service at every opportunity. He was known as the "praying Colonel."[5] After the war, Eliza (or "Grandma Garfield" or "the little white-haired mother") came to be part of Garfield's and Lucretia's family.[6] Garfield had remembered what his mother taught him when choosing his home in Hiram: his estate did not stand out from his neighbors except in the size of his library. He would say that his home "was

---

[1] West, *Search for the Ancient Order*, vol. 2.
[2] Boles, *Biographical Sketches of Gospel Preachers*.
[3] West, *Search for the Ancient Order*, vol. 2.
[4] Hosterman, *Life and Times of...*
[5] West, *Search for the Ancient Order*, vol. 2, p. 201.
[6] Hosterman, *Life and Times of...*, p. 94.

a place for 'plain living and high thinking.'"[1] When Garfield served in Congress in Washington, he rarely missed a service and was found at times teaching Sunday school.[2] His love for his savior and his mother's teachings was evident throughout his life.

On November 2, 1880, Garfield was elected President of the United States.[3] After he took the oath of office, he kissed the Bible and then turned to kiss his mother and his wife.[4] Eliza became the first mother in the history of the United States to attend her son's inauguration, and she lived at the White House for the short time he was there before his assassination. She probably enjoyed being carried by her strong son, who possessed the stature of his father, up and down the White House stairs.[5] How proud she must have been of her son the President, but even more proud of the man whose convictions inspired him to write this: "There is nothing that can make youth so shapeful, manhood so strong, and old age so beautiful, as the religion of Jesus Christ."[6] Garfield loved his Savior and his mother throughout his life. Eliza Ballou Garfield was a great woman of the Restoration Movement, a mother who through her son influenced a whole country.

JANE BREEDEN LIPSCOMB

Many of our Restoration mothers were step-mothers, yet a step-mother can be just as influential as a birth mother. Jane Breeden Lipscomb (1807-1885) is proof of this: as his step-mother, she was one of the "greatest influences" on young David

---

[1] *Ibid.*
[2] West, *Search for the Ancient Order*, vol. 2; Wasson, *James A. Garfield: Religion and Education.*
[3] Boles, *Biographical Sketches...*
[4] Green, *A Royal Life*, p. 194.
[5] Doenecke, *James A. Garfield: Family Life.*
[6] West, *Search for the Ancient Order*, vol. 2, p. 201.

Lipscomb's life.[1] Biographer Robert E. Hooper stated, "The character of Jane's entire family, whether stepchildren or her own, can be found in the character of the mother."[2]

David Lipscomb's father was Granville Lipscomb, and Jane was Granville's third wife. Late in the year 1826, the William Lipscomb family (David Lipscomb's paternal grandfather) left Louisa County, VA, for Franklin County, TN. Ellen Lipscomb, Granville's first wife, died soon after their arrival. Ann Lipscomb was Granville's second wife and the daughter of Granville's uncle, David Lipscomb Sr., from back in Louisa County. Ann was the mother of David Lipscomb, who was the namesake of his maternal grandfather.[3]

Ann's sister and her husband, the Lindsays from Hopkinsville, KY, were the first to put a copy of the *Christian Baptist*, a publication of Alexander Campbell's, in the hands of Granville Lipscomb. After studying the scriptures, Granville and his brothers decided to move to Sangamon County, Illinois, around Springfield, in order to set their slaves free. When the families found Illinois against freeing slaves, they just freed them over the state line in Indiana.[4] This part of their mission proved to find success. However, the Lipscombs' time in Sangamon County also brought heartache when Ann Lipscomb and three of her children were lost to malaria in 1835. Granville Lipscomb traveled back with the rest of the family to Franklin County, Tennessee, that same year without even securing the sale of his land.[5]

---

[1] Harp, *Early Church, Home Life & Parents of David & William Lipscomb*. TheRestorationMovement.com.
[2] Hooper, *Crying in the Wilderness*, p. 25.
[3] *Ibid.*
[4] West, *Search for the Ancient Order*, vol. 3.
[5] Hooper, *Crying in the Wilderness*.

Needing a mother for his three children, on April 11, 1837, Granville married Jane Breeden. David was only six years old at the time. Jane had moved from Spotsylvania County, Virginia, to Tennessee to help her brother teach school. She was influenced by several preachers in the area who believed in taking the Bible alone as one's only guide, and soon she became a member of the Salem Church, leaving her previous faith behind her. The Salem church met in Granville's home, and eventually Jane was introduced to Granville by a friend of theirs. Jane soon decided that she wanted to help take care of Granville's family, and she was also blessed with five children of her own.[1]

Early diary entries of Jane's are evidence of the type of Christian woman she committed herself to be. One entry on June 18, 1825, was entered after a day of memorizing scripture. She wrote, "O may I by the help of God be enabled not only to retain it in memory, but to let its sacred truths sink deep into my heart."[2] Jane Breeden was the type of person to make her own decisions based on God's word and not the preacher's. She was thoroughly convicted that His word was meant to be studied as truth and that people should defend themselves against false doctrines of men with His truths. She was definitely a Bible reader. In her later-recorded diary entries, we learn that she read the Bible through almost every year from 1870-1884.[3]

What a strong influence she must have been on David Lipscomb. She proved to be an anchor for him from the moment she walked into his life. The passing of his father in 1853 was a particular time where she proved to be a stronghold for Lipscomb. In reference to Proverbs 31, he called her "blessed" upon her

---

[1] *Ibid.*
[2] West, *Search for the Ancient Order*, vol. 3, p. 26.
[3] Hooper, *Crying in the Wilderness.*

death in 1885.[1] Lipscomb grew to be a great teacher, preacher, editor of the *Gospel Advocate* and founder of Nashville Bible College (now David Lipscomb University). Jane Breeden blessed countless numbers through her step-son. As we all strive to pursue our mission, restore truth and plant seeds, let us never forget the influential power we have as mothers and stepmothers to influence the world.

QUESTIONS

1. We see that the mothers in this chapter were great encouragers through prayer, Bible knowledge, steadfastness and consistency. Why are these qualities important in a mother?
2. Give examples from the Bible of mothers who had these qualities. Mary, Elizabeth, Dorcas, Priscilla?
3. When the apron strings are cut, what verses would you want to write down for your children to take with them on the rest of life's journey?
4. What life lessons did Garfield gain from his mother?
5. What important life lessons have you gained from a mother?

---

[1] *Ibid.*, p. 25.

Grave of Mary Potter, Mount Pleasant Cemetery, Warren County, Kentucky (6/29/2024)

Grave of Margaret Elam, Woodfin Cemetery/Shelbyville, TN (5/22/2024)

Grave of Mary "Miss Polly" Barnes, Fair Prospect Cemetery, Montgomery County, Alabama

Grave of Lucy Jane Beasley McCaleb, McCaleb Cemetery, Duck River, TN

*Grave of Jane Breeden,
Lipscomb Cemetery, Franklin Co. TN (5/4/2024)*

CHAPTER 12

Influential Wives of the Restoration

MARY CATHERINE CONN GANO

Mary Catherine Conn Gano lived from 1810-1891.[1] The Gano family that Mary Catherine married into has so much history that we have to start at quite a distance to appreciate it. The great, great, great, great grandparents of Wilbur and Orville Wright were Daniel and Sarah Gano.[2] This couple had a son by the name of John Gano. John was known as the "The Fighting Chaplain" in the Revolutionary War because he took up arms and ran to the front when he saw the Patriots turning to run at the Battle of White Plains.[3] In what J.B. Rushford called "a very interesting incident," George Washington, who looked to Gano as his friend and chaplain, was exposed to his preaching during the war.[4] According to numerous reports, Washington had approached Gano and requested a baptism of immersion, but he did not become a part of the Baptist church.[5] Rushford states, "This incident was unusual because the General was an Episcopalian, and the Chaplain was a Baptist."[6] John Gano used phrases such as "to make the word of God my only rule of faith and practice," but his life did not quite come in contact with the Restoration Movement as did his sons' and grandsons' lives.[7]

---

[1] *Mary Catherine Conn Gano 1810-1891*, FindAGrave.com.
[2] Rushford, *The Apollos of the West: The Life of John Allen Gano.*
[3] *Ibid.*, p. 18.
[4] *Ibid.*, p. 21.
[5] Childress, "John Gano 1736-1804: Was George Washington immersed?" *Firm Foundation*, April 1933.
[6] *Ibid.*, p. 21.
[7] *Ibid.*, p. 28.

One of Chaplain John Gano's grandsons was John Allen Gano. A young John Allen attended school under Barton W. Stone and then pursued a path to study law.[1] In 1823, while travelling on a steamer to Texas, he was put off with a lung hemorrhage to die. He made a promise to God then and there that he would eventually become a Christian and preach.[2]

It wasn't until 1827, when John Allen went to visit his friend, Mary Catherine Conn that he met up with his old teacher, Barton W. Stone.[3] John Allen began to attend meetings conducted by Stone and by a preacher named T.M. Allen. It was at one of T.M. Allen's meetings that the weight of John Allen's sins overtook him, and he decided that he wanted to become a Christian.[4] John Allen was baptized by T.M. Allen near Georgetown, Kentucky, on July 10th. Mary Catherine, who had been baptized a few days before, was there that day as well.[5]

In October of 1827, Mary Catherine Conn married John Allen Gano, with Stone performing the ceremony. Mary Catherine's mother had passed away just one year before her wedding, but her father, Captain William Conn, was there. He gave the newlyweds a farm near Georgetown just across the street from his home. The Conn family had settled that area in 1787 and had large landholdings. The new couple's home was a large Georgian house named Bellvue, and it remained their home together for fifty-nine years.[6]

The Ganos were very determined to remain unshaken in their Christianity. John Allen's convictions were so strong that

---

[1] Gano, "John Allen Gano," in Brown (ed.) *Churches of Christ*.
[2] Rushford, *The Apollos of the West*.
[3] *Ibid.*
[4] Gano, "John Allen Gano."
[5] Rushford, *The Apollos of the West*.
[6] *Ibid.*

when visited by Jacob Creath, Sr., who was sent upon the request of John Allen's sisters to straighten him out, he helped to turn Creath's thinking toward the Restoration Movement.[1] He said, "Elder Creath, if you show me in this book where it says, deny yourself, take up your cross and follow your grandfather, I will follow mine through life. But I read it, follow Christ, and I am determined to follow Him until death if it separates me from all kindred I have on earth."[2] John Allen went on to preach, baptizing more than 10,000 people and establishing churches while travelling with T.M. Allen and John T. Johnson.[3] James Challen said this about John Allen Gano's travels with John T. Johnson: "...hundreds obeyed the Gospel, as reports in the *Millennial Harbinger* and Christian Preacher for 1838 and 1839 will show, never before had such a state of things been witnessed in Kentucky for the triumph of the Gospel."[4] John Allen Gano also played a key role in the Restoration Movement by writing letters in report and defending Raccoon John Smith and John Rogers, who were chosen to help unite the Campbell and Stone movements.[5]

Mary Catherine spread her Christian influence by allowing John Allen to travel and preach, by entertaining at Bellevue and through her influence on her children. Like so many other wives of Restoration preachers Mary Catherine had to sacrifice and share her husband with those who needed the Gospel. Her son Richard described the demand for John Allen Gano's skills in the following statements:

---

[1] Gano, "John Allen Gano."
[2] *Ibid.*, p. 422.
[3] Challen, "Biographical sketch of John Allen Gano," in *Ladies' Christian Annual,* Oct. 1857.
[4] *Ibid.*, p. 308.
[5] Rushford, *The Apollos of the West.*

He was indeed, an able defender of the truth, a close adherent to God's Word, a remarkable exhorter; and his life came up so closely to his preaching that his influence was great, and he could quiet discordant elements to a remarkable degree, and was often called many miles to make peace between men. So universal was the feeling during the prime of his life, in Central Kentucky, that if we can only get Bro. Gano here we will have a good meeting.[1]

Mary Catherine unselfishly gave her husband to preach, but in later years, John Allen did stay in areas close to home in order to take care of her "long and protracted ill health.[2]"

Many preachers stayed at Bellevue. McGarvey called John Allen Gano "the one rich man among Kentucky preachers."[3] Therefore, Mary Catherine was blessed with the opportunity to bless these travelling preachers. Walter Scott once wrote his wife, Sarah, saying that Mrs. Gano was the "meekest of women."[4] T.M. Allen said that he was "received as ever with all Christian kindness by his amiable and beloved family."[5]

Nine children were born to Mary Catherine and John Allen (three died in infancy); Mary Catherine taught her six children with great care. Rushford states that she "was a Godly woman who instructed her children in the principles of the Christian faith."[6] However, life was hard on Mary Catherine as a mother. John Allen and Mary Catherine outlived all but two of their children. The Civil War years were especially hard on this mother. Mary Catherine lost her oldest son William to the war, and her

---

[1] Gano, "John Allen Gano," p. 422.
[2] Challen, "Biographical Sketch...," pp. 307-308.
[3] McGarvey, *The Autobiography of J.W. McGarvey*, p. 74.
[4] Baxter, *Life of Elder Walter Scott*, p. 334.
[5] Allen, "Progress of Reform," *Millennial Harbinger*, Jan. 1859, p. 57.
[6] Rushford, *Apollos of the West*, p. 207.

second son, Richard, or R.M., Gano gave his mother quite a few scares towards that end as well.[1]

R.M. Gano is still remembered in Texas history today. Gano earned rank of Brigadier General and was actually named Major General by General Robert E. Lee but decided not to accept.[2] Once, in 1862, R.M. rode up to Bellevue to have supper with his parents. The Ganos' close friends, the Hopsons, Mr. Conn and T.M. Allen were there that night. Mary Catherine's father heard someone and said, "That is Dick's voice." John Allen said, "They may send me to prison if they want to, but I will give Richard his supper" (John Allen was a pacifist during the war).[3] Mary Catherine told her son with tears in her eyes that the Yankees were at Lexington, Paris and Cynthiana, and to please let her hide him for a night. However, R.M. assured her that he had gotten in, so he could get out. The Ganos spent that night hardly able to even utter a prayer. John Allen was the only one who could speak. However, prayers were answered and their boy made it to safety.[4]

Another time, in 1863, R.M. and two more of his brothers (Frank and John) stayed with the Hopsons near McMinnville, Tennessee.[5] Dr. Hopson said, "Let us look in on the boys once more."[6] The boys lay sleeping on the floor with blanket and knapsack, and the Hopsons thought of the boys' mother and father in Kentucky praying so hard for their children.[7] Many prayers were offered on behalf of R.M. Gano, and perhaps his life was spared so he could live on to bring the Good News to others.

---

[1] *Ibid.*
[2] *Ibid.*
[3] Hopson, *Memoirs Dr. Winthrop Hartly Hopson*, pp. 105-106.
[4] Rushford, *Apollos of the West.*
[5] *Ibid.*
[6] Hopson, *Memoirs of Dr. Winthrop Hartly Hopson*, p. 128.
[7] Rushford, *Apollos of the West.*

After the war, R.M. Gano went on to become a great Restoration preacher like his father. R.M. is one who is remembered for being so disappointed and who "wept as a child" when the Missionary Society was brought to reality at a state meeting in Austin, Texas.[1] His sons as well contributed greatly to the soundness of the movement in Texas.[2] Mary Catherine was a wife, mother and grandmother of influence, and though not much material is recorded, we see the effect of her strong Christian faith throughout the Gano family.

SARAH I. TURNER SEWELL and ELIZABETH A. SEWELL

Sarah Sewell is a great example of the popular phrase, "The Power of One." Sarah lived from 1816 until 1862.[3] (David Lipscomb said this in regards to Sarah Sewell:

> God uses simple, unthought-of, and, as they appear to us, fortuitous circumstances to effect His ends. It teaches the lesson, that fidelity to God and man in the relations we are in is what God requires at our hands then he will overrule for good, and out of what seems to us small matters of life, bring the greatest results.[4]

Very little is known about the life of Sarah I. Turner Sewell. In his book on Jesse L. Sewell, David Lipscomb stated, "We know nothing of her, save that through her conversation her husband was won..."[5] This woman of the Restoration simply influenced the man in the relationship closest to her, the one God laid at her feet. She completed a task probably not considered by most

---

[1] West, *Search for the Ancient Order*, vol. 2, p. 423.
[2] Rushford, *Apollos of the West*.
[3] *Sarah Isabelle Turner Sewell 1816-1862*, FindAGrave.com.
[4] Lipscomb, *The Life and Sermons of Jessie L. Sewell*, p. 59.
[5] *Ibid.*

to be mountain-moving, yet Sarah Sewell was a woman of impact. Her simple deed snowballed and ended up impacting thousands, leading them to the simple gospel truth. Her life is a lesson to us all. What impact will she have on you?

Sarah I. Turner was a relative of Dr. J.M. Turner, the man who established the church in Willow Grove, Tennessee. This church is one of the oldest in the upper Cumberland area. Dr. Turner was the son-in-law of Squire John "Jack" Sevier, nephew of Governor John Sevier of Tennessee. This church, of which Sarah was a member, met in Squire Sevier's home during the winter months until a meeting house could be erected. Squire Sevier donated the land for the meetinghouse and served as an elder for many years.[1]

Sarah Turner married the oldest son of Stephen and Annie Sewell, William B. Sewell, in 1840.[2] "W.B. in deference to his wife's wishes, occasionally attended services with her and learned to appreciate them. Very shortly, he was partaking of the Lord's supper with these people."[3] He was attracted by the simplicity of the worship, the adoption of the Bible as the only rule of faith, and the laying of all "inventions of men" aside.[4]

W.B.'s conversion started a chain of events that led to a landslide of bringing others to the Gospel truth. As a clerk at the Wolf River Baptist Church, W.B. was immediately brought to trial before them after his conversion. William's uncle, W.D. Sewell, acted as moderator. Many members of the Sewell family, including William's father, were members at Wolf Creek.[5] On

---

[1] Goodpasture, "The Willow Grove (Tenn.) Meeting," *Gospel Advocate*, Sept. 1932.
[2] West, *Search for the Ancient Order*, vol. 2.
[3] *Ibid.*, p. 153.
[4] Lipscomb, *Life and Sermons of Jessie L. Sewell*, p. 57.
[5] *Ibid.*

the day of the trial, "William being the clerk of the church, had the Articles of Faith and Rules of Decorum; holding this in one hand and the New Testament in the other, he asked by which of the books would they try him?"[1] Those present proceeded in voting him out of the church before he was even tried at all.[2] Another uncle, J.A. Sewell, was among those who voted W.B. out of the Wolf Creek Church.[3] The impact of Sarah Turner Sewell upon William B. Sewell made quite an initial ripple in the Sewell family.

It was not long before W.B. was paid a visit by his brother Jesse, a preacher of the Baptist Church. Jesse thought William had made a mistake fellowshipping with the church at Willow Grove and wanted to show W.B. his error by using scripture.[4] William answered, "If you can show me by the Bible, I did wrong, I will gladly retract and confess my wrong."[5] The brothers studied for weeks, meeting regularly to discuss the scriptures. Jesse had not foreseen any difficulty in getting his brother to return to the Baptists. However, each meeting would leave Jesse feeling defeated about his own points and brought him to the simple truth of God's word.[6] "Finally, one day Jesse shut his Bible quickly and loudly, and exclaimed to his wife, 'Bettie, all the passages are William's.'"[7] It was not long after this event that Jesse too was cast out of the Baptist church for preaching "faith, repentance, and baptism for the remission of sins."[8] Jesse proceeded to carry the primitive gospel to all with whom he came in

---

[1] *Ibid.*
[2] West, *Search for the Ancient Order*, vol. 2.
[3] Goodpasture, "The Willow Grove (Tenn.) Meeting."
[4] Lipscomb, *Life and Sermons…*
[5] *Ibid.*, p. 58.
[6] Goodpasture, "The Willow Grove (Tenn.) Meeting."
[7] *Ibid.*, p. 1059.
[8] Lipscomb, *Life and Sermons…*, p. 71.

contact. Lipscomb wrote in his book that the "hold the Christian religion has upon the people of Middle Tennessee is due under God to Jesse Sewell more than any other one man."[1] Don't forget that behind that great preacher was his wife Elizabeth or Bettie, who was an active participant in Bible discussions and supporter of her husband preaching the truth from its pages.[2] According to Lipscomb, "She could remember more distinctly and accurately his different meetings and results than he (Jesse) could."[3] When Jesse L. Sewell was away preaching, Elizabeth was left to care for the children alone but determined to encourage him and to never be a deterrent. Out of her love for the Lord she conquered her fears on lonely nights, repaired fences, threshed her own oats and became the preferred miller among the neighbors.[4] Lipscomb wrote, "She says there is no kind of out-door work that she has not done."[5] Like her husband this strong, determined woman helped to spread the Gospel Truth out of self-sacrifice, but Sarah's influence did not stop with Jesse and Elizabeth.

Three other brothers of William B. Sewell's became preachers. Isaac C. Sewell, a brother who asked for his name to be stricken from the Wolf Creek Church at the same time that Jesse was excluded, became a preacher in Northeastern Tennessee. Caleb W. Sewell, baptized by his brother Jesse at age 20, attended Bethany College and was a favorite of Mrs. Campbell's.[6] Through Caleb, Mrs. Campbell (Selina) sent "Mother Sewell" a gift of a silk cap. Mrs. Annie Sewell never wore this precious gift

---

[1] *Ibid.*, p. 119.
[2] Sewell, "Biographical Sketches of Restoration Preachers," *The Harding College Lectures 1950.*
[3] Lipscomb, *Life and Sermons...*, p. 91.
[4] *Ibid.*
[5] *Ibid.*
[6] Goodpasture, "The Willow Creek Meeting."

until she passed away because she was buried in it.[1] Caleb preached in Louisville, Kentucky, and then returned to Tennessee. The youngest Sewell brother that became a preacher was Elisha G. Sewell. He edited the *Gospel Advocate* for over 50 years and influenced people far and wide.[2] Four out of seven of the Sewell boys became preachers, and then all of Jesse Sewell's sons became preachers. Joseph preached in Missouri. William A. preached in Tennessee and Texas. Caleb also preached in Texas, and L.R. preached around Nashville.[3] As we continue to trace Sarah Sewell's influence down through history, William A. Sewell's son, Jesse P. Sewell, was a prominent preacher and the president of Abilene Christian College from 1912-1924.[4]

Now, these are just the well-known preachers of the Sewell family. Many other members preached, married preachers, or labored in the church as devoted workers in God's Kingdom.[5] Sarah Sewell impacted thousands of people in her own quiet way, through which she brought the gospel to her husband. Ladies, one never knows the impact that we can have on others, no matter how small the action. The crucial point to remember is to stay active in our mission to take the gospel to others, because our job is to plant the seed and to water; God will do the rest (1 Cor. 3:6-7).

ELIZABETH CAMPBELL STONE and CELIA WILSON BOWEN STONE

Two more Restoration wives hardly mentioned in recorded history are those of Barton W. Stone. Leroy Garrett, author of

---

[1] *Ibid.*, pp. 1059, 1067.
[2] Goodpasture, "The Willow Creek Meeting."
[3] Harp, *The Sewell Family—The Beginning.* TheRestorationMovement.com.
[4] West, *Search for the Ancient Order*, vol. 3.
[5] Harp, *The Sewell Family...*

The Stone-Campbell Movement, said that Stone's marriage to Elizabeth Campbell at age 28 must have been a "close second" behind the Cane Ridge Revival on the measure of major lifetime events for Stone.[1] Before this, he was too busy for women because he was "eluding robbers, Indians, poverty and Calvinism."[2] However, the only line written about Elizabeth in Stone's autobiography was, "My companion was pious, and much engaged in religion."[3] Elizabeth only lived about nine years after their marriage. The couple had four daughters, and their only son, Barton W. Stone, Jr., died shortly after birth along with his mother.[4]

MRS. CELIA WILSON BOWEN STONE

Stone's second wife was Celia Wilson Bowen (1793-1857), Elizabeth's cousin. Celia was the youngest daughter of Captain William Bowen (1742-1804) of Mansker's Creek.[5] Celia married Stone in her childhood home (in Goodlettsville) in 1811, and the Stones lived there for a short time around 1814.[6] Today many school children visit the two-story brick home on field trips

---

[1] Garrett, *The Stone-Campbell Movement*, p. 102.
[2] *Ibid.*, p. 103.
[3] Stone, *The Autobiography of Barton W. Stone, with Additions and Reflections by Elder John Rogers*, p. 35.
[4] Garrett, *Stone-Campbell Movement.*
[5] Harp, *Celia Wilson Bowen Stone August 26, 1793-April 23, 1857,* TheRestorationMovement.com.
[6] Harp, *The Homes of Barton W. Stone,* TheRestorationMovement.com.

because it is considered the oldest brick home in Middle Tennessee.[1]

From this union six more children were born, including another son named after his father. Describing Celia, Scott Harp said, "She remained cohort and promoter of her beloved husband throughout the remaining days of his life."[2] Celia must have had a great influence on all of her children, but it was certainly evident in her daughter, Mrs. Amanda Bowen, the wife of Captain Samuel S. Bowen of Hannibal, Missouri. Amanda was one of the first members of the Hannibal church, and according to Scott Harp she was "a committed Christian."[3] Celia moved to Hannibal near her daughter after Stone's death and lived out her remaining years there. Her grave was only recently rediscovered in 2009 by some of our brethren (Scott Harp, Tom Childers, and Wayne Kilpatrick) in an old, run down cemetery in Hannibal.[4]

Celia's grandsons, Barton, Sam and Will Bowen, were playmates and lifelong friends of Samuel Clemens (a.k.a. Mark Twain). It's also interesting that Barton and Sam were the ones who instructed Samuel Clemens in becoming a riverboat pilot. Another connection Clemens had to the Restoration Movement is evidenced in the fact that he wrote in his autobiography about a meeting that Alexander Campbell held in Hannibal. This path of knowledge suggests that Mark Twain probably at least knew about the Church.[5]

The wives of Stone were great influences on their family and probably the many others they came in contact with in their

---

[1] Slater, "Bowen-Campbell House," *Tennessee Encyclopedia*.
[2] Harp, *Celia Wilson Bowen Stone*, para. 2.
[3] Harp, *Restoration Movement scenes around Hannibal, Missouri*, para. 5, TheRestorationMovement.com.
[45] Harp, *Celia Wilson Bowen Stone*
[5] Harp, *Restoration Movement scenes around Hannibal, Missouri*.

lifetimes. Stone influenced thousands upon thousands. However, despite the influence of a strong Christian family, one grandson of Stone's, C.C. Moore, left the faith and became the editor of one of the first atheistic journals in the U.S. He is also regarded by atheists as a father of atheism. According to Scott Harp, this man reminds us that God gave everyone the right to choose and we are always "one generation away from apostasy."[1]

MARGARET E. VICK HOLBROOK

Joseph H. Holbrook's first wife was Margaret E. Vick (1841-1891).[2] Margaret, like Sarah Sewell, demonstrated the "The Power of One" with her Godly influence. She was a remarkable woman who not only encouraged her husband in the Christian faith, but also everyone that her life touched.

Margaret met her future husband before his enlistment in the Confederate Army. Joseph was captured at the Battle of Nashville and remained at Camp Douglas in Chicago, Illinois, a northern prisoner of war camp, until the end of the Civil War. He returned home with hardly a scrap of clothes on, in debt and without a single penny to his name. His state of mind regarding religion was not much better. He was still not settled on the topic of God's salvation and how one received it. As a young boy from Hickman County, Tennessee, he had grown up around his mother's faith of the Primitive Baptists and their strong Calvinistic doctrines.[3] It worried Joseph when he would listen to the religious experiences of those who preached and heard them expound upon how "wicked" they had been before their

---

[1] Harp, *Charles Chilton Moore 1837-1906*, para. 3, TheRestorationMovement.com.
[2] Srygley, "Death of a Noble Woman," *Gospel Advocate*, Oct. 1891.
[3] Srygley, *Biographies and Sermons*.

experience.[1] A lot of these experiences Joseph heard in his own home, because his mother invited many preachers home in hopes that her husband would be blessed with "the call." Joseph knew that his father wanted to be saved and that he was an upright man. Yet why had God saved these formerly "extremely wicked" people and not his good father?[2]

Margaret was just what Joseph needed. Upon his return from the war, ragged and poor, Joseph saw that it was past time for spring planting; so he borrowed a coat and two dollars and set off to marry Margaret. Joseph described Margaret as a girl "who had nothing but a pure heart and a good stock of religion."[3] Margaret was a member of the Church of Christ and was baptized at age 16 by Wade Barrett.[4]

Margaret used her Godly influence to break through to her tough-skinned, war-torn soldier, and Joseph soon responded to the Gospel. He was baptized by E.A. Land, and it wasn't long before Joseph decided that he wanted to preach. However, he found that he needed to start from ground zero. His Biblical knowledge was scarce, he had little opportunity to be around other educated preachers and money to buy books was just not available.[5] Nevertheless, he did begin to study the New Testament on his own, and Boles said "…within a few years no other preacher in that country knew more of the word of God than did J.H. Halbrook."[6] Joseph also worked very hard to accumulate funds for a home and extra land stock in order to reach a comfortable place of financial security. However, upon reaching this

---

[1] Boles, *Biographical Sketches of Gospel Preachers*, p. 318.
[2] *Ibid.*
[3] Srygley, *Biographies and Sermons*, p. 53.
[4] *Ibid.*
[5] *Ibid.*
[6] Boles, *Biographical Sketches…*, p. 319.

point and after much deliberation between the two, the couple decided to sell everything to allow Joseph to attend school under T.B. Larimore at Mars Hill in Florence, Alabama.[1] Srygley states that "his desire to preach was so great he could not feel satisfied to enjoy the fruit of his labors and live at ease."[2]

After reaping the knowledge of his great teacher, Larimore, Joseph began to preach all over the countryside of his new home in Fayette County, Alabama, taking the gospel to the poor. His reputation spread, and he eventually preached throughout Alabama, Arkansas, Missouri, Texas, Mississippi and Tennessee, establishing churches and baptizing thousands.[3] Boles stated:

> "There are prosperous churches in all of these States now which are the result of his preaching. He seldom went into a new section that he did not establish a congregation there. The joy of his life was to plant churches in new territory."[4]

In 1891, due to health reasons, the Holbrooks made a move from Fayette County, Alabama, to Levy County, Florida. However, Margaret died of consumption shortly after the move.[5]

Margaret was Joseph's helpmeet as he ministered to others. She spread her influence whether she stayed at home or travelled with him. After meeting Margaret when she and her husband attended a meeting at the Rock Creek church in Northern Alabama, F.D. Srygley wrote, "She was then the efficient and earnest

---

[1] Srygley, *Biographies and Sermons*.
[2] *Ibid.*, p. 53.
[3] *Ibid.*
[4] Boles, *Biographical Sketches...*, p. 320.
[5] Srygley, *Biographies and Sermons*.

helper of her ever faithful husband in his labors as an evangelist in that rugged region."[1] Reflecting upon her death, F.D. stated:

> She knows now, what perhaps she never fully understood in this world, though I often tried to make her understand it, how much her steadfast faith, consuming zeal and earnest words of private admonition and exhortation during that meeting help to decide me and others to turn to the Lord and trust him for salvation.[2]

Up to that point, Srygley had heard a lot of great preaching growing up (especially from T.B. Larimore), but he just couldn't submit himself fully to the Lord. He wrote this:

> But when that Godly woman came to me with the light of purified heart shining in her face, and the tear drops of a baptized soul trembling in her eyes I began to see my way clearer. Somehow she seemed to reach across the chasm, grasp my hand and nerve my heart for the leap.[3]

F.D. Syrgley became a great gospel preacher and writer. Looking back at his baptism he said that he just couldn't explain what Margaret Holbrook did for him to help him decide that he could be a Christian and how she led him into that decision. Continuing to describe her, he said:

> She was not fluent of speech, her vocabulary was meager, her diction faulty, her grammar defective, her information limited. She was not even a good reader. In truth, she read nothing but the Bible and religious books and papers, and it was with difficulty she spelled out the harder words in them. Her appearance was by no means prepossessing.

---

[1] Srygley, "Death of a Noble Woman," p. 626.
[2] *Ibid.*
[3] *Ibid.*

> Her dress was plain calico made by her own hands and evidently cut with an eye to comfort and economy rather than gaudy display. She wore no jewelry, assumed no social airs, and courted no homage. She seemed always prayerful, occasionally heart-burdened, rarely despondent, and never frivolous. She talked constantly of the things pertaining to the kingdom of God and the name of Jesus Christ and never gossiped.[1]

Margaret, with her Pollyanna attitude, always found something for which to be thankful. Once, F.D. Syrgley held a meeting near her home. His body was so weak from disease and pain that he could hardly stand in the pulpit.[2] Margaret said, "Thank the Lord Brother Syrgley, for your afflictions. You never could have preached such a sermon as that or moved such hardened sinners as came forward today, if you had not been under the chastening hand of God."[3] Another time, when Joseph was out preaching, Margaret was brought news that her husband's horse had fallen up in the hills and had caused Joseph to break his leg. She said in all seriousness, "Thank the Lord for ever for his goodness. I am so glad it was not his neck instead of his leg that was broken."[4]

Margaret never had children. She did raise a niece, but one might think it was lonely keeping house and tending her garden, while most days her husband was away preaching. She continued on "full of joy at the thought that Joseph was winning souls to Christ."[5]

In 1891, after Margaret's death, F.D. Syrgley wrote an article in the *Gospel Advocate* about this "noble woman."[6] He

---

[1] *Ibid.*
[2] *Ibid.*
[3] *Ibid.*
[4] *Ibid.*
[5] *Ibid.*
[6] *Ibid.*

credited Margaret as being the one who had encouraged him to go to Mars Hill College and the one who kept alive his love of doing God's work to save souls through her letters. Syrgley said:

> I shall not forget her hallowed influence, nor cease to thank the Lord that ever it was my good fortune to be a co-worker with her in the best of all cases, and if but I finish my course and keep the faith not the least of my joys at the time of my departure will be the confident hope of meeting her in heaven.[1]

After reading Syrgley's description, how could we ever diminish our sense of the importance of our roles as Christian women? How can we come up with so many excuses after witnessing the harvest of Margaret's influence? Teresa Hampton, a lady dear to this author's heart and an author of many of our popular ladies' books, tells the story of her husband Gary's Christian roots, starting with Margaret Holbrook. Margaret influenced her husband, Joseph, to become a Christian. Joseph baptized a young man by the name of Charlie Wheeler. Among the 6,000 that Charlie Wheeler baptized was a man by the name of Gus Nichols, and Gus Nichols baptized Gary Hampton's mother, who in turn taught Gary.[2] Today, Gary and Teresa have proven to be a strong, Christian power couple who have influenced countless more. Never underestimate what one woman can do.

---

[1] *Ibid.*
[2] Hampton, "The Power of One," sermon.

QUESTIONS

1. How was Mary Catherine Gano a rock of Christian influence to her husband and her sons?
2. How did Sarah Sewell and Margaret Holbrook demonstrate the "The Power of One" by just influencing those closest to them? Do you remember the "The Power of One" in the little things that you do for others?
3. Why is it important to be engaged in our religion and to be cohorts/promoters to our husbands' Christian work as Stone's wives were?
4. Describe Margaret Holbrook's "Pollyanna" attitude in her Christian walk.
5. Have these ladies inspired you to take the Gospel to others and to pray for opportunities?

Grave of Mary Catherine Gano, Lexington Cemetery, Lexington, Kentucky ( )

Grave of Margaret E. Holbrook, Ebenezer Baptist Church Cemetery, Outside of Bronson, FL

204

*Grave of
Elizabeth Sewell
Cemetery at Old
Philadelphia, Viola, TN (5/4/2024)*

*Grave of Sarah Sewell,
St. Johns Cemetery, Clay County, TN (6/14/2024)*

*Grave of Elizabeth
Campbell Stone,
Cane Ridge Cemetery,
Cane Ridge, Kentucky
(6/25/2024)*

*Grave of Celia Bowen Stone,
Old Baptist Cemetery,
Hannibal, MO*

CHAPTER 13

Wives of Influence Continued

HETTY DE SPAIN CLARK

Hetty De Spain Clark (1824-1894) was the wife of Restoration preacher, Joseph A. Clark.[1] The background stories of Hetty and her husband are filled with historical figures and events. Though Hetty is not historically famous, her act of leading her husband to Christ led many others to obey the Gospel. She pointed Joseph A. Clark towards his life's purpose, and purpose only made this man on the move want to move around more to share the Good News. Let's look at Hetty's background first and then her husband's.

Hetty's grandfather, Benjamin Lynn, started a distillery with two friends in 1771 near what is today Bardstown, Kentucky, a town still known for its liquor production. After the local Native Americans were stirred up by the British in the Revolutionary War, the countryside was devastated, and many people fled to Fort Harrodsburg for refuge, including Lynn. Here he met up with his good friend George Rogers Clark, the brother of William Clark of "Lewis and Clark." For six months, the Native

---

[1] Harp, *Joseph Addison Clark 1815-1901.* TheRestorationMovement.com

Americans surrounded this fort, hoping to starve its inhabitants. However, Benjamin Lynn, who had lived with Native Americans in his younger days and knew their language, would slip out at night to talk with them, learn their plans and collect food to take back to the fort. Thanks to Lynn, the settlers in the fort survived.[1]

After the war, Lynn began to preach the scriptures that he had been so diligently studying during the time of the Native American raids. He heard tell of a man named Barton W. Stone who preached the Bible alone, and he decided to travel 80 miles to be baptized by him. Following this event, he moved his family (including his daughters, Esther and Rachel) to Huntsville, Alabama. After Lynn's death, Esther and her husband, John Chisholm, along with the Despains soon moved just north of Florence where they established what would be the Stony Point Church of Christ, the oldest Church in Northwest Alabama still meeting today. A few years later, it was here that Tolbert Fanning was baptized after hearing B.F. Hall, Esther's son-in-law (he married her daughter Dorinda), preach baptism for the remission of sins.[2] Rachel and her husband, Marshall Despain, moved to Waterloo, Alabama, and established another church. Any record of this church seemed to have vanished until a letter was discovered at Texas Christian University explaining that the whole church left in a wagon train for Texas. Hetty Esther Despain, daughter of Rachel and namesake of her aunt, was a small child when her brother, now-widowed mother and over 300 members of the Waterloo Church of Christ from Alabama moved to the Mexican controlled land of Texas. In Clarksville, they established the first known church patterned after the New Testament

---

[1] *Ibid.*
[2] *Ibid.*; Harp, *John and Esther Chisholm*, TheRestorationMovement.com.

in Texas.[1] Their wagon train was originally assigned Davy Crockett as their scout. However, when the travelers reached Memphis, Crockett left for the Alamo. He had become too impatient with the wagon train stopping every Sunday for all-day worship. Scott Harp makes the point that Crockett certainly heard the Gospel, but we do not have evidence that he obeyed it.[2]

Now let's take a look at the life of Hetty's husband. Joseph A. Clark seems to have been always on the move since his birth. After his birth in Shawneetown, Illinois, in 1815, his family moved close to the Ohio River near what would become Louisville, Kentucky. Then the family settled in Hopkinsville, Kentucky, followed by Columbia, Tennessee. As a young boy, Joseph took a special trip to Nashville with his father, where he saw his first steamboat. The steamboat was carrying Lafayette, the French patriot who helped the Continental Army during the Revolutionary War. Joseph's father died a year later and his mother moved the family to Selma, Alabama. Here Clark learned to be a printer.[3]

From Selma, Alabama, Joseph followed his family to Columbus, Mississippi, and eventually back to Kentucky, where he served as principal for a school at Mount Pleasant. Upon his younger brother's death, he followed his mother and two sisters to Texas. Soon after their arrival, Clark's mother died. When the oldest sister married, Clark followed both sisters to Austin. Austin held its first congressional meeting for the new Republic of Texas while he resided there.[4] Keeping busy, Clark, along with John Henry Brown, worked on a book called, "Topographical

---

[1] Harp, *Joseph Addison Clark*; Harp, *Addison Clark 1842-1911*. TheRestorationMovement.com.
[2] Harp, *Joseph Addison Clark*.
[3] Srygley, *Biographies and Sermons*.
[4] *Ibid.*

Description of Texas."[1] Having no means to bind books sufficiently in Austin, Joseph travelled by boat to New Orleans. On his return trip, he found himself stranded at a stop in Lynnville because Comanches had just burned the town and scattered the people. Joseph Clark, always having to be on the move and having no way back to Austin but to walk, left his books in Lynnville and walked two hundred miles through Native American land; he never saw his books again.[2]

This brings us up to his next move in 1841 to Nacogdoches, where he fell in love with Hetty. J.A. Clark married this young Christian girl in 1842.[3] Srygley mentioned, "The purity of her life and simplicity of her faith in Christ soon made an impression on him, and in less than a year he confessed his faith in the Lord Jesus and was baptized into Christ."[4] Hetty and J.A. Clark had moved to Titus County by the time of Joseph's conversion, and he soon began to preach.[5]

Marriage to Hetty did not stop Joseph from moving. Since there were already two preachers spreading the gospel in Titus County, Clark decided that he needed to travel far and wide across Texas taking the gospel light to all he could possibly reach.[6] Srygley states, "He travelled over many parts of Texas, held many successful meetings, baptized hundreds of people, and established a number of congregations."[7] Hetty Clark helped Joseph find his purpose on this earth in living his life for the Lord. Her influence spread through him all over Texas, and through all

---

[1] *Ibid.*, p. 81.
[2] *Ibid.*
[3] *Ibid.*
[4] *Ibid.,* p. 82.
[5] *Ibid.*
[6] *Ibid.*
[7] *Ibid.*, pp. 84-85.

of his writings in the *Gospel Advocate* and the *Firm Foundation*.[1] Hetty—having been surrounded by examples of strong Christian leadership in her grandfather's preaching; her aunt, uncle and parents helping to establish churches; and her brother, Lynn Despain, becoming a gospel preacher—only passed along the Gospel treasure that had been given to her. Hetty was probably delighted to add to this list her two sons, who decided to become preachers as well as prominent educators.

In 1869, Joseph and his two sons, Addison and Randolph, directed The Male and Female Seminary of Fort Worth. By the end of 1873, Joseph's family and Addison's family joined Randolph's family, who had left earlier upon learning about Thorp Spring, Texas, and the opportunity to move their school away from the "worldly influence" of Fort Worth.[2] It was decided that the new school should be named in memory of Addison's firstborn, Addran, Hetty's and Joseph's first grandchild, who was lost to diphtheria at the age of three.[3]

Addran College was one of the first coeducational schools in the Southwest run by Restoration leaders.[4] It eventually became a university and proved to be a forerunner of Texas Christian University, first in Waco and then in Fort Worth.[5] Addran-Jarvis College, a small college that continued in Thorp Spring, was renamed Thorp Spring Christian College in 1910.[6]

There, Joseph finally stayed put, remaining in Thorp Spring until his death. Hetty and Joseph are buried in the Thorp Spring

---

[1] Roberts, *Joseph Addison Clark (1815-1901)*.
[2] Harp, *Addison Clark*, para. 5.
[3] Harp, *Addran Clark 1869-1872*, TheRestorationMovement.com.
[4] Thomas, "Thorp Springs Christian College," *Enclyclopedia of the Stone-Campbell Movement*.
[5] Harp, *Addran Clark*.
[6] West, *Search for the Ancient Order*, vol. 3.

Cemetery.[1] However, due to the controversy over the instrument that hit Texas just as it did other regions of the U.S., Joseph and Hetty did not retire peacefully. About five months before Hetty's death, a sad event occurred much like the one that made R.M. Gano cry "as a child."[2] At a meeting at the Thorp Spring Church, Joseph presented a petition against the use of the instrument in worship. His two sons conversed quietly with each other, and then Addison said to the pianist, "Play on Miss Bertha!"[3] "When the accompaniment began, the old Joseph Clark, now in his 80s, got up, and with cane in hand, slowly walked out of the church building with 2/3rds of the congregation following behind him. The other 1/3 left was in tears at the sad parting."[4] It is debated how many members left, but the incident did prove detrimental to Addran College and its enrollment.[5] As for Joseph, "the founder and builder of the work, he had died broken-hearted."[6] And who can imagine what Hetty went through, a mother in the middle of the instrument controversy within her own family.

Hetty died in 1894, and her gravestone simply states, "We loved her."[7] Though not a famous figure of history, she should be remembered for her influence on a husband who was hard to keep in one place and on all that were reached by the Gospel through his work.

---

[1] Harp, *Joseph Addison Clark*.
[2] West, *Search for the Ancient Order*, vol. 2, p. 423.
[3] Griffith, *Play On, Miss Bertha!* (term paper), TheRestorationMovement.com
[4] Harp, *Joseph Addison Clark*, The Incident at Thorp Springs Church section.
[5] Griffith, *Play On, Miss Bertha!*
[6] West, *Search for the Ancient Order*, vol. 3, p. 290.
[7] Harp, *Joseph Addison Clark*, Thorp Spring Cemetery Section.

LAVINIA CAMPBELL PENDLETON

Another woman of influence was Campbell's daughter and the wife of W.K. Pendleton, Lavinia Campbell Pendleton (1818-1846).[1] Lavinia's epitaph reads:

> Beautiful in person, pure in heart, warm in her affections, ardent in her mind and ever ready to do good, her friends might well have prayed the good Lord to lend her a little longer to soothe and lighten the sorrows of earth; but he had taken her where there is fullness of joy and though we raise this stone to her memory we know she sleeps not here, but rejoices as an angel in the presence of God.[2]

How many of us have let the world tell us that outward beauty was needed for self-worth? I Samuel 16:7 says, "But the Lord said to Samuel, 'Do not look at his appearance or at his physical stature, because I have refused him. For the Lord does not see as man sees; for man looks at the outward appearance, but the Lord looks at the heart'" (NKJV). Sometimes women with great beauty struggle in putting their heart right with God, just as some do who own great riches. Lavinia Campbell Pendleton, even though beautiful, set her eyes on the Lord at a young age and kept them fixed there throughout her short life. Let's take a look at her husband's life and how the couple met.

According to West, out of all the pre-Civil War preachers, William Kimbrough Pendleton was one of the "most influential." "His broad knowledge and calm, deliberate consideration of every issue made him a natural leader in the earlier days of the restoration."[3] Brother McGarvey said he was "one of the clearest

---

[1] *Lavinia M. Campbell Pendleton1818-1846*, FindAGrave.com.
[2] Philips, *A Medley of the Restoration*, p. 34.
[3] West, *Search for the Ancient Order*, vol. 1, p. 89.

headed men he had ever known."[1] Pendleton was brought up in a well-to-do family; he had one of the best cultural backgrounds and was offered one of the best educations of any of the Restoration preachers. After reading Campbell's *Christian Baptist* and *Millennial Harbinger* publications, Pendleton's parents and older brother were baptized and became part of the Mt. Gilboa church in Louisa County, Virginia. Pendleton was soon influenced by his family, and while studying law at the University of Virginia, he read Campbell's publications and studied his Bible searching for religious truth.[2]

Meanwhile, Lavinia went on a tour with her father to Charlottesville, Virginia, in 1838.[3] Campbell would often take one of his daughters along on his preaching tours, and sometimes young men would ask his permission to court them before "paying their addresses" to the daughters.[4] Pendleton, being a student at the University of Virginia, may have had the chance to meet Lavinia at the time of this tour, but he was sick.[5] After Pendleton's friends saw this "young lady of great beauty and an unusual buoyant personality," they poked fun around his bedside at what he had missed.[6] Pendleton assured his friends that he would get the best of them, and that is just what he did. He soon met this young lady of beauty in "church circles."[7] Then it wasn't long before he captured Lavinia's heart, and the two made plans to marry.[8]

---

[1] McGarvey, "W.K. Pendleton," *Christian Standard*, Sept. 1899, p. 1193.
[2] West, *Search for the Ancient Order*, vol. 1.
[3] S. Campbell, *Home Life and Reminisces of Alexander Campbell*.
[4] *Ibid.*, p. 24.
[5] West, *Search for the Ancient Order*, vol. 1.
[6] *Ibid.*, p. 91.
[7] Duke, "Pendleton, William Kimbrough," *Encyclopedia of the Stone-Campbell Movement*, p. 591.
[8] West, *Search for the Ancient Order*, vol. 1.

In 1840, Pendleton was baptized by Campbell near his family's church and married Lavinia in October of that same year at the Campbell mansion in Bethany. Pendleton became a co-worker with Campbell, helping to establish a school at Bethany and teaching there. Pendleton and Lavinia had one daughter, Campbellina, in 1841.[1] However, Lavinia's health grew increasingly worse over the next five years, and this "brought many anxious hours to Pendleton."[2] In 1846, Lavinia died of consumption at the age of 29. Pendleton later married Clarinda, another daughter of Campbell's.[3] According to West, Clarinda was a woman a lot like her sister but "quieter and more reserved" than Lavinia.[4] Clarinda also died of consumption, in 1850. Pendleton married his third wife, Catherine Huntington King, in 1855.[5]

Lavinia was blessed by God as a woman of beauty. It was a beauty that made people take notice. However, she is not remembered for her outward beauty in death. Since she was only 29 when she died, her beauty had not faded; but still, she was remembered for her beauty in being "pure in heart," "warm in her affections," "ardent in her mind" and "ever ready to do good."[6] Lavinia was a woman of influence, not only to her husband, but to all women to help them remember that outward beauty is not what is important in the end. The Godly qualities of our inward souls should be our top priority as we prepare to meet our maker.

---

[1] *Ibid.*
[2] *Ibid.*, p. 92.
[3] *Ibid.*
[4] *Ibid.*, p. 93.
[5] *Ibid.*
[6] Phillips, *A Medley of the Restoration*, p. 34.

ANNIE BACON FALL

The next wife is Mrs. Annie Bacon Fall (1800-1888), the wife of Philip Slater Fall.[1] P.S. Fall was the older brother of Charlotte Fanning, who was discussed in a previous chapter.[2] Annie was a woman of influence, because like so many other Restoration wives, she helped her husband.

P.S. Fall came with his family from England in 1817. Both parents died soon after their arrival in Kentucky, and Philip, at age 19, was left to care for ten siblings. Legally he became the caretaker of just two sisters and four brothers, but this was still a great responsibility set upon the shoulders of such a young man.[3] In 1818, Fall established a school near Louisville and identified himself with the Baptist church.[4] In 1819, he began to preach, and in 1821, he married Miss Annie Bacon, daughter of a "distinguished Kentucky family."[5]

Fall preached for a small Baptist church in Louisville while reading the writings of Campbell and studying the New Testament. After coming to the knowledge of the simple New Testament pattern, P.S. fall took his stand to follow the Bible alone and put creeds away. The whole congregation at Louisville was convinced to join him in following Restoration principles.[6] West states, "P.S. Fall himself became the first resident Baptist preacher in the state to accept the ancient order of things."[7]

In 1825, Fall and Annie moved to Nashville in order for Fall to teach at the Nashville Female Academy. Fall explained ahead

---

[1] *Anne Apperson Bacon Fall 1800-1888*, FindAGrave.com
[2] Jenkins, "The Legacy of Charlotte Fanning," *Gospel Advocate*, July 2003.
[3] Doran, "Philip Slater Fall," *World Evangelist*, Sept. 1991.
[4] Boles, *Biographical Sketches of Gospel Preachers.*
[5] *Ibid.*, p. 87.
[6] *Ibid.*
[7] West, *Search for the Ancient Order*, vol. 1, p. 238.

of time to the Baptist church there that he would use the Bible as his guide and not a creed.[1] Boles states, "Soon the congregation in Nashville, with but few exceptions, adopted his views and from that beginning a church after the New Testament order began..."[2] In 1831, Fall and his wife moved to Frankfort, where he taught at the Female Eclectic Institute for 26 years. Again Fall was successful in convincing the congregation there to use the Bible as their only guide.[3] This church later became the church that lost their building to fire, and which Emily Tubman from Augusta, Georgia, donated the money to rebuild.[4]

Very little is recorded about Annie. West said, "She was of great assistance to her husband in his preaching, and stood faithfully by him."[5] These words, though few, say a lot about this woman of influence. She was his faithful helpmeet as he took a stand to follow the Bible alone in Tennessee and Kentucky. A faithful wife who took a stand beside her husband would have meant the world to any Restoration preacher of yesteryear, and would mean the same to any Gospel preacher of today.

OTWAYANNA FRANCES HIX MCGARVEY

Another Restoration wife who has very little recorded history is J.W. McGarvey's wife, Otwayanna Frances Hix McGarvey (1834-1911).[6] We again must look at the story of the husband to see the wife who contributed to the cause by working behind the scenes. As a boy in Hopkinsville, Kentucky, McGarvey lost his father when he was only four. His mother, who had been a

---

[1] *Ibid.*
[2] Boles, *Biographical Sketches...*, p. 88.
[3] West, *Search for the Ancient Order*, vol. 1, pp. 238-239.
[4] Nunnelly, *Emily Harvey Thomas Tubman: a Disciple Wonder Woman,* TheRestorationMovement.com.
[5] West, *Search for the Ancient Order*, vol. 1, p. 236.
[6] *Otwayanna Frances Hix McGarvey 1834-1911*. FindaAGrave.com

student of Barton W. Stone as a girl, then married Gurdon F. Saltonstall. He was the husband of her deceased sister and a father of nine children. McGarvey's mother had four children of her own, plus she bore six more to this second marriage, making the couple parents of 19 children.[1] In 1839, Saltonstall moved his family to Illinois, where McGarvey attended an excellent "Yankee" school.[2]

At age 18, he was off to Bethany. Saltonstall was a good step-father to McGarvey. He had supplied his son's tuition by previously donating money to the support of Bethany.[3] He also travelled with his son to enroll him. From his autobiography, we know that McGarvey enjoyed spending time with girls while he was a student at Bethany. He thought it was a good pastime as long as it didn't interfere with studies.[4] He enjoyed walks along the Buffalo Creek and serenading with his flute and "fair" singing voice.[5]

While at Bethany, McGarvey was baptized by W.K. Pendleton, and he soon determined to become a preacher.[6] After graduating, McGarvey travelled to Fayette, Missouri, where his family had relocated. Here he opened a boys' private school and preached at the Fayette Church while being mentored by T.M. Allen. In January of 1853, McGarvey accepted an invitation from a church in Dover, Missouri, and made the move to begin an extended ministry there.[7] However, McGarvey had met a young girl upon his leaving Fayette and soon became engaged.[8] Her name

---

[1] McGarvey, *The Autobiography of J.W. McGarvey*.
[2] *Ibid.*, p. 6.
[3] West, *Search for the Ancient Order*, vol. 1.
[4] McGarvey, *Autobiography*.
[5] *Ibid.*, p. 10.
[6] West, *Search for the Ancient Order*, vol. 1.
[7] *Ibid.*
[8] McGarvey, *Autobiography*.

was Otwayanna Frances Hix, or "Ottie." Ottie's son described her as "a girl of eighteen, with bright face, perfect form, a high school education and was also a sweet singer."[1] W.C. Morro, a biographer of McGarvey's, said, "Mrs. McGarvey's appearance when she was well past sixty suggests that the son had not overdone the praise of his mother."[2] Her father was a "prominent citizen of Fayette" and she was related to many influential people through her mother's side of the family as well.[3] Ottie and McGarvey arranged their marriage to occur on March 23rd so the couple could attend a convention in Louisville, Kentucky, on Bible revision while on their honeymoon. The ceremony was performed by Alexander Proctor. McGarvey and Ottie then resided in Dover nine years.[4]

By the first year of the Civil War, McGarvey decided he needed to support his family, now including three children, more fully. Therefore, he accepted an invitation to go to the Main Street Church in Lexington, Kentucky. McGarvey's name had been suggested to the church by Dr. Winthrop H. Hopson, a former preacher who felt that McGarvey's neutrality stance between North and South would benefit the church.[5] McGarvey described his and Ottie's parting from their home and friends, "who had become as dear to us as life," as a severe "trial."[6] But the couple settled in Lexington, and in 1864, the couple had to endure another trial: the death of their firstborn, Loulie, a sweet girl who only reached the age of ten.[7] Imagine Ottie carrying the loss of her daughter, yet still being a faithful helpmeet of a dedicated

---

[1] Morro, *Brother McGarvey: The Life of President J.W. McGarvey*, p. 69.
[2] *Ibid.*
[3] *Ibid.*; McGarvey, *Autobiography*.
[4] McGarvey, *Autobiography*.
[5] *Ibid.*
[6] *Ibid.*, p. 26.
[7] *Ibid.*

Gospel preacher and soon to be a very busy, influential teacher for many years to come.

In 1865, Kentucky University moved to Lexington, and McGarvey was invited to teach at the College of the Bible under Robert Milligan's presidency.[1] West states, "McGarvey's name had by now become a household word among members of the church. His commentary on Acts of The Apostles was already before the public and widely acclaimed."[2] Eventually McGarvey resigned from preaching at Main Street due to increasing responsibilities at the school. Nevertheless, in 1870, McGarvey began a twelve year span of preaching for the Broadway church.[3] J.J. Halley, one of McGarvey's Bible students, said this about his teacher:

> If at any time his place had been vacant, it would have taken two first class men to contrive his work. He had four classes in college. He contributed regularly to two or three of our periodicals. He was the preacher of the Broadway Congregation for a number of years. He had always one book and sometimes two or three in preparation. Every letter was answered with his own hand. There was the family and business interest that always takes a considerable slice out of a man's time.[4]

Hicks states, "In addition he brought to his students the fruits of dedicated study which caused him to be recognized as the most thorough student of the English Bible in the world."[5] Phillips included a quote by *The London Times*: "In all probability John W.

---

[1] West, *Search for the Ancient Order*, vol. 2.
[2] *Ibid.*, p. 113.
[3] McGarvey, *Autobiography*.
[4] Quoted in Phillips, *A Medley of the Restoration*, p. 60.
[5] Hicks, "John W. McGarvey," *The Restoration Principle: Abilene Christian College Annual Bible Lectures 1962*, p. 369.

McGarvey is the ripest Bible scholar on earth."[1] In regard to his trip to the Holy Lands, the guide reported that, "The Little Man from Kentucky measured every hole in Palestine with a tape-line."[2]

All this being said about McGarvey, how do we learn anything about Ottie? We just know that she was there with him, taking care of the family and allowing McGarvey to do all the work, all the studying and all the good that he did. She was also with him through all of the turmoil caused by decisions made by the Regent of Kentucky University, John B. Bowman. To understand the circumstances, we need to look back at Kentucky University's history, beginning with Bacon College of Georgetown, Kentucky. Bacon College had been moved to Harrodsburg in 1839 due to financial trouble. The college continued there for ten years under President James Shannon, but later fell to ruin. In 1858, Bowman raised funds in order to revive Bacon College, and it was decided that the name would change to Kentucky University. You may recall from the previous chapter on Mattie Carr that after a fire in the main building of the Harrodsburg campus, the university was moved to Lexington, where it merged with Transylvania University.[3] By this time, Transylvania University had accepted a deal from Congress for a large land grant and an annex of a secular A&M college. Bowman bought even more land in his excitement to grow the university. Eventually a war of newspaper and journal articles broke out. The brotherhood sensed that Bowman and his curators were pulling the school away from them and the principles laid down for the school. J.W. McGarvey and his friend Moses Lard were not pleased with

---

[1] Phillips, *A Medley of the Restoration*, p. 60.
[2] *Ibid.*
[3] Harp, *The History of Bacon College*, TheRestorationMovement.com.

Bowman and found themselves right in the middle of the fight.[1] (According to West, Bowman accused them of starting a conspiracy to "oust" him, resulting in McGarvey's dismissal, which itself disillusioned the brotherhood.[2] Deciding that Kentucky University just wasn't their "Bacon College of 1847," the brotherhood did not support the College of the Bible now controlled by the churches, even upon its separation from Kentucky University and the rehiring of McGarvey.[3] West explains that the separation wasn't "organically separate."[4] Therefore, the brotherhood created their own independent College of the Bible with McGarvey teaching there. However, Bowman fought back and made Lard the President of his College of the Bible. Later it was discovered that McGarvey's friend Lard took the position because Bowman promised he would step down after a year if Lard would join them. After a year, Bowman's attempt at another College of the Bible failed, and Kentucky University let McGarvey's school use their classrooms once again.[5] McGarvey had been through the tumbler, including the seeming deception by his friend, yet all we know is that Ottie was there struggling with him.

Another rare mention of Ottie is during another troubling time when instrumental music was about to be introduced at the Broadway Church. "McGarvey and his wife promptly changed their membership" to the Chester St. Church, where they could worship with a good conscience.[6] It was another sad time, but Ottie was with him.

---

[1] West, *Search for the Ancient Order*, vol. 2.
[2] *Ibid.*, p. 118.
[3] *Ibid.*
[4] *Ibid.*, p. 125.
[5] *Ibid.*
[6] *Ibid.*; West, *Search for the Ancient Order*, vol. 3, p. 45.

Even in death, Ottie was close to him: She passed one month after her husband. Although there is very little information on Ottie McGarvey, we can take a lesson that sometimes our influence is strongest by just being there for those we love.

QUESTIONS

1. Hetty Clark stood for truth alongside her husband. Discuss someone you may know who had to stand against family and friends for truth.
2. How did Lavinia Campbell possess true beauty? Can outer beauty be a pitfall to the Christian walk?
3. Annie Bacon Fall worked alongside her husband as he converted whole churches to the New Testament pattern. How can wives support and spur their husbands to do great things for the Lord?
4. McGarvey went through many trials in his life, but his wife was always at his side. How is our Christian influence affected at times by just being there for others?

Grave of Hetty Esther D'Spain Clark, Thorp Spring Cemetery, Thorp Spring, Texas

Grave of Esther Chisholm, Chisholm Cemetery, Lauderdale County, AL (7/2/2024)

225

Grave of Dorinda Hall, Chisholm Cemetery, Lauderdale County, AL (7/2/2024)

Grave of Lavinia and Clarinda Campbell-Pendleton, God's Acre Cemetery, Bethany, WV (6/28/2024)

Grave of Annie Bacon Fall,
Frankfort Cemetery, Frankfort, Kentucky (6/24/2024)

Graves of Otwayanna, Loulie and J.W. McGarvey,
Lexington Cemetery, Lexington, Kentucky (6/26/2024)

CHAPTER 14

Influential Aunts, Mother-in-laws, Sister-in-laws, Sisters, Grandmothers, Adopted Moms, Daughters and Close Friends

MARY GOFORTH GANO
(Aunt and Mother-in-law)

Women are just as responsible as men to impart the truth to others within the unique roles God has given them. One does not have to be a mother or a wife to be an influence. God's plan for you may come in the role of aunt, like John Allen Gano's aunt. Mary Goforth Gano (1768-1857) was the first of the Gano family to become associated with the Restoration Movement when she decided to be baptized in 1824.[1] This was a decision that influenced not only her children and grandchildren, but also her extended family and their children.[2]

In 1788 Mary Goforth, then a young girl traveled under hostile conditions from Pittsburg on flatboats with 28 others to reach an outpost in Columbia, Ohio. Cincinnati was then "a dense forest only inhabited by wild beasts." Mary eventually became one of the first settlers of Cincinnati. Appointed by George Washington, her father, Judge Goforth, became the first judge in the Northwest. Mary cherished the memories of dining with Generals Washington and Lafayette in her father's "native" home in New York, and I'm sure she was full of stories of her adventures. However, she probably cherished memories of sharing her faith with her family more.[3]

---

[1] *Mary Goforth Gano 1768-1857*, FindAGrave.com; Rushford, *The Apollos of the West: The Life of John Allen Gano*.
[2] Rushford, *The Apollos of the West*.
[3] "Death of a Venerable Lady," *The Washington Union*, July 4, 1857, p. 3.

Maybe God has planned for you to be influential in the role of mother-in-law. Mary Goforth Gano's daughter, Mary, who was baptized by Jeremiah Vardeman in 1827, was married to D.S. Burnett.[1] He was the "boy preacher" of Cincinnati and another prominent pre-Civil War preacher of the Restoration.[2] According to Rushford, Mary Burnett was "a devoted wife and a strong support to her husband throughout his ministry."[3] She often travelled with her husband as well. D.S. Burnett was blessed to have strong support in his Restoration pursuits from his wife and his mother-in-law.[4]

D.S. Burnett wrote in his mother-in-law's obituary that she was a "consistent professor of religion" and stayed in his house for over two decades as his "constant adviser."[5] Mary Goforth Gano "lived to be the oldest pioneer remaining in Cincinnati," and she was regarded by her son-in-law as "remarkable."[6]

ANNA LIPSCOMB
(Sister-in-law)

Maybe your influence will be spread as a sister-in-law. As a young man, David Lipscomb spent more time at his brother William's and sister-in-law Anna's home than he did his own. Anna Lipscomb lived from 1833-1875.[7] William was a remarkable teacher alongside Tolbert Fanning at Franklin College and helped to start the publication of the *Gospel Advocate.*[8] William may have been a great influence on young Lipscomb, but sister-in-law

---

[1] Rushford, *Apollos of the West.*
[2] West, *Search for the Ancient Order*, vol. 1, pp. 95-97.
[3] Rushford, *Apollos of the West*, p. 42.
[4] *Ibid.*
[5] Burnett, "Obituary Notices," *Millennial Harbinger*, August 1857, p. 480.
[6] *Ibid.*; Rushford, *Apollos of the West*, p. 44.
[7] *Sarah Anna Fulgham Lipscomb 1833-1875*, FindAGrave.com
[8] West, *Search for the Ancient Order*, vol. 1.

Anna certainly made a profound impact. Lipscomb wrote in Anna's obituary, "But one or two deaths during life have touched my feelings so nearly as this... She became my most intimate and confidential friend and advisor. She was gentle kind and sympathetic. Her influence was always mild, but for good.[1] Lipscomb admired how "she aimed to rule only through love" in her home, but he also admired her deep desire and determination to make all people around her happy whether they were family, friends or those in need. She loved: no matter the color of skin or station in life. She loved them and they loved her. One can truly see the Christian influence she had on David Lipscomb's life.[2]

DOROTHEA CAMPBELL BRYANT and JANE CAMPBELL MCKEEVER (Sisters)

One may also be an influence for God in the role of sister. One of Alexander Campbell's sisters was Dorothea Campbell. According to Richardson, "She was well versed in the scriptures, having a fine memory..." and possessed an "understanding resembling in this respect her brother Alexander more than any of the family."[3] After Campbell's first child was born, he went into a deep study on infant baptism and found it to be unauthorized by the scriptures. Determined to be baptized himself into a believer's baptism of immersion, he sought out the help of Matthias Luce to administer the baptism. On his way to Luce's home, he stopped at the home of his parents. "Soon after he arrived, his sister, Dorothea, took him aside and told him that she had been in great trouble for some time about her baptism. She could find, she said, no authority whatsoever for infant baptism and could

---

[1] Lipscomb, "Obituary," *Gospel Advocate*, Feb. 1875, pp. 217-218.
[2] *Ibid.*
[3] Richardson, *Memoirs of Alexander Campbell*, vol. 1, pp.96-97.

not resist the conviction that she never had been scripturally baptized."[1] Dorothea wanted Campbell to talk to her father about it for her. Campbell smiled at his sister when she shared this with him and told her about where he was headed. He assured her that he would talk to their father (Thomas Campbell) for both of them. Dorothea had been studying the scriptures as well and maybe she was there that day to back Campbell up and lend him support in this important decision.[2] On June 12, 1812, the Campbells, members of the Brush Run Church, and others of curiosity journeyed out to a deep pool in Buffalo Creek located on David Bryant's farm. Dorothea's and Alexander's mother, Jane Corneigle Campbell, brought a change of clothes for her and her husband. We know from Richardson's account that Jane's ancestors were French Huguenots: She grew up "in the nurture and admonition of the Lord" and "had become noted for her sincere devotion to religious duties."[3] Campbell's first wife, Margaret, had also come to the conclusion of a believer's baptism. Richardson describes how Campbell often discussed his thoughts with Margaret, "who also became much interested in them, and finally came to the same conclusions with himself."[4] After Thomas and Alexander Campbell spoke on their reasons for being at the creek side that day, seven were immersed. [The meeting lasting seven hours allowed Joseph Bryant time to attend a muster meeting concerning the onset of the War of 1812 and still return in time for an hour of preaching]. Campbell, Margaret, Dorothea, Campbell's parents, and a husband and wife by the name of Haven were all baptized on that momentous day.[5] Dorothea was not just a follower

---

[1] *Ibid.*, p. 395.
[2] *Ibid.*
[3] *Ibid.*, pp. 19-20.
[4] *Ibid*, p. 395.
[5] *Ibid.*

in her family. She searched the scriptures for herself and acted upon them.

Alexander had another sister, Jane Campbell McKeever, who acted upon her convictions, but on the subject of slavery the siblings did not always see eye to eye. Both agreed upon the evils of the institution, but not in the method of its abolishment. Campbell believed in a gradual decline that could be played out by the rules of government policy. Jane was an abolitionist who was not afraid to take action.[1] What led Jane to possess such courage?

At a young age Jane learned to withstand trials. She was born June 25, 1800, the fourth child of Thomas and Jane Campbell.[2] At the age of six her father sailed from Ireland to America for health reasons. Her mother and six other siblings were to follow that same year, but smallpox infected the younger Campbells, and Jane came out of the trying ordeal with lifelong scars upon her face. Another attempt to sail for America was made in October but resulted in a shipwreck off the coast of Scotland where

---

[1] White, "Jane Campbell McKeever (1800-1871): A Brief Biography with Comparison to Her Brother Alexander Campbell on the Issue of Slavery and Abolition," *Stone-Campbell Journal* 13.1.
[2] Richardson, *Memoirs of Alexander Campbell*, vol. 1, p. 46.

the family remained until finally reaching America in September of 1809.[1] Describing the family reunion with their father, Richardson states:

> When Jane was presented to him, so much changed in appearance by the effect of the small-pox that he would not have recognized her, he said, in a tone of the kindest sympathy, as he took her into his arms, 'And is this my little white-head?' a phrase of endearment amongst the Irish, and kissing her affectionately, gave thanks to God for her recovery, and for the kind Providence which had at length brought them all once more together.[2]

At a young age Jane learned to respect education, especially a spiritual education. She grew up tutored extensively by her well-educated father and sometimes brother as the family moved from place to place allowing Thomas Campbell to spread the Gospel.[3] Jane's mother would "keep up the regular order of religious worship and instruction in the family" when her husband was away.[4] This helped the Campbell children consistently feed on the Word of God. They were usually expected to prepare a recitation of scripture at their time of meeting. Richardson mentions one instance when Jane was eleven; she wanted to choose just the right passage to honor her brother's marriage to Margaret Brown. Jane memorized and recited the verses about the Virtuous Woman beautifully. Margaret thanked young Jane with a kiss "expressing the hope that she might herself be enabled, in some measure, to practice its teachings."[5]

---

[1] White, "Jane Campbell McKeever."
[2] Richardson, *Memoirs of Alexander Campbell*, vol. 1, pp. 217-218.
[3] White, "Jane Campbell McKeever."
[4] *Ibid.*, p. 36.
[5] Richardson, *Memoirs of Alexander Campbell*, vol. 1, pp. 363-364.

Young Jane also learned to take action in pursuing her goals. At the age of 18 Jane was successfully helping her father with his school in Burlington, Kentucky. According to Richardson she "soon became distinguished for her ability as a teacher, rendering the school quite popular…"[1] However, Jane's work had to take a new path when prejudicial Kentucky policy concerning the teaching of slaves frustrated her father enough to move them back to Pennsylvania. In 1819, Jane pursued her goals by opening her own school in West Middleton. Then a couple of years later she married Matthew McKeever, a man who wholeheartedly supported her educational endeavors. At first Jane's school was a day-school for girls and boys, but eventually it evolved into Pleasant Hill Female Seminary, a female counterpart to Campbell's Bethany College. Both schools with similar programs of study proved prestigious and sometimes even shared instructors. Five of Campbell's daughters had the opportunity to attend their aunt's school, and glean from her Christian influence. Jane saw that all students attended a daily program of Bible study, and she especially made it a point to have individual conferences with each of her girls concerning their relationships with the Lord.[2]

Jane took all that she had learned and mustered a great courage. She used her courage to speak out against slavery with great passion. She just didn't understand how the Golden Rule and slavery could ever mesh. Matthew, who came from a family of abolitionists, shared her views and together they looked for ways to stand against the evil institution. One day the path was opened to them to help on a dangerous but grand scale. The McKeever's were associated with the abolitionist John Brown through his wool business, and according to White, "It was probably through

---

[1] *Ibid.*, p. 494.
[2] White, "Jane Campbell McKeever."

Brown's influence that the McKeever farm became a station on the Underground Railroad, helping escaped slaves on their way to freedom in Canada."[1] Jane was presented with another opportunity to spread her influence, and she seized it. Jane and Matthew risked their lives to help other people have better lives. She was a sister that made an impact. Her venerable courage, demonstrated in all that she accomplished, made her an example not only to her family but to us all.

ANN DAY LIPSCOMB
(Grandmother)

One could be a grandmother of influence like David Lipscomb's grandmother, Ann Day Lipscomb (1778-1870).[2] Ann Day Cook from Louisa County, Virginia, married William Lipscomb in 1796. Probably looking for a better life financially, the couple moved their family in 1826, after thirty years of marriage, to Bean's Creek Valley in Tennessee. This was the same valley where Davy Crockett set up his "Old Kentuck Farm."[3] (Ann Day lost her oldest child, Mary, just before the move, and a daughter-in-law just after the move. Then, in 1829, Ann's husband William was killed by a falling tree.[4] Ann was a strong woman though. Hooper states, "…the quality of character that caused William and Ann Lipscomb to leave their home in Virginia when approaching old age might have been the edge that turned the family toward success."[5] Lipscomb expressed that his grandmother's trials "served to develop fully her quiet strength of will, her calm, modest self-reliance, her sound discriminating judgement, her

---

[1] *Ibid*, p. 11.
[2] Lipscomb, "Obituaries: Ann Day Lipscomb," *Gospel Advocate*, April 1870.
[3] Hooper, *Crying in the Wilderness*, p. 18.
[4] *Ibid.*
[5] *Ibid.*

wonderful energy and untiring perseverance."[1] Lipscomb also mentioned her impatient streak, which ran through the family, but overall his grandmother was a woman of sound influence.[2]

In 1842, Ann Day Lipscomb united with the Church of Christ near Salem, Tennessee.[3] Remember from Chapter Eleven that the Salem Church was the one that started in the home of David Lipscomb's father after the Lipscombs no longer attended the Bean's Creek Baptist church.[4] In regards to Ann's religious habits, Lipscomb described his grandmother as one who rarely missed a service and would walk two to three miles there round-trip. She was not idle and wanted to provide for all those around her, including the poor. She held great empathy for others. When the Civil War began and the first report of casualties reached her ears, someone informed her that the boys were not from their side.[5] Ann Day said, "No, but they are somebody's boys, that will sadly mourn for them."[6] In regards to Ann's great empathy for others, do you see her influence on her grandson from events described in chapter eight?

Lipscomb described his grandmother's hospitality and home in glowing terms. Ann Day kept a simple home and had simple tastes, but loved to spoil her guests, especially the children. She loved to be surrounded by children. Lipscomb called her home a "fond resort" for family.[7] Ann had 56 grandchildren and 76 great-grandchildren. At age 84, Ann Day was bedridden when Sherman's army came through and robbed her home of all that she had built. They took so much that she did not even have enough

---

[1] Lipscomb, "Obituaries: Ann Day Lipscomb."
[2] *Ibid.*
[3] Hooper, *Crying in the Wilderness*, p. 26.
[4] *Ibid.*
[5] Lipscomb, "Obituaries: Ann Day Lipscomb."
[6] *Ibid.*, p. 401.
[7] *Ibid.*

food left for one meal for herself. Her daughter came to move her that very day, and she spent the remainder of her days enjoying her grandchildren.[1]

Ann Day Lipscomb was a grandmother of influence to all of her little ones. Her strength, her faith in her Lord, her warm hospitality and her love reached far. It especially influenced the grandson who reached so many through his preaching and writing, David Lipscomb.

LUCINDA KUYKENDALL SEWELL
(Adopted Mother or Adopted Aunt)

Another way to be an influence is to be an adopted mother. You may not have adopted children in the legal sense of the word, but you can be an influence to someone who looks to you as a mother, as in the case of Lucinda Sewell and T.F. Bonner. Bonner greatly appreciated the influence his "adopted" mom had on him.

Lucinda Kuykendall was married to E.G. Sewell, the youngest Sewell boy whose family was influenced toward Restoration principles by his sister-in-law, Sarah Sewell. E.G. Sewell became a great gospel preacher and a co-editor of the *Gospel Advocate* with David Lipscomb, writing "regularly for the Advocate a little more than fifty years."[2] Boles states, "Brother Sewell did more to encourage the churches in the South to remain faithful to the New Testament than any other man."[3]

Lucinda married E.G. Sewell in November of 1853. The couple moved in with Lucinda's parents who lived just north of Cookeville, Tennessee. Lucinda's father helped continue Sewell's education by helping to send him to Burritt College. Her

---

[1] *Ibid.*
[2] Boles, *Biographical Sketches of Gospel Preachers*, p. 240.
[3] *Ibid.*, p. 241.

brother helped with Sewell's next step in education by opening a boarding house and giving Lucinda and the children the job of running it while Sewell attended Franklin College. Sewell then began to travel and preach, but as his family grew Lucinda began to struggle at taking care of the family on her own. Therefore, when David Lipscomb offered Sewell the opportunity to help him with the *Gospel Advocate*, he accepted and settled in Edgefield, Tennessee, east of Nashville.[1]

As a young man, T.F. Bonner lived at the Sewell residence in Nashville for several years, and he continued to visit their home after he was married. He felt like Lucinda and her husband were like a mother and father to him, especially after his own parents passed. Bonner lovingly called Lucinda, "Aunt Lucy." In a *Gospel Advocate* article written upon Aunt Lucy's death, Bonner described his adopted mom in glowing terms, saying that it was hard to find even one flaw in Aunt Lucy. She was not one to gossip or talk down to anyone, always giving the benefit of the doubt, saying, "It may be they don't know any better, or perhaps you misunderstood them."[2] Bonner explained that she was not tolerant of wrong deeds, "but she was so pure and correct in her own life that she did not condemn anyone 'on suspicion'; and when it became necessary for her to reprove any one she did so in the spirit of Christ."[3]

Aunt Lucy was also very talented in serving others. According to West, "The Sewell home became known for its hospitality."[4] It was always open to travelling preachers that came through the Nashville area.[5] Bonner admired Aunt Lucy's

---

[1] West, *Search for the Ancient Order*, vol. 1.
[2] Bonner, "Aunt Lucy," *Gospel Advocate*, Jan. 1927, p. 85.
[3] *Ibid.*
[4] West, *Search for the Ancient Order*, vol. 2, p. 156.
[5] *Ibid.*

housekeeping abilities and described her ability to be thrifty and organized. He states, "She did not waste anything. If she prepared more for a meal than was used, she would then prepare it in some other way that was just as appetizing, and I have often thought more so, if possible, than at first."[1] Many preachers and guests of the Sewell home probably enjoyed Aunt Lucy's service and influence towards the Lord's work.

S.H. Hall, who also wrote an article in the *Gospel Advocate* about Sister Sewell, felt like women should look to Sister Sewell as a "model" or "pattern." He said that "her life has been one continuous sermon..." and "The sermon she preached made Satan tremble."[2] T.F. Bonner loved and admired his adopted mom, Aunt Lucy, a woman of influence. Bonner states, "She has passed from us, but her influence will still live."[3]

LAVINIA CAMPBELL AND HER SISTERS
(Daughters)

You could also be a daughter of influence like Lavinia and her sisters, who travelled with their father, Alexander Campbell, as he preached on his tours.[4] They were probably a great encouragement to their father while he worked for the Lord.

LOULIE MCGARVEY
(Daughter)

Loulie McGarvey was also a great encouragement to her parents, J.W. and Ottie McGarvey. Even though she only lived to be ten years old, she was a good example to her peers. McGarvey states, "Though but ten years and six months of age she had read

---

[1] Bonner, "Aunt Lucy," p. 85.
[2] Hall, "A Most Beautiful Life," *Gospel Advocate*, 1926, p. 1180.
[3] Bonner, "Aunt Lucy."
[4] S. Campbell, *Home Life and Reminisces of Alexander Campbell.*

nearly 200 of the small volumes composing the Sunday school library and could sing from memory a large number of hymns then popular with children. She was admired and loved by all who knew her."[1] Even young girls choosing to walk in the path of the Lord and studying His ways are an encouragement to all those around them. A young person should never think their age a hindrance to spreading her influence for the Lord. Remember, Paul told Timothy, "Let no one despise your youth, but be an example to the believers in word, in conduct, in love, in spirit, in faith, in purity" (1 Timothy 4:12, NKJV).

MRS. DABNEY
(A Friend)

All women have the opportunity to spread their influence as a close friend. David Lipscomb found encouragement in a close friend of the family by the name of Mrs. Dabney. His first try at preaching resulted in discouragement, and he needed someone with which to share his story: After entering the pulpit, Lipscomb had read his text and then found his mind to be empty of any material that he had prepared. He read the text again and still could not remember a word. Therefore, he asked his preacher companion that day, who had preached for 50 years, to take over.[2] Caught by surprise, the older gentleman couldn't utter a word. On the way home, when the elder preacher said, "Brother David, I hope you will not let this discourage you."[3]

Lipscomb said, "Well Brother Stroud, I will not be discouraged if I can help it; but I confess that it is enough to discourage

---

[1] McGarvey, *Autobiography of J.W. McGarvey*, pp. 24-25.
[2] Hooper, *Crying in the Wilderness*.
[3] Srygley, *Biographies and Sermons*, p. 157.

a young man to see a man who has been preaching for 50 years make such a failure as you made to-day."[1]

Lipscomb related his story to Mrs. Dabney who "sympathized" with him, and in the process of telling the story, he preached a sermon.[2] Mrs. Dabney sang his praises and encouraged him. She probably never knew the extent to which she had influenced the young man before her that day. Throughout his lifetime, David Lipscomb struggled and felt embarrassed to speak in front of people, but thanks to Mrs. Dabney's influence, he forced himself to climb into the pulpit again and again.[3] You never know the good you can do by just being a friend.

Who Has Influenced You?

This author has been greatly influenced by many women of my church. Specifically, I had two older ladies that encouraged me during my quest to find the nerve to present my first Ladies' Day talk. Ms. Lois, who formulated the idea of me speaking, wouldn't take no for an answer, and Ms. Charlotte, a huge Star Trek fan, said, "You can do this. You are Kirk and I am your Spock."

I've also been influenced by Christian women that do not go to my home church or live nearby. One woman who encouraged me to write a book is Teresa Hampton. She said, "If you can write a series of lessons, you can put those together and write a book." Carole Childers, the dear wife of Tom Childers, was a great woman of encouragement to me. Besides my dad, I wanted to dedicate this book to Carole because of her words of

---

[1] *Ibid*, p. 158.
[2] Hooper, *Crying in the Wilderness*, p. 51.
[3] *Ibid*.

encouragement as I finished a ladies' lecture at the Southeast Institute for Biblical Studies. Carole gave me the confidence, not only in my ability to prepare and present lectures, but in my ability to finish this book. Jane Washington is another lady who constantly checks on me and encourages me. Never underestimate the influence you may have with just a few lines of encouragement to a friend, to those your own age, those older, or, like Lipscomb's story to the younger generation.

There is no certain age required to be a woman of influence. There is not a specific situation necessary for a woman to spread her Christian influence: it can happen in the role of mother, wife, aunt, sister, daughter, "adopted" mom or friend. The important thing to remember is to always be looking for ways to be about our Father's business. Never underestimate the wonders that God may choose to work through you.

QUESTIONS

1. Is being an influence in the role of mother and wife the only way for women to have an impact on others? Who besides his wife was a great influence on D.S. Burnett?
2. Who did David Lipscomb consider to be his closest friend and advisor when he was a young man?
3. Who was Dorthea Campbell, and whom did she influence by her study of scripture? Discuss your thoughts on the courage of Jane Campbell Mckeever.
4. How much influence can a grandmother have? What did David Lipscomb say about the trials of his grandmother, and

how do you think her trials influenced him? Discuss more attributes that Ann Day Lipscomb had that would have influenced her many grandchildren.

5. Discuss the admirable attributes of Lucinda Sewell. Do we have to be a certain age to influence others toward the Lord? (Discuss Loulie McGarvey)

6. Do you think Mrs. Dabney realized how much she affected Lipscomb's life with her encouragement? Do we always realize the effect our words may have on others?

7. Who has been a great spiritual influence in your life?

*Grave of Mary Goforth Gano,
Spring Grove Cemetery, Cincinnati, Ohio (6/26/2024)*

243

*Grave of Dorothea
Campbell Bryant,
God's Acre Cemetery,
Bethany, WV
(6/28/2024)*

*Graves of Thomas
Campbell and Jane
Corneigle Campbell,
God's Acre Cemetery,
Bethany, WV (6/28/2024)*

Grave of Jane Campbell McKeever, God's Acre Cemetery/Bethany, WV (6/28/2024)

Jane Corneigle Campbell, wife of Thomas, and mother of Alexander Campbell

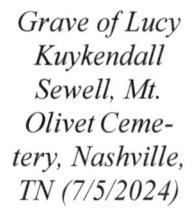

Grave of Lucy Kuykendall Sewell, Mt. Olivet Cemetery, Nashville, TN (7/5/2024)

CHAPTER 15

"Faults They Had, But Faults Have We"
(Alexander Campbell)

Remember that one should never place Restoration ladies upon a pedestal. Yes, most of these women had great zeal for the Lord. They seem to be so strong living through the hardships of the 1800's and working so hard while their husbands were out preaching. However, Restoration women were not perfect. Alexander Campbell said, "Ah me! Live not their virtues in our memory? Faults they had, but faults have we."[1] Restoration women were women with temptations, struggling to walk with God, like all Christian women. What is sad is when some of our Restoration women already had very little recorded about them, and what was recorded highlighted a negative feature. Written records, like funeral commemorations, generally highlight the most becoming qualities of a person. However, again because of the scarcity of their recorded history a few ended up with their unbecoming qualities being recorded.

MARY PERSONETT FRANKLIN

Mary Personett (1809-1888) was one such lady given very little attention in the pages of history.[2] Her husband, Ben Franklin, was an editor of *The American Christian Review* and a major influence on the Restoration Movement in the North. Like McGarvey's wife, Mary was in the background supporting her busy husband and taking care of home and family. Thanks to her

---

[1] Richardson, *Memoirs of Alexander Campbell*, vol. 2, p. 652.
[2] *Mary Personett Franklin 1809-1888.* FindAGrave.com

son, Joseph, who wrote a book with J.A. Headington we know this:

> His wife was two and a half years older than he, but belongs to a family who live longer. She went with him through all his long career, bore him eleven children, and cared for them with a mother's patient and tender care, through many long years of privation and sorrow, keeping up courage and hope where many a woman would have sunk under the heavy burden.[1]

In regards to their financial circumstances, Joseph also said this about his mother:

> Such darning and patching, turning and shifting, as were necessary to make the meager income satisfy the actual wants of the family cannot be described. The situation can only be comprehended by the wife and mother who has gone through the trying ordeal.[2]

The following story illustrates Mary's trials as a preacher's wife in regards to the meager compensation supplied to her family: At one point, the Franklins lived in an area where a deal was made for a house to be given to the Franklins by one church member and provisions were to be supplied by the other members. During hog-killing time, many members remembered their preacher.[3] "Back-bones very neatly trimmed, spare-ribs (very spare indeed), and uncleaned heads and feet, came in such abundance that the wife and mother, already weary and half sick, was thoroughly disgusted."[4] There was no smokehouse to store and preserve the offering, so the Franklins worked together to turn

---

[1] Franklin & Headington, *Life and Times of Benjamin Franklin*, p. 9.
[2] *Ibid.*, p. 69.
[3] *Ibid.*
[4] *Ibid.*, p. 68.

many of the bones to soap. A sister known to be a busy-body paid the Franklins a visit and then reported to the community that the Franklins had been given too much and that the preacher was wasting time over a soap kettle when he ought to be working for the Lord. She also said in regards to Mary that she "didn't see why some women had to be waited on so much, anyway." Mary was strong and did not shed a tear, until another sister with wisdom and empathy blessed Mary with a great store of fresh meat for the family.[1]

The Franklin family, including eight children at the time, still struggled financially when they moved to the Cincinnati area. Franklin had worked as a partner with D.S. Burnett on two papers and had preached with him around the area.[2] D.S. Burnett was the husband of Mary Gano Burnett mentioned earlier. He was also the son of a great mayor of Cincinnati.[3] The Burnetts secured a home across the road from the Franklins, and some of the only lines about Mary recorded by West are as follows:

> There was some self-pity mixed with envy when Franklin's wife looked across the road to Burnett's lovely home. From her point of view there was only one satisfactory fact of life: her husband was a popular and successful evangelist. She took sole pride in this knowledge.[4]

The envy Mary struggled with is something many women would struggle with. At least we know enough from recorded history to know what Mary' life was like before living near the Burnett's, and we also know that the social classes of the two

---

[1] *Ibid.*, p. 69.
[2] West, *Elder Benjamin Franklin: Eye of the Storm*.
[3] West, *Search for the Ancient Order*, vol. 1.
[4] West, *Elder Benjamin Franklin*, p. 97.

families were vastly different.[1] Mary's son wrote, "The grace of God may teach a family to endure without complaint such a state of things. But it would require a miracle to make them feel at ease."[2] Nevertheless, Mary probably did not want her struggle concerning the Burnetts to be what she was remembered for in Restoration history.

Mary supported her husband and made it possible for him to be a great influence for the Restoration cause. She in turn can be remembered as a great influence on Restoration women today. She can remind us that Restoration women can be greatly admired for their Godly self-sacrifice, but they were not perfect.

LUCRETIA RUDOLPH GARFIELD

James A. Garfield's wife was Lucretia Rudolph Garfield (1832-1918). This couple consisted of exact opposites. Rushford states that Garfield "married into a strong Stone-Campbell family in Hiram, and became 'a favorite preacher' among Western Reserve Disciples."[3] Both Lucretia and Garfield attended Geauga Seminary, but the courtship really began at the Western Reserve Eclectic Institute in Hiram, Ohio, a school that Lucretia's father helped to start. Garfield first noticed Lucretia in Greek class. She was a "petite, delicate, pretty girl with deep set eyes."[4] Garfield began courting Lucretia through letters. Over the course of their relationship, the couple sent 1,200 letters back and forth. Lucretia felt more at ease expressing herself in letters, but when not using her pen, she came across as very quiet and reserved. The couple did share a great love for books and learning, and this brought

---

[1] Franklin & Headington, *Life and Times of Benjamin Franklin.*
[2] *Ibid.*, p. 194.
[3] Rushford, "James A. Garfield," *Encyclopedia of the Stone-Campbell Movement*, p. 349.
[4] Weinkamer, *James and Lucretia's Love Story*, the Blog of the James A. Garfield National Historic Site, para. 6.

them together. The two were married on November 11, 1858. However, Garfield wasn't sure that he had made the right decision.[1]

Garfield and Lucretia spent very little time together in their early years of marriage, and their relationship struggled. They called these years "The Dark Years." Garfield was only home about 20 weeks out of five years. Eventually, Lucretia decided to change her attitude about her relationship and met some of her childhood issues, brought about by non-affectionate parents, head-on. She was also able to show Garfield her true feelings for him by letting him read her diary. As the couple endured the Civil War years, plus horrible trials including the loss of children, the Garfields found that they grew through these hardships. Lucretia was determined to make a happy home, and Garfield as well determined to devote himself to his family and Lucretia. They leaned on their faith and they went back to sharing their love for books and learning. They were also able to spend more time together when Garfield moved his family to Washington and began his political career. In a letter to Lucretia from December 1867, Garfield said, "We no longer love because we ought to, but because we do. Were I free to choose out of all the world the sharer of my heart and home and life, I would fly to you and ask you to be mine as you are."[2]

Hosterman stated, "The match was a love-match and has turned out very happily."[3] According to Weinkamer, Lucretia kept all of her and her husband's letters to show their children the path of their relationship. She wanted them to gain an understanding that relationships develop over time and take work. Lucretia's

---

[1] *Ibid.*
[2] *Ibid*, para. 13.
[3] Hosterman, *The Life and Times of James Abram Garfield*, p. 94.

and Garfield's relationship turned into a true love story.[1] Again, marriage troubles are something many women would not want recorded as history, but Lucretia overcame her struggles, and she is a wonderful Christian example to all.

ELIZA SANDIDGE SCOTT

Now, poor Walter Scott and his third wife are a different story. Proverbs 21:19 says, "Better to dwell in the wilderness than with a contentious and angry woman" (NKJV). Walter Scott was an early and important Restoration preacher who brought Restoration principles to the Western Reserve. Scott baptized so many (about 1,000 a year) between the years of 1827-1829 that he gained the label of "Golden Oracle."[2] Alexander Campbell said this about Walter Scott: "Next to my father, he was the most cordial and indefatigable fellow laborer in the origin and progress of the present Reformation. His whole heart was in his work."[3] John P. Simpson stated, "Alexander Campbell provided the intellectual direction, while Walter Scott provided the evangelistic fervor for the Restoration Movement."[4] Scott was also called "the five-finger preacher."[5] He taught his students the steps of faith, repentance, baptism, remission and Holy Spirit, and they in turn would go home and teach their parents using their five fingers.[6]

Scott's first wife was Sarah Whitsett. She was a wife who inspired his preaching and helped him face the challenges presented by his work on the Western Reserve. According to Baxter,

---

[1] Weinkamer, *James and Lucretia's Love Story*.
[2] Phillips, *A Medley of the Restoration*, p. 68.
[3] Quoted in Phillips, *A Medley of the Restoration*, p. 58.
[4] Simpson, "Restoration Leaders: Walter Scott," *Church Growth—A Blueprint for Stronger Churches, Freed-Hardeman College Lectures 1981*, p. 328.
[5] Phillips, *A Medley of the Restoration*, p. 16.
[6] *Ibid.*

she "animated her husband to persevere when these difficulties had well-nigh overcome his faith."[1] Sarah had her own difficulties with Scott not having the best money sense about him, but she loved him anyway and made the most of the small amount that they had.[2] Upon her death in 1849, Scott wrote, "Best of wives, tenderest of mothers, the most faithful of friends, a Christian in faith, works and charity."[3] Scott's second wife, Nannie B. Allen, or "Annie," also loved Scott for who he was.[4] She said once, "I would rather be Walter Scott's widow than the wife of any other man."[5]

It was Scott's third marriage to a rich widow named Eliza Sandidge that brought him so much misery. Scott believed that money was to use or to give away. Daniel Hayden once said to Scott, "Bro. Scott, you ought not to handle a dollar; whatever means you have, ought to be in the hands of someone with less sympathy and more judgement than yourself..."[6] Eliza thought differently about money. She believed that possessions were to be respected.[7] Scott would go to the store for groceries and give them all away on his way home. Another time, he gave away a cow because he had two and a neighbor needed one.[8] As a result, Eliza would "storm at him and run him out of the house"; often, "he spent the night sitting on the doorstep of a neighbor."[9] Once, when no one knew Scott's whereabouts, two elders found him wandering the streets of Cincinnati. When the elders insisted that

---

[1] Baxter, *Life of Elder Walter Scott*, p. 262.
[2] Simpson, "Restoration Leaders: Walter Scott."
[3] Baxter, *Life of Elder Walter Scott*, p. 262.
[4] West, *Search for the Ancient Order*, vol. 1.
[5] As cited in Stevenson, *Walter Scott: Voice of the Golden Oracle*, p. 202.
[6] Baxter, *Life of Elder Walter Scott*, p. 106.
[7] Stevenson, *Walter Scott: Voice of the Golden Oracle*.
[8] West, *Search for the Ancient Order*, vol. 1.
[9] *Ibid.*, p. 86.

he go home he said, "Very well. I will go back, but not alone. You must go with me."[1] It is sad that Walter Scott spent his final years on Earth in a miserable marriage. It is also sad that Eliza, in the few words of history recorded about her, is remembered for her contribution to Scott's misery. From what we know, Eliza may not have been a good influence for the cause of the Restoration.

SUSAN MITCHUM BALL HALL

Finally, we come to B.F. Hall's second wife, Susan Ball (1803-1868).[2] This woman proved to be probably the worst hindrance to the restoration cause out of any of the Restoration women. Let's take a look at B.F. Hall's life to understand more about his circumstances.

B.F. Hall, a preacher, doctor and dentist, was one of the earliest Restoration leaders who taught that baptism was essential to salvation. His first wife, Dorinda C. Chisholm, daughter of Esther Chisolm from a previous chapter, died after four years of marriage.[3] Dorinda was baptized for the remission of her sins, and so were their twin daughters at the age of 12. The twins were only two years old when Dorinda died, but Hall said that they imitated their good mother.[4]

B.F. Hall's second marriage to Susan Ball was not at all like his first marriage. It proved to be very demanding and discouraging to Hall. He said of this marriage:

> Instead of enlarging the sphere of my usefulness by increasing my facilities for preaching as I had anticipated it

---

[1] Stevenson, *Voice of the Golden Oracle*, p. 213.
[2] *Susan Mitchum Ball-Hall 1803-1868*, FindAGrave.com.
[3] Harp, *Dr. Benjamin Franklin Hall*, TheRestorationMovement.com
[4] Hall, *Autobiography of B.F. Hall, MD and DDS*. TheRestorationMovement.com

would do, it increased the burden of my cares, and for a time forced me from the field evangelical in order to carry out the worldly program of my wife which she had determined upon prior to our marriage, and which was in an attitude not then to be changed.[1]

Hall started his marriage on rocky ground. He found himself mixed up in a fraud over numerous notes for land that he did not want in the first place: First, Susan had tried to get B.F. Hall to sign a prenuptial, which he refused. Evidence suggests that she put all of her landholdings in her brother's name just an hour before the wedding. She then proceeded to send Hall to purchase land in Mississippi that she had verbally contracted in his name. She told him to use the money from the sale of her farm in Kentucky. Remember, however, that she put her farm in her brother's name, probably as insurance since the prenuptial was not signed. Hall was forced to use credit for bank notes totaling $9,000. Eventually, after not being able to pay it back, a suit was brought against him. He was humiliated and unsure if his wife had orchestrated it.[2]

One problem led to another and eventually Susan wanted a separation of the two families. He would be responsible for educating his children, and she would be responsible for her own. However, after the separation, Susan said that if Hall would open his dentistry practice in Lexington, Kentucky, she would return, but she never did. Then she said if he would open his dentistry practice in Nashville, she would join him; she stayed six weeks and said she was going back to Kentucky. Meanwhile, Hall continued to preach and to travel. When a request came to help brethren in Chicago with building a meeting place, Susan refused to

---

[1] *Ibid.*, para. 189.
[2] *Ibid.*

go with him, and Hall had to decline the work. Selfishly, Susan eventually divided all her property among her children from her previous marriage, leaving $8,000 for Hall that she had obtained in a lawsuit from him in the first place. Again, she told Hall if he would buy a place in Texas, she would follow.[1] At this point, Hall let her know that he would make the decisions as the head of the house, but that she would be his "beloved wife."[2] Susan wanted nothing to do with this.[3]

Scott Harp said, "The second wife might be kindly described as difficult."[4] Susan came across as deceptive, selfish and in pursuit of worldly gain for herself and her own. She got Hall mixed up in embarrassing debt and lawsuits, not to mention the negative influence she had on her husband's reputation concerning his marital status. Dealing with this for years, Hall tried to preach in between one fiasco after another, and also tried to be a good husband to her. Eventually, Hall stayed in Texas, not knowing if Susan was alive or dead.[5]

Married to a great Restoration preacher Susan not only looked out for herself instead of the cause of the Restoration, she was a hindrance to the Lord's work. Yes, we all fall down, making mistakes and getting up to try again, but may we all strive never to be a negative influence and hindrance to the Lord's work. Let us deny ourselves and take up our cross daily and follow Him. Let us take the Bible as our only guide and share these truths as women of influence for God and not a negative influence for Satan.

---

[1] *Ibid.*
[2] *Ibid.*, para 270.
[3] *Ibid.*
[4] Harp, *Dr. Benjamin Franklin Hall,* para. 11.
[5] Hall, *Autobiography of B.F. Hall, MD and DDS.*

SOPHIA LEWIS JOHNSON

Let our lives more resemble the life of Sophia Lewis Johnson (1796-1849), wife of John T. Johnson.[1] Johnson was an early Restoration preacher who had a lot to do with uniting the Stone group and the Campbell group by helping them to see their similarities.[2] Sophia was saddened when J.T. Johnson was absent so much from home to preach and labor in the work of the Lord, but she persevered with a cheerful resignation. In a letter to Campbell upon Sophia's death, Johnson said, "For some eight years, the sacrifice of personal happiness, owing to my absence from home, preyed heavily upon my wife, and seemed to be more than she could bear. But the cause was dearer to her than life."[3] Sophia was an influence to all, especially to her family. Johnson called her his "heaven on earth."[4] Upon her deathbed, she charged her children "to lead a Godly life and meet her in heaven."[5] This particular quote drew this author's heart close to Sophia's, because my favorite phrase growing up, often stated by my softball coaches was, "Remember where we are going to meet." In turn I have said this over and over to my children and my ball players.

Sophia's life left an impact on us all. Let us conquer our faults and lean on the Lord so that one day our epitaph reads like hers: **"She left the world a strong example of Christian piety, fortitude and resignation. May we all profit by it."**[6]

---

[1] *Sophia E. Lewis Johnson 1796-1849*, FindAGrave.com.
[2] Boles, *Biographical Sketches of Gospel Preachers*.
[3] Rogers, *The Biography of J.T. Johnson*, p. 296.
[4] *Ibid.*, p. 299.
[5] *Ibid.*, p. 297.
[6] *Sophia E. Lewis Johnson 1796-1849*, FindAGrave.com.

QUESTIONS

1. When this book was taught to my ladies' class, at times the historical accounts of the glowing attributes of some of the Restoration women seemed almost too good to be true. Why is it important to remember that we all have faults and struggles?

2. There may be more historical record of Mary Franklin than this author found, and we should realize that she was a great wife that supported Ben Franklin. However, we are left only with a short description of one fault. If only one attribute could be recorded about you, what would it be? Would you like to be remembered more like Sophia Lewis Johnson?

3. Like Lucretia Garfield, what issues from childhood have you had to overcome in your marriage? What were some other things Lucretia did to help her marriage? Garfield was a busy man in the limelight of life. Compare Lucretia to an elder or a preacher's wife.

4. What verses come to mind about the negative influence of a woman? How were Eliza Sandidge Scott and Susan Ball Hall a negative influence, or even a detriment to the Lord's work?

257

Grave of Mary Franklin, West Maplewood Cemetery, Anderson, IN

Sephulcher of Lucretia and President Garfield, Lake View Cemetery, Cleveland, OH

Lucretia Garfield

Grave of Sophia Lewis Johnson, Lexington Cemetery/ Lexington, Kentucky (6/26/2024)

CHAPTER 16

Conclusion: Looking Forward

Now it's time to look forward. What will you leave to the world as your influence? Will you be a woman of submission like Elizabeth Rogers, a woman of character like Nancy Smith, a woman that gives of herself to His cause like Emily Tubman or a woman of usefulness like Selina Campbell? Will you be a woman that teaches like Charlotte Fanning, a woman of motherly love like Nancy Larimore or a woman of positive invention like Margaret Lipscomb? Will you be a woman with a song in her heart like Esther Larimore, a woman on a mission like Mattie Carr or a woman of impact like Sarah Sewell? Will you be a woman of influence for the Lord's work, like so many of the Restoration women that worked behind the scenes to further the Kingdom?

No one can say that women are limited in the Biblical role God has given us if they have read about these Restoration Women. Know how much these women of the Restoration accomplished for the Lord and reflect on what has been done before this present time by women just like you. Reflect, and then begin your journey to restore all things to God through your influence by moving forward with a plan to be about your Father's business. Realize that lost souls are at stake. This is your precious time God has blessed you with to be useful to the Him. How will you put your talents to work for your Creator and carry on the Restoration cause, bringing souls to the simple gospel truth through your influence? Phillips said:

> The Lord's church is always one generation from apostasy, as teaching the truth is a constant must. Restoration must be discovered anew by each generation. It is still true that God has no grandchildren, only children... Nothing remains won; the jungle must be constantly beaten back.[1]

We can take three steps to help us with our plan to look and move forward in our mission to be Restoration women in our time. We should remember three R's: **Reflect, Reconcile and Restore**.

Step 1 is to Reflect: First, we need to be women of the word. We need to reflect upon the Lord's teaching and His truths. "But his delight is in the law of the Lord, and in his law doth he meditate day and night" (Psalm 1:3, KJV). "Study to shew thyself approved unto God, a workman that needeth not to be ashamed, rightly dividing the word of truth" (2 Timothy 2:15, KJV). Then, if reading about Restoration women inspires you, reflect upon their zeal for the Lord's work—but remember not to take anything as your guide except the Bible. Remember they were simply people; they were good people with human faults just like us.

Step 2 is to Reconcile: We should reconcile ourselves to our commitment to "Listen to God." This author has committed to memory this amazing excerpt of Restoration theology from one of Scott Harp's sermons:

> Truth is a wonderful thing to pray for; it's a wonderful thought, and a wonderful commitment to have...That's one of the things I have long appreciated: Commitment to the desire to preach and teach the Gospel and nothing but the Gospel of Jesus Christ. Not to go to the left or to the

---

[1] Phillips, *A Medley of the Restoration*, p. 1.

right but to stay right in the middle of the book and do Bible things in Bible ways. Try to speak where the Bible speaks and have the desire to remain silent where the Bible is silent, and just always do things the way God wants us to do them. Those are truly great challenges for us. They're not always easy to do. It's not always an easy thing to accomplish because sometimes when personalities get involved it presents more and more of a challenge. But God's way is always the best way. It's always the right way, and when you do them His way then you can't go wrong... As far back as men can remember God has always appealed to man to listen to Him. **Listen to Me...** Can you remember in Genesis chapter four when He was talking with Cain? Why has your countenance fallen? Listen to me! If you do the right thing everything will be okay, but if you don't, sin lies at the door. And that's always a challenge for man. What Cain was really dealing with in his heart and mind is what every man has to deal with...

But yet it is a challenge for us all. Am I going to do things my way, or am I going to do things God's way? If you look down through the history of time, that's always been the challenge...as far back as the days of the New Testament, as far back as time goes, God has always called upon us to remember His way and to do His things in His way...that was the challenge of the first century. That's the challenge of the twenty-first century. And as long as man lives upon this earth that will always be the challenge because we know the word of God is going to last forever. As long as we are here upon the earth we have no worry that the Word is going to be here.[1]

---

[1] Harp, "Adhering to the Restoration Plea," *Gospel Advocate*, July 2012.

> Isaiah 40:8—The grass withers, the flower fades, but the word of God stands forever. (NKJV)

If you have **reconciled** yourself to listen to God and you find there is something in your practice of following God that you just cannot find in His book, go back and **reflect** on His word. Then if you have caught that insatiable zeal to be a woman of Restoration, than look forward to step 3.

Step 3 is to Restore: Remember your mission to <u>restore</u> God's truths to the world. Remember the mission God has so sacredly blessed you with during your short time on this earth. Let the honor and the gravity of the mission with which we have been entrusted sink into your soul. Like Charlotte Fanning taught, there is no time to waste, and like Selina Campbell believed, we all need to be useful towards His cause. Keep your mission and His truths ever before you. As Charlotte Fanning said:

> Let the Bible have its influence in our everyday life. Lay up the precepts of God's word in your hearts, and let it mold your characters. Teach its truths with earnestness and simplicity. The life of women should be earnest. They are capable of doing good that others cannot affect. Will you not walk thoughtfully, remembering that your influence may lead others to the Savior whom you have elected to follow, or may render them careless of the things that concern their peace?.[1]

God gave women a mission to restore truth and lost souls back to Him. Like Margaret Holbrook, never underestimate what one woman can do. Don't let Satan put any doubt in your mind that you cannot be the one to make a difference. You may be a

---

[1] Larimore, *The Life Work of Mrs. Charlotte Fanning*, p. 10.

restoration woman that influences thousands or you may influence that one lost sheep that was so important to the Shepherd. You may be the one that just influences those closest to you, like Sarah Sewell, and in the process unknowingly influence thousands. Remember what David Lipscomb wrote in regards to Sarah Sewell:

> God uses simple, unthought-of, and, as they appear to us, fortuitous circumstances to effect His ends. It teaches the lesson, that fidelity to God and man in the relations we are in is what God requires at our hands then he well over rules for good, and out of what seems to us small matters of life, brings the greatest results.[1]

Choose this day to look forward and to be a Restoration woman for this time and age.

> Yet who knows whether you have come to the
> kingdom for such a time as this?
> (Esther 4:14b, NKJV)

Let us be restorers of the truth and do "Bible things in Bible ways."

> For we cannot do anything against the truth, but
> only for the truth. For we are glad when we are
> weak and you are strong. Your restoration is
> what we pray for (2 Corinthians 13:8-9, ESV).

God desires Restoration. Let us stand for the truth and carry out our mission from the Lord to reach others. Christ is the strongest in our weaknesses so don't let anything hold you back.

---

[1] Lipscomb, *The Life and Sermons of Jessie L. Sewell*, p. 59.

It is no small matter that we too as women are "ambassadors for Christ."

> Now then, we are ambassadors for Christ as
> though God were pleading through us…
> (2 Corinthians 5:20a).

QUESTIONS

1. In regard to looking forward and becoming women of Restoration for this generation, discuss the three R's that can be helpful in this journey (Reflect, Reconcile, Restore).
2. Who was your favorite Restoration woman and why?
3. What are your plans for becoming a woman of the ongoing Restoration Movement of today, to do "Bible things in Bible ways" and to take God's truths to the world?

REFERENCES

Allen, T.M. (1859, January). Progress of Reform. *Millennial Harbinger, 2*(1) 56-57.

Anderson, N. (2003, July). Tolbert Fanning: A Spiritual Giant. *Gospel Advocate, 145*(7), 3.

Anne Apperson Bacon Fall (1800-1888)—Find a Grave. (2012, October). www.findagrave.com. Created by Tina Toles Wingate, https://www.findagrave.com/memorial/98529062/ann_apperson_fall

Augusta Chronicle. (2021, March 21). March 21, 1794: Emily Tubman, Augusta's great benefactor, is born. *The Augusta Chronicle*, https://www.augustachronicle.com/story/news/2021/03/21/emily-tubman-augusta-ga-benefactor-freed-slaves-time-machine/4692336001/

Barclay, J.T. (1882). The City of the Great King, or, Jerusalem as it was, as it is, and as it is to be. W.H. Thompson.

Baxter, William (2017) Life of Elder Walter Scott: with sketches of his fellow-laborers, William Hayden, Adamson Bentley, John Henry, and others. Cobb Publishing. Reformatted from the original edition of 1874.

Boles, H. Leo (1932). Biographical Sketches of Gospel Preachers, including the pioneer preachers of the Restoration Movement and many other preachers through decades down to the present generation who have passed to their reward. Gospel Advocate.

Bonner, T.F. (1927, January 27). Aunt Lucy. *Gospel Advocate, 69*(4), 85.

Brown, J.T. (Ed.). (1904). Churches of Christ: A historical, biographical and pictorial history of churches of Christ in the United States, Australasia, England and Canada. John P. Morton & Co.

Burnett, D.S. (1857, August). Obituary Notices. *Millennial Harbinger*, 7(7), 479-480.

Campbell, Alexander (1839, June). Schools and Education No. II. *Millennial Harbinger, 3*(6), 278-280.

Campbell Selina (1878, July 27). Woman's Work. *Christian Standard,* p. 238.

Campbell, Selina (1880, December 18). Women Preachers. *Christian Standard*, p. 402.

Campbell, Selina H. (1882). Home Life and Reminisces of Alexander Campbell. John Burns.

Carr, O.A. (1907, November 28). In Memory of Mrs. O.A. Carr. *Gospel Advocate* 49(48), 762.

Challen, James (Ed.). (1857, October). Biographical Sketch of John Allen Gano. *Ladies' Christian Annual.* 6(10), 305-310, https://webfiles.acu.edu/departments/Library/HR/restmov_nov11/www.mun.ca/rels/restmov/texts/jchallen/lcab/GANOJA.HTM

Childress, J.H. (1933, April) John Gano 1736-1804: Was George Washington immersed? *Firm Foundation, 50(15)*, 1, 3. https://www.therestorationmovement.com/_states/kentucky/gano,john.htm

Colley, G. (1989). John Moody McCaleb (1861-1953). *Glory to God: Freed-Hardeman College Lectures 1989*, (pp. 62-66).

Coombs, J.V. (1911). *The Basis of Christian Unity.* Stone-Campbell Books. 331 http://digitalcommons.acu.edu/crs_books/331

Cox, J.D. (1951). *A Concise Account of Church History.* Dehoff Publications.

Darsie, G. (1904). Mrs. Emily H. Tubman. In J.T. Brown (Ed.), Churches of Christ: a historical, biographical, and pictorial history of Churches of Christ in the United States, Australasia, England and Canada, (pp. 442-443). J.P. Morton & Co.

Death of a venerable lady. (1857, July 4). *The Washington Union.* p. 3. -Find a..., (2007, April 17). Image by A. Beard. https://www.findagrave.com/memorial/18990547/mary-gano

Doenecke, Justus. (2019) *James A. Garfield: Family life*. UVA Miller Center. https://millercenter.org/president/garfield/family-life

Donaldson, E. (1993). Raccoon John Smith: Frontiersman and Reformer. Wind Publications.

Doran, A. (1991, September). Philip Slater Fall. *The World Evangelist, 20(2)*, 5.

Duke, J.O. (2004). Pendleton, William Kimbrough (1817-1899). In D.A. Foster, P.M. Blowers, A.L. Dunnavant, & D.N. Williams (Eds.), *The encyclopedia of the Stone-Campbell movement*. (pp. 134-138). William B. Eerdmans.

Elam, M.L. (1926, April 22). Association with Sister Lipscomb: A Benediction. *Gospel Advocate, 68*(16), 363.

Eldon S. Potter (1871-1899)—Find a... (2012, April 15). Created by Pat, www.findagrave.com/memorial/88555892/eldon-s-potter

Eldon S. Potter (1899, November 9). *Gospel Advocate, 41*(45), 710.

Ellis, J.B. (1910). *The Story of a Life.* Reynolds-Parker. https://www.gutenberg.org/files/37677/37677-h/37677-h.htm

Ernst, J. (2001). *From Augusta to Africa part—1: Journey to freedom*. Issue. https://issuu.com/augustachronicle/docs/from_augusta_to_africa_-_part_1. (This article can also be located in the Augusta Chronicle Archives)

Ferguson, E. (1967). Way of Life series: No. 107. *Church History Reformation and Modern* (J.D. Thomas Ed.). (2nd ed.).

Floyd, J.D. (1907, March 14). A Noble Woman Gone to Rest. *Gospel Advocate,* 49(11), 166.

Franklin, J. & Headington, J.A. (1956). *The Life and Times of Benjamin Franklin*. Old Paths Book Club.

Gano, R.M. (1904). John Allen Gano. In J.T. Brown (Ed.), Churches of Christ: a historical, biographical, and pictorial history of

Churches of Christ in the United States, Australasia, England and Canada, (pp. 421-423). J.P. Morton & Co.

Gardner, E.C. (2004, July). Tolbert Fanning: The Successor to Alexander Campbell. *Gospel Advocate, 146(7)*, 12-16.

Garrett, L. (1981). The Stone-Campbell Movement: An anecdotal history of three churches (3rd ed.). College Press.

Georgia Women of Achievement. (2016). *Emily Harvie Thomas Tubman: Business woman, founder, philanthropist.* https://www.georgiawomen.org/copy-of-thomas-ella-gertrude-clanto

Gifford, J.M. (1975, Spring). Emily Tubman and the African Colonization Movement in Georgia. *The Georgia Historical Quarterly,* 59(1), 10-24. https://www.jstor.org/stable/40580141

Goodpasture, B.C. (1932, September). The Willow Grove (Tenn.) Meeting. *Gospel Advocate,* 1059, 1067. https://www.therestorationmovement.com/_states/tennessee/sewells.htm

Green, F.M. (1882). A Royal Life: or, the Eventful History of James A. Garfield, Twentieth President of the United States. Central Book Concern.

Griffith, Kevin. (2001, August). *Play on, Miss Bertha.* [Term Paper]. The Restoration Movement. https://www.therestorationmovement.com/_states/texas/clark3.htm

Hagger, T. (1938). *Heralds of Christian Unity,* 74-78. https://therestorationmovement.com/_states/texas/carr,oa.htm

Hall, B.F. (n.d.) *Autobiography of B.F. Hall, M.D. and D.D.S.* The Restoration Movement. http://www.therestorationmovement.com/_states/texas/hallautobio.htm

Hall, S.H. (1926). A Most Beautiful Life. *Gospel Advocate 68(50)*, 1180-1181.

Hampton, G. (n.d.). The Power of One: sermon notes. [Power Point Slides].

Hampton, T. (2003). *Come to the Garden.* Publishing Designs.

Harp, S. (n.d.-a). *Celia Wilson Bowen Stone August 26, 1793—April 23, 1857*. The Restoration Movement. http://www.therestorationmovement.com/_states/missouri/stone,c.htm

Harp, S. (n.d.-b). *Charles Chilton Moore 1837-1906*. The Restoration Movement. http://www.therestorationmovement.com/_states/kentucky/cc_moore.htm

Harp, S. (n.d.-c). *Chronology of the Life of Alexander Campbell, 1788-1866*. The Restoration Movement. http://www.therestorationmovement.com/_states/wv/cmblachronology.htm

Harp, S. (n.d.-d). *Early Church, Home Life & Parents of David & William Lipscomb*. The Restoration Movement. https://www.therestorationmovement.com/_states/tennessee/lipscomb,granville.htm

Harp, S. (n.d.-e). *Joseph Addison Clark 1815-1901*. The Restoration Movement. http://www.therestorationmovement.com/_states/texas/clark,ja.htm

Harp, S. (n.d.-f). *Oliver Anderson Carr 1845-1912: Carr-Burdette College* section. [Notes from *History of Texas Christian University*]. The Restoration Movement. https://www.therestorationmovement.com/_states/texas/carr,oa.htm

Harp, S. (n.d.-g). *Restoration Movement Scenes around Hannibal, Missouri*. The Restoration Movement. http://www.therestorationmovement.com/_states/missouri/hannibal.htm

Harp, S. (n.d.-h). *The History of Bacon College*. [PowerPoint slides]. The Restoration Movement. http://www.therestorationmovement.com/lessons/RM History of Bacon College.pptx

Harp, S. (n.d.-i). *The Homes of Barton W. Stone*. The Restoration Movement. https://www.therestorationmovement.com/_states/kentucky/stonehomes.htm#bowenhome

Harp, S. (2011, June). *Dr. Benjamin Franklin Hall*. The Restoration Movement. http://www.therestorationmovement.com/_states/texas/hall,bf.htm

Harp, S. (2012a, July). Adhering to the Restoration Plea. *Gospel Advocate, 154(7)*, 18-20.

Harp, S. (2012b, September 16). The Life of N.B. Hardeman [Audio Sermon]. The Restoration Movement. https://www.therestorationmovement.com/audio/SDH-TheLifeOfNBHardeman.mp3

Harp, S. (2013a, November). *John and Esther Chisholm*. The Restoration Movement. https://www.therestorationmovement.com/_states/alabama/chisholm.htm

Harp, S. (2013b, September 21). *The Sewell Family—The Beginning*. The Restoration Movement. https://www.therestorationmovement.com/_states/tennessee/sewells.htm

Harp, S. (2018a, July). *Addison Clark 1842-1911*. The Restoration Movement. http://www.therestorationmovement.com/_states/texas/addison_clark.html

Harp, S. (2018b, July). *Addran Clark 1869-1872*. The Restoration Movement. http://www.therestorationmovement.com/_states/texas/addran_clark.html

Hicks, O. (1962). John W. McGarvey. The Restoration Principle: Abilene Christian College annual Bible lectures. ACU Student's Exchange. 363-372.

Holman, Selina M. (1907, April 4). A Good Mother. *Gospel Advocate, 49(14)*, 210.

Hooper, R.E. (1979). *Crying in the wilderness.* David Lipscomb College.

Hopson, E.L. (1887). *Memoirs of Dr. Winthrop Hartly Hopson*. Standard Publishing.

Hosterman, A.D. (1881). Life and Times of James Abram Garfield: Twentieth President of the *United States*. Farm and Fireside. https://archive.org/stream/lifetimesofjameshost/lifetimesofjameshost_djvu.txt

Jenkins, A. (2003, July). The Legacy of Charlotte Fanning. *Gospel Advocate, 145(7)*, 16-18.

Jenkins, A. (2013, July). Franklin College: The Shadow of a Great Man. *Gospel Advocate,* 155(7), 18-20.

J.M. McCaleb. (1971). The Gospel is for All. In A.H. Howard (Ed.), *Songs of the Church*. (p. 88). Howard Publishing.

Kenney, D.R. (2013, March). Light from Above. *Gospel Advocate, 155(3),* 38-39.

Kimbrough, Earl. (2014, March). *"Miss Polly" A History of Mary Lumpkin Barnes 1811-1891* [PDF Lecture]. Faulkner University. Friends of the Restoration. 1-9. http://www.therestorationmovement.com/classes/pollybarnes.pdf Also appears in the book, Miss Polly, by the same author, Cobb Publishing, 2021.

Lane, J.J. (1903). *History of education in Texas. (No. 35).* Washington: Government Printing Office. https://texaslegalguide.com/images/History_of_Education_in_Texas.pdf

Larimore, T & Page, E. (1910). *Letters and sermons of T.B. Larimore Vol. III*. Stone-Campbell Books. https://digitalcommons.acu.edu/crs_books/155

Larimore, E.P. (2012). *The Life Work of Mrs. Charlotte Fanning*. Memphis, TN: General Books LLC, RareBooksClub.com (Reprinted from 1907 ed., McQuiddy Printing).

Larimore, T.B. (1915, December 2). What I Owe My Mother. *Gospel Advocate, 57*(48), 1204-1205

Larimore, E.P. (2006). *Life, Letters, and Sermons of T.B. Larimore*. Guardian of Truth. (Reprinted from 1931 ed., *Gospel Advocate* Co.).

Lavinia M. Campbell Pendleton (1818-1846)—Find a... (2006, July 26). www.findagrave.com, Created by Cheryl Behrend, https://findagrave.com/memorial/15048083/Lavinia-m-pendleton

Lewis, J.T. (1926, April 22). A True Helpmate. *Gospel Advocate, 68*(16), 377.

Lipscomb, A.B. (1926, April 22). Thank Her and Thank God. *Gospel Advocate, 68*(16), 363-364.

Lipscomb, D. (1866, November 27). A Word to Our Southern Brethren. *Gospel Advocate, 8*(48), 756-758.

Lipscomb, D. (1870, April 28) Obituaries: Ann Day Lipscomb. *Gospel Advocate, 12*(17), 400-402

Lipscomb, D. (1875, February 25). Obituary. *The Gospel Advocate, 17*(9), 217-218.

Lipscomb, D. (1891). The Life and Sermons of Jessie L. Sewell. *Gospel Advocate*.

Long, L.M. (2001). *The Life of Selina Campbell*. University of Alabama Press.

Long, L.M. (2004). Campbell, Selina Huntington Bakewell (1802-1897). In D.A. Foster, P.M. Blowers, A.L. Dunnavant, & D.N. Williams (Eds.), *The Encyclopedia of the Stone-Campbell Movement*. (pp. 134-138). William B. Eerdmans.

Loyd, D. (2012, July). The beginning of the Gospel Advocate. *Gospel Advocate*, 154(7). 24-26.

Lucy Jane Beasley McCaleb (1832-1882)—Find a... (2012, December 12). www.findagrave.com. Created by Larry Orr. https://www.findagrave.com/memorial/102078498/lucy-jane-mccaleb

Mary Catherine Conn Gano (1810-1891) Find a... (2012, April 17). www.findagrave.com. Created by Tom Childers. https://www.findagrave.com/memorial/88686270/mary-catherine-gano

Mary Goforth Gano (1768-1857)—Find a..., (2007, April 17). www.findagrave.com, Created by K Guy. https://www.findagrave.com/memorial/18990547/mary-gano

Margaret Lingow Elam (1835-1907)—Find a... (2011, February 13). www.findagrave.com. Created by Scott & Priscilla Butler

Fraser, https://www.findagrave.com/memorial/65613113/margaret-elam

Mary Personett Franklin (1809-1888)—Find a…, (2015, October 4). www.findagrave.com. Created by Eric McGuire, https://www.findagrave.com/memorial/153276475/mary-franklin

Mattie F. Myers Carr (1846-1907)—Find a… (2015). www.findagrave.com. Created by Don Rubarts, https://www.findagrave.com/memorial/141096097/mattie-f-carr

Maxwell, J.O. (2013). *Let's go back…way back!: Black presence in the Restoration Movement.* Terrell, TX: James Maxwell.

McCaleb, R.L. (2008, June 30). *John Moody McCaleb* [Email update from family member Dr. R.L. McCaleb]. The Restoration Movement. https://www.therestorationmovement.com/_states/california/mccaleb.html

McDonald, B. (n.d.) *The Gentle Lady of Mars Hill*. Lindsey McDonald Collection [McDonald's personal copy of article] (UNA) Collier Library Archives, Florence, AL, United States.

McGarvey, J.W. (1899, September 16). W.K. Pendleton. *Christian Standard*, 1193.

McGarvey, J.W. (1960). *The Autobiography of J.W. McGarvey*. The College of the Bible.

McQuiddy J.C. & Harding, J.A. (1909, December 2). Potter Bible College. *Gospel Advocate*, 51(48), 1512.

Meeks, R.P. (1903, January 8). "Grandmamma Larimore." *Gospel Advocate, 45*(2), 27.

"Mrs. Alexander Campbell." (1874, June 13). [Reprinted article from May 27, 1874 Memphis Appeal]. *Christian Standard*, 187.

Merriam-Webster. (n.d.). Restore. In *Merriam-Webster dictionary*. Retrieved March 11, 2024, from https://www.merriam-webster.com/dictionary/restore

Morgan, Lynne. (1999, Winter). *Emily Tubman: Christian, Emancipator, Humanitarian. We're History* 4(3), 6, https://webfiles.acu.edu./departments/Library/HR/rest-mov_nov11/www.mun.ca/rels/rest-move/texts/etubman/ETCEH.HTM

Morro, W.C. (2016). *Brother McGarvey*. Charleston, AR: Cobb Publishing. Reformatted and edited edition of the 1940 original.

NKAA. (2017, September 14). *Tubman, William V.S.* Notable Kentucky African Americans Database. March 26, 2024 from https://nkaa.uky.edu/nkaa/items/show/749

Nunnelly, D.A. (n.d.). *Emily Harvey Thomas Tubman: a Disciple Wonder Woman*. The Restoration Movement. http://therestorationmovement.com/ states/kentucky/tubman,emily.htm

Olbricht, Tom. (2019, July). Where sin has gone must go his grace: John Moody McCaleb (1861-1953). *Gospel Advocate,* 161(7), 12-14.

Otwayanna Francis Hix McGarvey (1834-1911)—Find a... (2011, January 22). www.findagrave.com, Created by Margaret, https://www.findagrave.com/memorial/64529122/otwayanna-francis-mcgarvey

Owen, D.R. (2006, January). Is "Restoration" a Valid Principle? *Gospel Advocate*, 148(1), 38-39.

Page, E. (1907, July 18). Julia Esther Gresham Larimore. *Gospel Advocate 49(29)*, 451.

Peskin, A. (1978). *Garfield: a Biography*. Kent State University Press.

Phillips, D. (1978). *A Medley of the Restoration*. Bible & School Supply.

Powell, J.M. (2002). *The Man from Mars Hill: the Life and Times of T.B. Larimore.* 21st Century Christian.

Richardson, R. (1897). *Memoirs of Alexander Campbell* (Vol. 2). Religious Book Service.

Roberts, R.L. (1952). *Joseph Addison Clark (1815-1901)*. Texas State historical association: Handbook of Texas Online. https://tshaonline.org/handbook/online/articles/fcl10

Rogers, J. (1956). *The Biography of J.T. Johnson,* Gospel Advocate.

Rogers, S. (1880). *Toils and Struggles of the olden times* (Rev ed.). Standard Publishing.

Rushford, J.B. (1972). *The Apollos of the West: The Life of John Allen Gano.* [Thesis, Abilene Christian College]. http://www.therestorationmovement.com/books/gano.pdf

Rushford, J. (1977). *Political Disciple: The Relationship between James A. Garfield and the Disciples of Christ* [Doctoral dissertation, Pepperdine University]. Digital Commons. https://digitalcommons.pepperdine.edu/cgi/viewcontent.cgi?article=1006&context=heritage_center

Rushford, J.B. (2004). James A. Garfield. In D.A. Foster, P.M. Blowers, A.L. Dunnavant, & D.N. Williams (Eds.), *The Encyclopedia of the Stone-Campbell Movement,* (pp. 690-691). William B. Eerdmans.

Santayana, G. (1905). *The Life of Reason: Reason in Common Sense vol. 1* (Dover ed.). https://www.gutenberg.org/files/15000/15000-h/15000-h.htm#vol1

Sarah Anna Fulghum Lipscomb (1833-1875)—Find a… (2017). www.findagrave.com. Created by Tom Childers, https://www.findagrave.com/memorial/181235353/sarah_anna_lipscomb

Sarah Isabelle Turner Sewell (1816-1862)—Find a… (2008). www.findagrave.com. Created by Roots and Branches, https://www.findagrave.com/memorial/29957559/sarah-isabelle-sewell

Schaff, P. (1910). *History of the Christian Church: The History of the Reformation Vol. 7* (2nd ed.). http://www.ccel.org/ccel/schaff/hcc7.html

Scobey, J.E. (1954). *Franklin College and its Influences*. Gospel Advocate.

Sewell, E.G. (1874, May 21). Brother T. Fanning. *Gospel Advocate*, 16(21), 492-495.

Sewell, J.P. (1951). Biographical Sketches of Restoration Preachers. *The Harding College Lectures 1950*. Harding College Press. (pp. 66-75).

Shields, B.E. (2004). Smith, "Raccoon" John (1784-1868). In D.A. Foster, P.M. Blowers, A.L. Dunnavant, & D.N. Williams (Eds.), *The Encyclopedia of the Stone-Campbell Movement*. (pp. 690-691). William B. Eerdmans.

Simpson, J.P. (1981) Restoration Leaders: Walter Scott. Church Growth—A Blueprint for Stronger Churches. Freed-Hardeman College Lectures 1981, (pp. 324-328).

Slater, D.M. (2017, October 8). Bowen-Campbell House. *Tennessee Encyclopedia*. Tennessee Historical Society. https://tennesseeencyclopedia.net/entries/bowen-campbell-house/

Sophia E. Lewis Johnson (1796-1849)- Find a…, (2009, August 14). www.findagrave.com, Created by Dave Johnston, https://www.findagrave.com/memorial/40672147/sophia-e-johnson

Srygley F.D. (1891, October 7). Death of a Noble Woman. *Gospel Advocate, 33(40)*, 626.

Srygley, F.D. (1961). *Biographies and Sermons*. Gospel Advocate.

Srygley, F.D. (1955). *Larimore and His Boys* (5th ed.). Gospel Advocate.

Stevenson, D.E. (1980). Walter Scott: Voice of the Golden Oracle. College Press.

Stone, B. W. (2019). *The Autobiography of Barton W. Stone, with Additions and Reflections by Elder John Rogers*. Charleston, AR: Cobb Publishing. Originally titled "The Biography of Elder Barton Warren Stone," first published in 1847.

Stroop, Z.D. (2003, July). The Pioneer Spirit of Aunt Mag Lipscomb. *Gospel Advocate, 145*(7), 12-15.

Susan Mitchum Ball-Hall (1803-1868)—Find a… (2011, September 24). www.findagrave.com. Created by Christine Keene

Shallcross, https://www.findagrave.com/memorial/77030810/susan-ball-hall

Taylor, B.F. (1956) *History of Potter Orphan Home and Genealogy of the Potter Family.* Potter Orphan Home and School.

Thayer, J.H. (2003, October). Hupotasso. In *Thayer's Greek-English Lexicon of the New Testament.* (4th ed., p. 645).

Thomas, T.N. (2004). Thorp Spring Christian College. In D.A. Foster, P.M. Blowers, A.L. Dunnavant, D.N. Williams (Eds.), *The Encyclopedia of the Stone-Campbell Movement.* (pp. 742-743). William B. Eerdmans.

Tidwell, G.A. (2012, July). Building a Heritage of Faith. *Gospel Advocate*, 154(7), 21-23.

Walker, W., Norris, R. A., Lotz, D. W., & Handy, R.T. (1918). *A History of the Christian Church* (4th ed.). Charles Scribner's Sons.

Washington, E.K. (1866, December). In Memory of Alexander Campbell. *Millennial Harbinger, 37*(12), 529-539.

Wasson, W.W. (1952). *James A. Garfield: His Religion and Education.* Tennessee Book Company.

Weinkamer, D. (2017, February). *James and Lucretia's Love Story.* The Blog of James A Garfield National Historic Site. https://www.nps.gov/articles/000/james-lucretia-garfield-s-love-story.htm

West, D.G. (2003, July). Selina Campbell: Keeper of the Home. *Gospel Advocate*, 145(7), 21-22.

West, E.I. (1949). *The Search for the Ancient Order* (Vol. 1). Gospel Advocate.

West E.I. (1950). *The Search for the Ancient Order.* (Vol. 2). Religious Book Service.

West, E.I. (1954). *The Life and Times of David Lipscomb.* Henderson, Religious Book Service.

West, E.I. (1979). *The Search for the Ancient Order.* (Vol. 3). Religious Book Service.

West, E.I. (1984). *Elder Ben Franklin: Eye of the Storm*. Delight, AR: Gospel Light.

White, E.B. (2010). Jane Campbell McKeever (1800-1871): A Brief Biography with Comparison to Her Brother Alexander Campbell on the Issue of Slavery and Abolition. *Stone-Campbell Journal*, *13*(1), 3–16.

Williams, D.N. (2004). Stone, Barton Warren (1772-1844). In D.A. Foster, P.M. Blowers, A. L. Dunnavant & D.N. Williams (Eds.), *The Encyclopedia of the Stone-Campbell Movement* (pp. 701-720). William B. Eerdmans.

Williams, D.S. (2008). *From Mounds to Megachurches: Georgia's Religious Heritage*. University of Georgia Press. http://site.ebrary.com/id/10367022

Williams, J.A. (1870). Life of Elder John Smith: with some account of the rise and progress of the current reformation. R.W. Carroll & Co. Reformatted and republished by Cobb Publishing, 2016.

Young, Norvel M. (1949). *A History of Colleges Established and Controlled by Members of the Churches of Christ*. Old Paths Book Club.

A SPECIAL THANK YOU

Thank you to all of the South Knoxville ladies in our Wednesday night ladies class. The following ladies worked hard to create the questions included at the end of each chapter:

Darlene White—Thank you for taking my chapters home to proofread.

Brenda Jones (Mom)—Thank you for proofreading and typing questions.

Carolyn Art—Thank you for your encouragement in expressing how the book has affected your life and for your enthusiasm for a Restoration trip.

Sandy Bauman, Lorle Art, Jane Walker, Charlotte Haviland, and Nita McDaniel—Thank you all for your encouragement and for making excellent questions.

Thank you to the South Knoxville teenage girls for inspiring excellent discussion in class.

Thank you to David Anguish for handing me my first *Ancient Order* off the church library shelves.

Thank you to Sam Hester for being the best Restoration teacher at Freed-Hardeman.

Thank you to Scott Harp and Tom Childers for encouraging me to write a book on Restoration history.

Thank you to Hillary Broome and TCC for encouraging me and allowing me to work on my book at camp.

Thank you to Barb Henbest at Potter Children's Home for all the help. I truly wish you could spend the day drinking lemonade with Mary on her front porch.

I want to say thank you to my dear husband, Geoff, for coming up with the idea and title of the book. He was there for me the whole way.

Finally, I want to say thank you to Abigail Buchanan for working on the majority of the edits to this book. If you are looking for an editor who encourages you through the whole editing process she is a jewel.

Final Notes

Most of the pictures of the Women of the Restoration found in this book are used by permission of Scott Harp, curator of TheRestorationMovement.com.

The photo of Lucy Jane Beasley McCaleb comes from findagrave.com, and is used by permission of Gary Waddey. The photo of her tombstone comes from the same website, and is used by permission of Leonard J. McCown.

The photo of Mattie Carr comes from John T. Brown's 1904 book, the Church of Christ.

The photo of Eliza Garfield comes from the National Park Service website. https://www.nps.gov/people/eliza-ballou-garfield.htm. The photo of Lucretia Garfield is from the Library of Congress website: https://loc.getarchive.net/topics/james+garfield. Both photos are in the public domain.

Any other photos of tombstones that do not include the author are taken from TheRestorationMovement.com, and are used by permission.